WRITER: REGINALD HUDLIN

"WORLD TOUR"
PENCILERS: SCOT EATON & MANUEL GARCIA
INKERS: ANDREW HENNESSY, MARK MORALES,
SANDU FLOREA & JAY LEISTEN
WITH SEAN PARSONS
COLORISTS: DEAN WHITE & MATT MILLA

"WAR CRIMES"
PENCILERS: KOI TURNBULL & MARCUS TO
INKERS: DON HO, SAL REGLA,
JEFF DE LOS SANTOS & NICK NIX
COLORIST: J.D. SMITH

LETTERER: VC'S RANDY GENTILE
COVER ARTISTS: SCOT EATON, ANDREW HENNESSY,
DEAN WHITE, ESAD RIBIC, GARY FRANK,
MIKE DEODATO JR. & MICHAEL TURNER

COLLECTION EDITOR: JENNIFER GRÜNWALD
ASSISTANT EDITORS: MICHAEL SHORT & CORY LEVINE
ASSOCIATE EDITOR: MARK D. BEAZLEY
SENIOR EDITOR, SPECIAL PROJECTS: JEFF YOUNGQUIST
SENIOR VICE PRESIDENT OF SALES: DAVID GABRIEL
PRODUCTION: JERRON QUALITY COLOR
PRESIDENT OF CREATIVE: TOM MARVELLI

ASSISTANT EDITOR: DANI͏
EDITOR: AXEL ALO͏

EDITOR IN CHIEF: JOE QUESADA
PUBLISHER: DAN BUCKLEY

PREVIOUSLY:

There are some places you just don't mess with. Wakanda is one of them. Since the dawn of time, that African warrior nation has been sending would-be conquerors home in body bags. While the rest of Africa got carved up like a Christmas turkey by the rest of the world, Wakanda's cultural evolution has gone unchecked for centuries, unfettered by the yoke of colonization. The result: a high-tech, resource-rich, ecologically-sound paradise that makes the rest of the world seem primitive by comparison.

Ruling over all of this is the Black Panther.

The Black Panther is more than just the embodiment of a warrior cult that's served as Wakanda's religious, political and military head since its inception. The Black Panther is the embodiment of the ideals of a people. Anyone who'd dare to make a move on Wakanda must go through him.

Despite conflict amongst his allies in America, the Black Panther was able to enjoy his marriage to Storm of the X-Men. Yet, as soon as the celebration concluded, T'Challa and his queen were thrust into the new reality of their world—one where Wakanda is in the precarious position of navigating a political minefield. And to further complicate matters, the couple was approached with a startling proposition: an alliance with their adversary, Dr. Doom!

BLACK PANTHER
CIVIL WAR

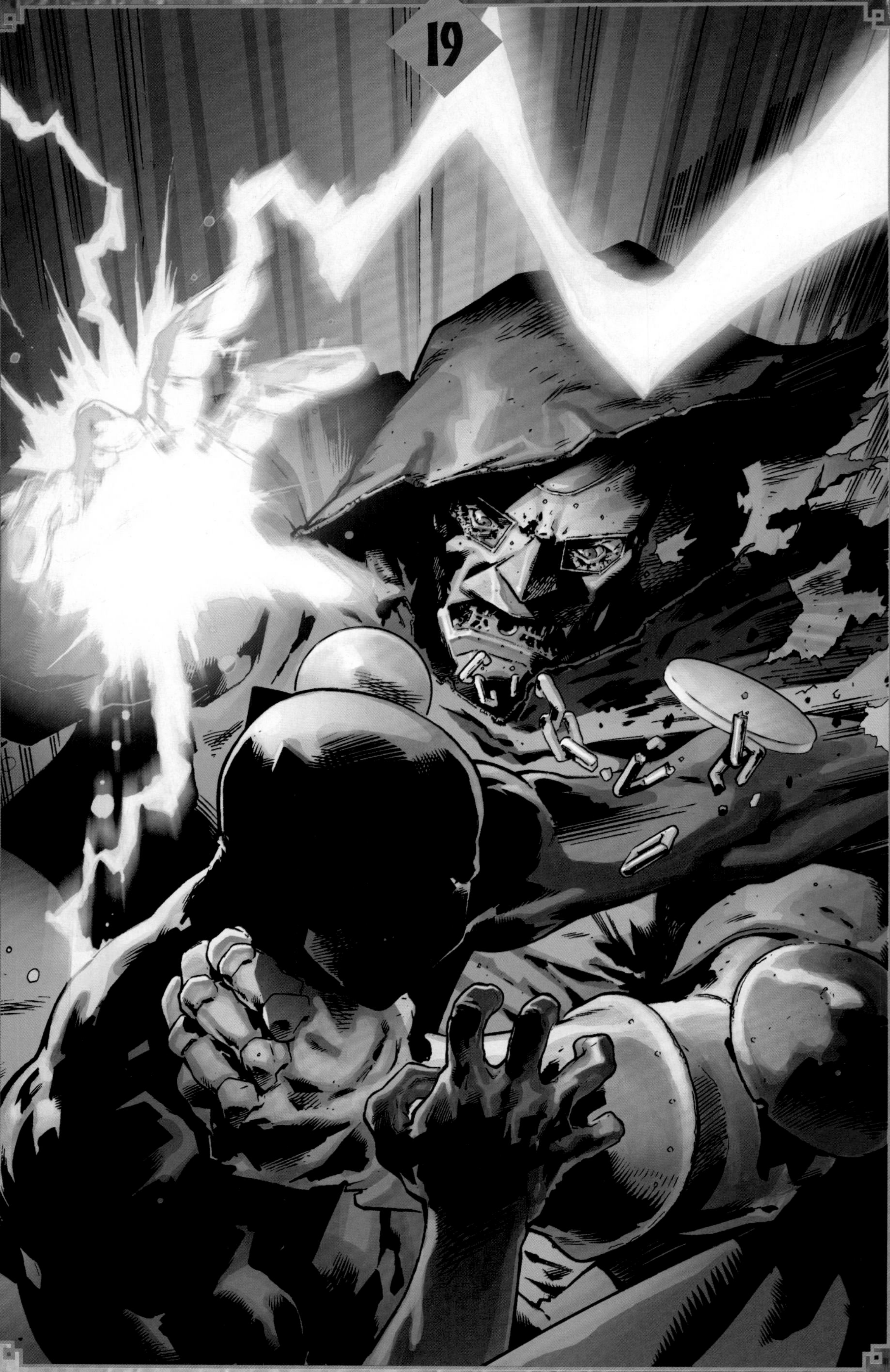
19

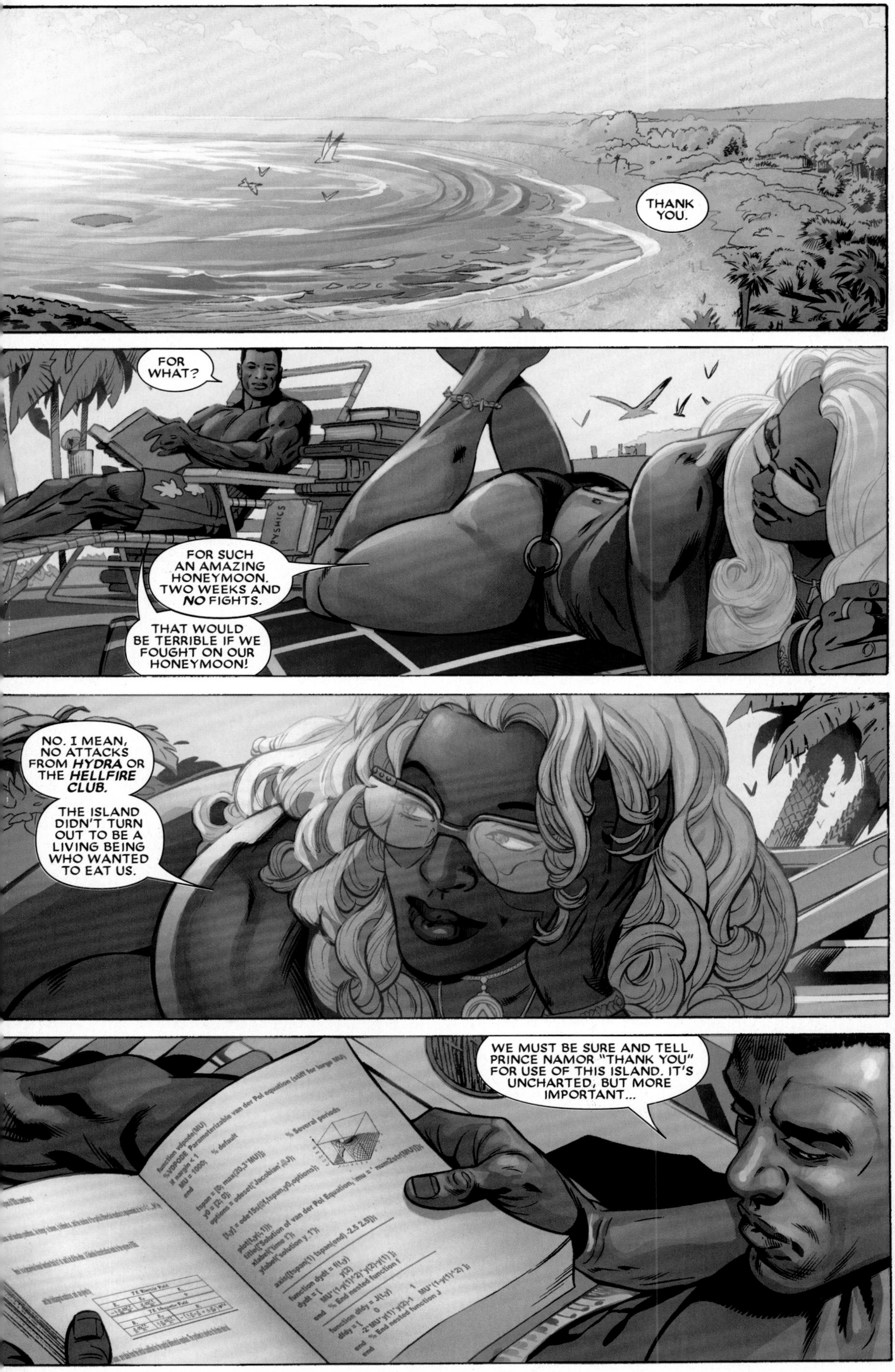
THANK YOU.
FOR WHAT?
FOR SUCH AN AMAZING HONEYMOON. TWO WEEKS AND *NO* FIGHTS.
THAT WOULD BE TERRIBLE IF WE FOUGHT ON OUR HONEYMOON!
NO. I MEAN, NO ATTACKS FROM ***HYDRA*** OR THE ***HELLFIRE CLUB.***
THE ISLAND DIDN'T TURN OUT TO BE A LIVING BEING WHO WANTED TO EAT US.
WE MUST BE SURE AND TELL PRINCE NAMOR "THANK YOU" FOR USE OF THIS ISLAND. IT'S UNCHARTED, BUT MORE IMPORTANT...

"...HE'S GOT THE MOST DANGEROUS SEA CREATURES ON EARTH PATROLLING THE WATERS AROUND THE ISLAND FOR MILES."

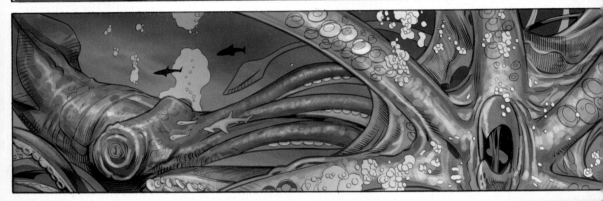

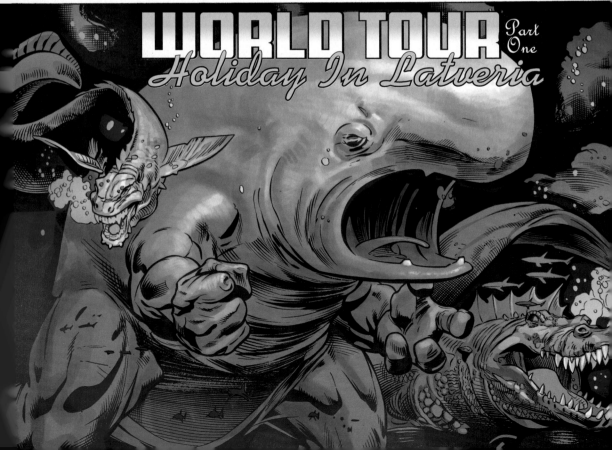

WORLD TOUR Part One
Holiday In Latveria

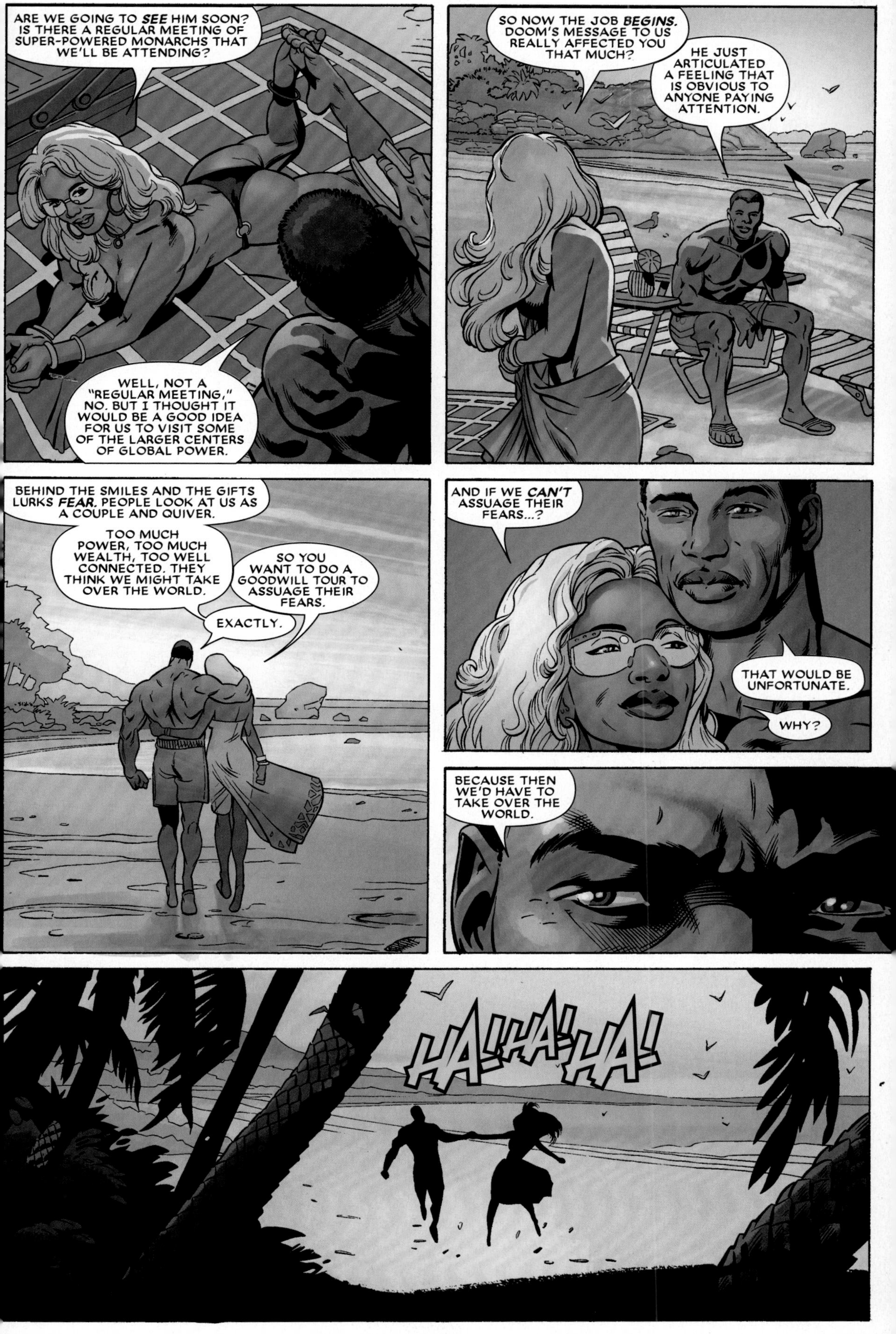
ARE WE GOING TO SEE HIM SOON? IS THERE A REGULAR MEETING OF SUPER-POWERED MONARCHS THAT WE'LL BE ATTENDING?
WELL, NOT A "REGULAR MEETING," NO. BUT I THOUGHT IT WOULD BE A GOOD IDEA FOR US TO VISIT SOME OF THE LARGER CENTERS OF GLOBAL POWER.
SO NOW THE JOB BEGINS. DOOM'S MESSAGE TO US REALLY AFFECTED YOU THAT MUCH?
HE JUST ARTICULATED A FEELING THAT IS OBVIOUS TO ANYONE PAYING ATTENTION.
BEHIND THE SMILES AND THE GIFTS LURKS FEAR. PEOPLE LOOK AT US AS A COUPLE AND QUIVER.
TOO MUCH POWER, TOO MUCH WEALTH, TOO WELL CONNECTED. THEY THINK WE MIGHT TAKE OVER THE WORLD.
SO YOU WANT TO DO A GOODWILL TOUR TO ASSUAGE THEIR FEARS.
EXACTLY.
AND IF WE CAN'T ASSUAGE THEIR FEARS...?
THAT WOULD BE UNFORTUNATE.
WHY?
BECAUSE THEN WE'D HAVE TO TAKE OVER THE WORLD.
HA! HA! HA!

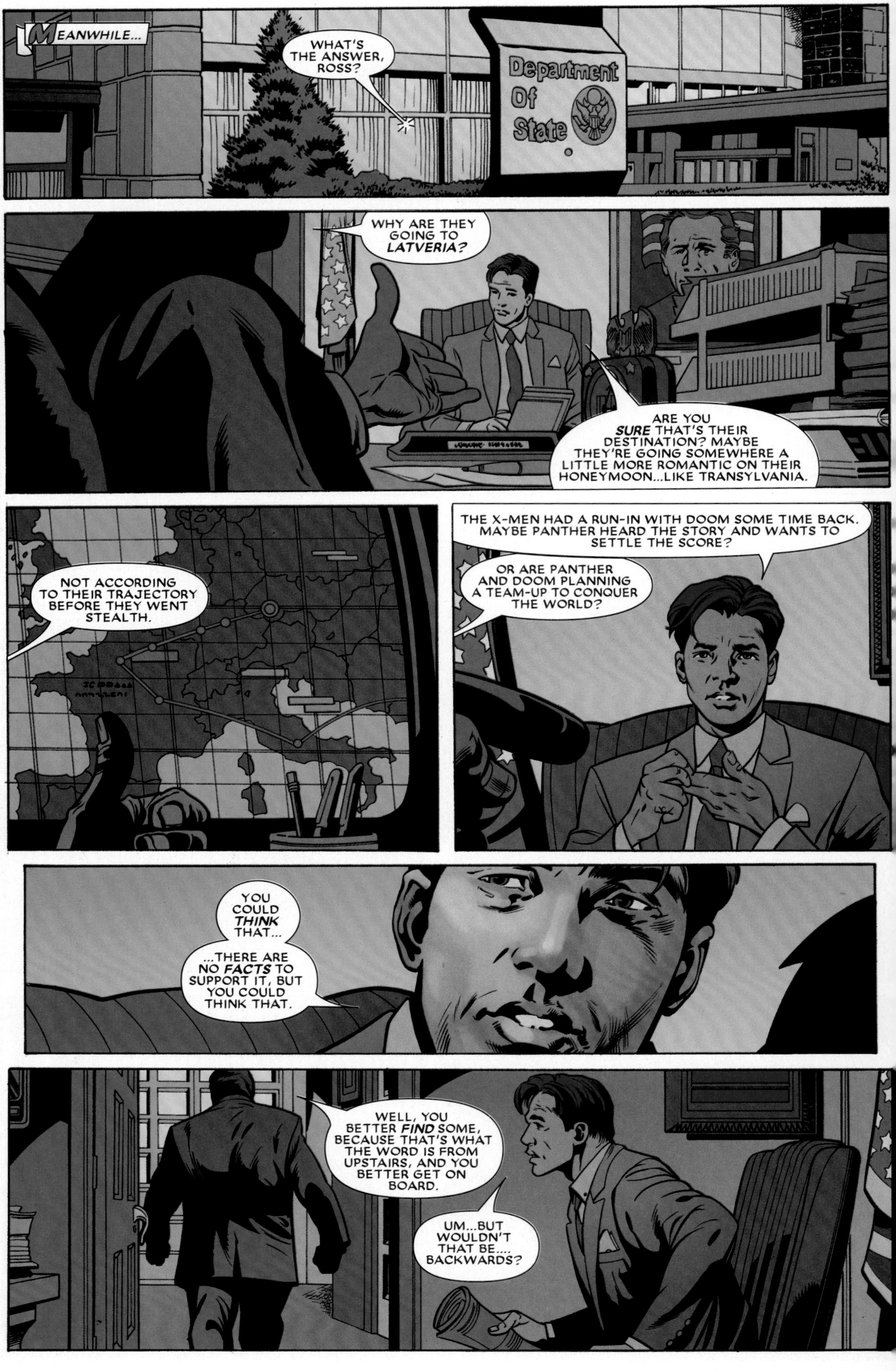
MEANWHILE...
WHAT'S THE ANSWER, ROSS?
Department Of State
WHY ARE THEY GOING TO LATVERIA?
ARE YOU SURE THAT'S THEIR DESTINATION? MAYBE THEY'RE GOING SOMEWHERE A LITTLE MORE ROMANTIC ON THEIR HONEYMOON...LIKE TRANSYLVANIA.
NOT ACCORDING TO THEIR TRAJECTORY BEFORE THEY WENT STEALTH.
THE X-MEN HAD A RUN-IN WITH DOOM SOME TIME BACK. MAYBE PANTHER HEARD THE STORY AND WANTS TO SETTLE THE SCORE?
OR ARE PANTHER AND DOOM PLANNING A TEAM-UP TO CONQUER THE WORLD?
YOU COULD THINK THAT...
...THERE ARE NO FACTS TO SUPPORT IT, BUT YOU COULD THINK THAT.
WELL, YOU BETTER FIND SOME, BECAUSE THAT'S WHAT THE WORD IS FROM UPSTAIRS, AND YOU BETTER GET ON BOARD.
UM...BUT WOULDN'T THAT BE.... BACKWARDS?

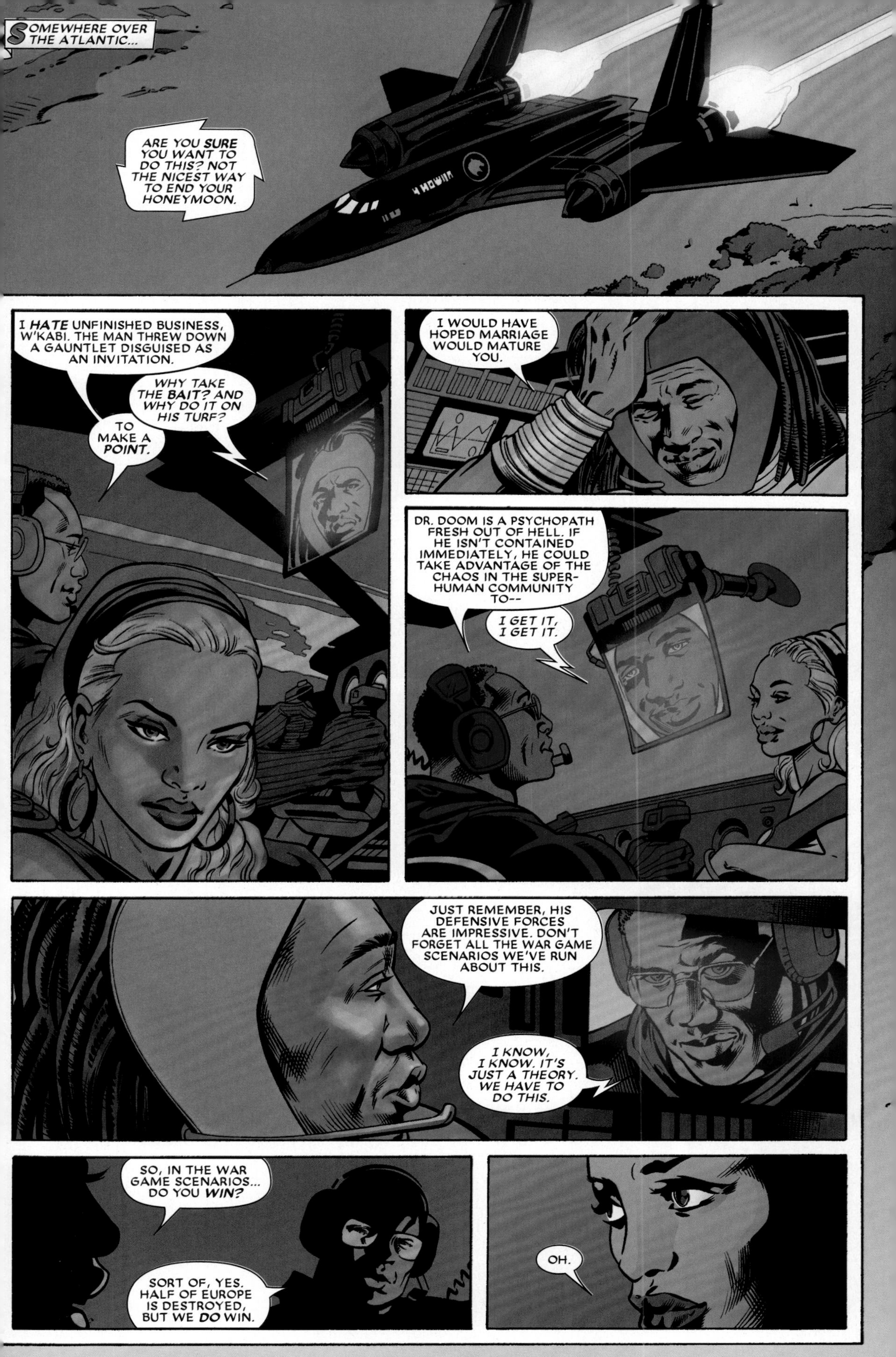
SOMEWHERE OVER THE ATLANTIC...
ARE YOU SURE YOU WANT TO DO THIS? NOT THE NICEST WAY TO END YOUR HONEYMOON.
I HATE UNFINISHED BUSINESS, W'KABI. THE MAN THREW DOWN A GAUNTLET DISGUISED AS AN INVITATION.
WHY TAKE THE BAIT? AND WHY DO IT ON HIS TURF?
TO MAKE A POINT.
I WOULD HAVE HOPED MARRIAGE WOULD MATURE YOU.
DR. DOOM IS A PSYCHOPATH FRESH OUT OF HELL. IF HE ISN'T CONTAINED IMMEDIATELY, HE COULD TAKE ADVANTAGE OF THE CHAOS IN THE SUPER-HUMAN COMMUNITY TO--
I GET IT, I GET IT.
JUST REMEMBER, HIS DEFENSIVE FORCES ARE IMPRESSIVE. DON'T FORGET ALL THE WAR GAME SCENARIOS WE'VE RUN ABOUT THIS.
I KNOW, I KNOW. IT'S JUST A THEORY. WE HAVE TO DO THIS.
SO, IN THE WAR GAME SCENARIOS... DO YOU WIN?
SORT OF, YES. HALF OF EUROPE IS DESTROYED, BUT WE DO WIN.
OH.

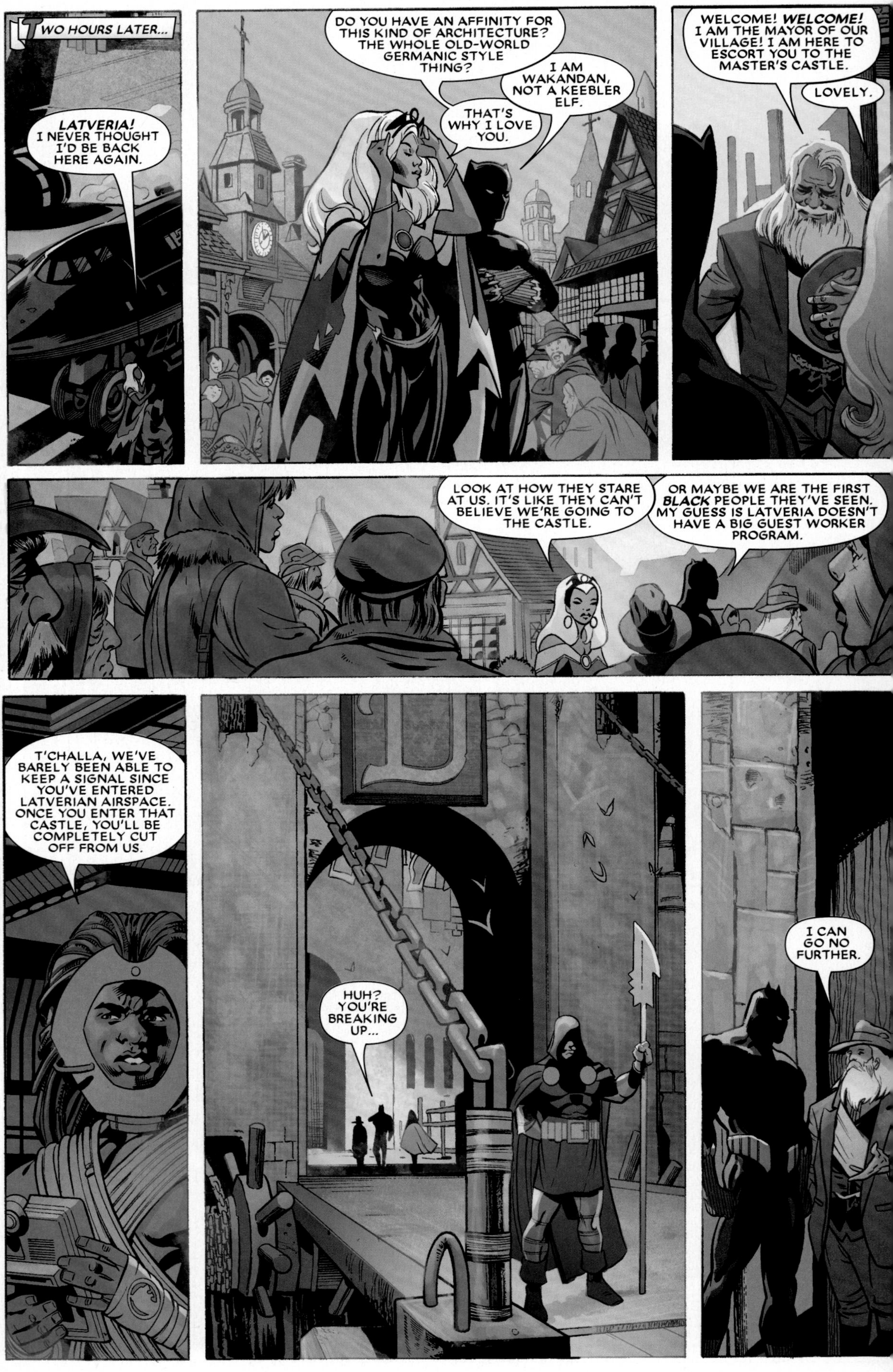
TWO HOURS LATER...
LATVERIA! I NEVER THOUGHT I'D BE BACK HERE AGAIN.
DO YOU HAVE AN AFFINITY FOR THIS KIND OF ARCHITECTURE? THE WHOLE OLD-WORLD GERMANIC STYLE THING?
I AM WAKANDAN, NOT A KEEBLER ELF.
THAT'S WHY I LOVE YOU.
WELCOME! WELCOME! I AM THE MAYOR OF OUR VILLAGE! I AM HERE TO ESCORT YOU TO THE MASTER'S CASTLE.
LOVELY.
LOOK AT HOW THEY STARE AT US. IT'S LIKE THEY CAN'T BELIEVE WE'RE GOING TO THE CASTLE.
OR MAYBE WE ARE THE FIRST BLACK PEOPLE THEY'VE SEEN. MY GUESS IS LATVERIA DOESN'T HAVE A BIG GUEST WORKER PROGRAM.
T'CHALLA, WE'VE BARELY BEEN ABLE TO KEEP A SIGNAL SINCE YOU'VE ENTERED LATVERIAN AIRSPACE. ONCE YOU ENTER THAT CASTLE, YOU'LL BE COMPLETELY CUT OFF FROM US.
HUH? YOU'RE BREAKING UP...
I CAN GO NO FURTHER.

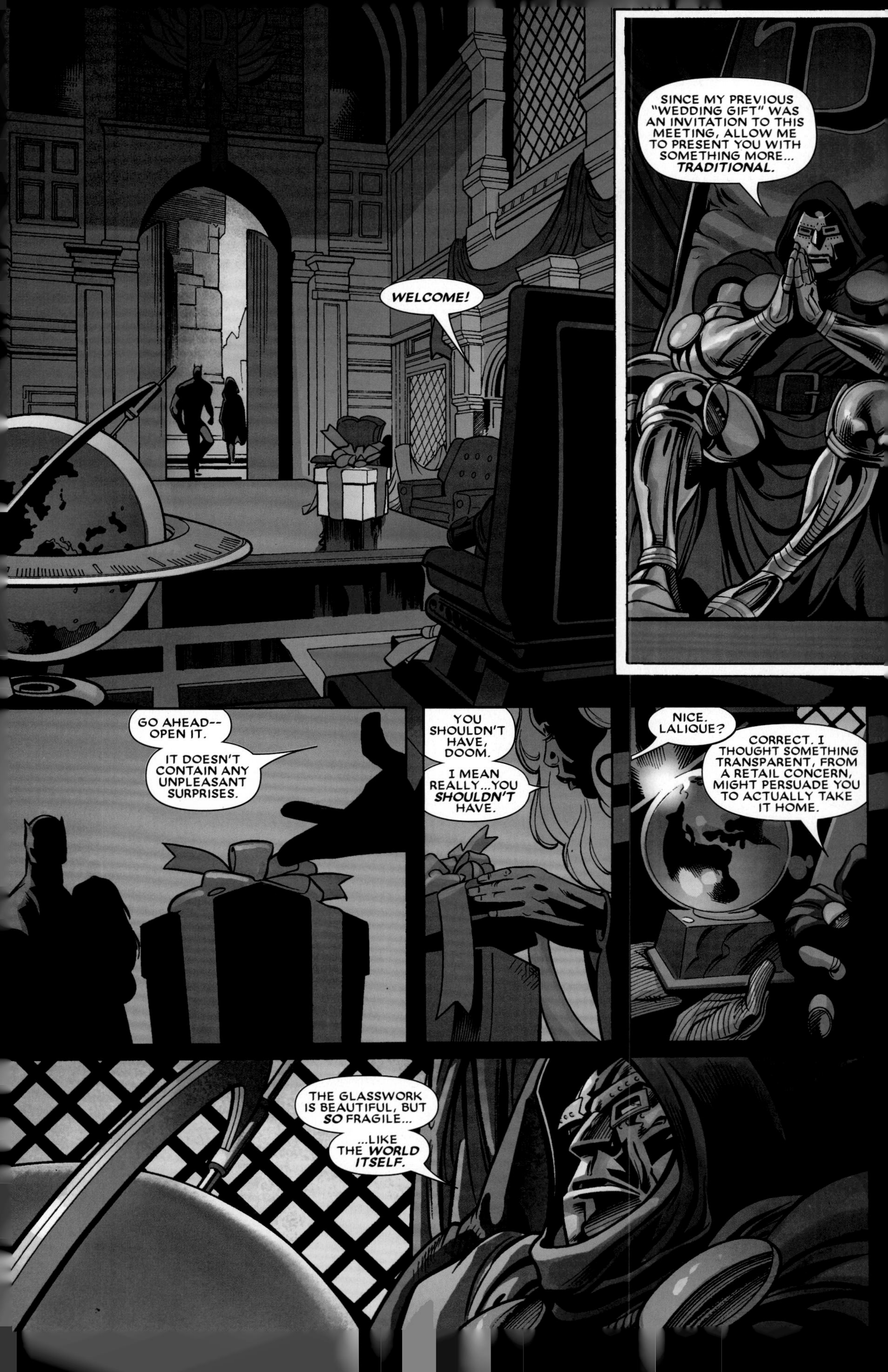
WELCOME!
SINCE MY PREVIOUS "WEDDING GIFT" WAS AN INVITATION TO THIS MEETING, ALLOW ME TO PRESENT YOU WITH SOMETHING MORE... *TRADITIONAL.*
GO AHEAD-- OPEN IT.
IT DOESN'T CONTAIN ANY UNPLEASANT SURPRISES.
YOU SHOULDN'T HAVE, DOOM.
I MEAN REALLY...YOU *SHOULDN'T* HAVE.
NICE. LALIQUE?
CORRECT. I THOUGHT SOMETHING TRANSPARENT, FROM A RETAIL CONCERN, MIGHT PERSUADE YOU TO ACTUALLY TAKE IT HOME.
THE GLASSWORK IS BEAUTIFUL, BUT *SO* FRAGILE...
...LIKE THE *WORLD ITSELF.*

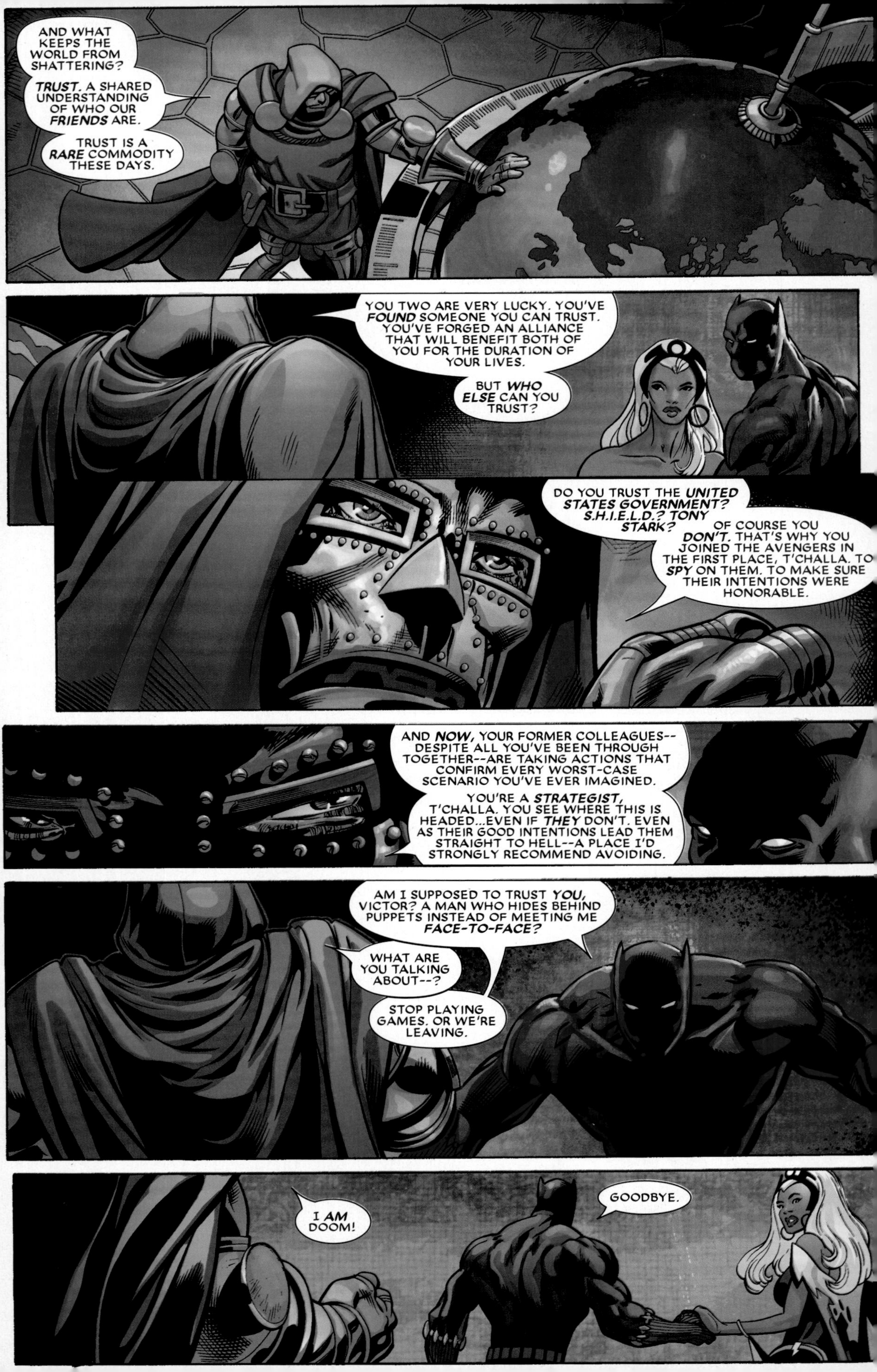
AND WHAT KEEPS THE WORLD FROM SHATTERING?
TRUST. A SHARED UNDERSTANDING OF WHO OUR FRIENDS ARE.
TRUST IS A RARE COMMODITY THESE DAYS.
YOU TWO ARE VERY LUCKY. YOU'VE FOUND SOMEONE YOU CAN TRUST. YOU'VE FORGED AN ALLIANCE THAT WILL BENEFIT BOTH OF YOU FOR THE DURATION OF YOUR LIVES.
BUT WHO ELSE CAN YOU TRUST?
DO YOU TRUST THE UNITED STATES GOVERNMENT? S.H.I.E.L.D.? TONY STARK?
OF COURSE YOU DON'T. THAT'S WHY YOU JOINED THE AVENGERS IN THE FIRST PLACE, T'CHALLA. TO SPY ON THEM. TO MAKE SURE THEIR INTENTIONS WERE HONORABLE.
AND NOW, YOUR FORMER COLLEAGUES--DESPITE ALL YOU'VE BEEN THROUGH TOGETHER--ARE TAKING ACTIONS THAT CONFIRM EVERY WORST-CASE SCENARIO YOU'VE EVER IMAGINED.
YOU'RE A STRATEGIST, T'CHALLA. YOU SEE WHERE THIS IS HEADED...EVEN IF THEY DON'T. EVEN AS THEIR GOOD INTENTIONS LEAD THEM STRAIGHT TO HELL--A PLACE I'D STRONGLY RECOMMEND AVOIDING.
AM I SUPPOSED TO TRUST YOU, VICTOR? A MAN WHO HIDES BEHIND PUPPETS INSTEAD OF MEETING ME FACE-TO-FACE?
WHAT ARE YOU TALKING ABOUT--?
STOP PLAYING GAMES. OR WE'RE LEAVING.
I AM DOOM!
GOODBYE.

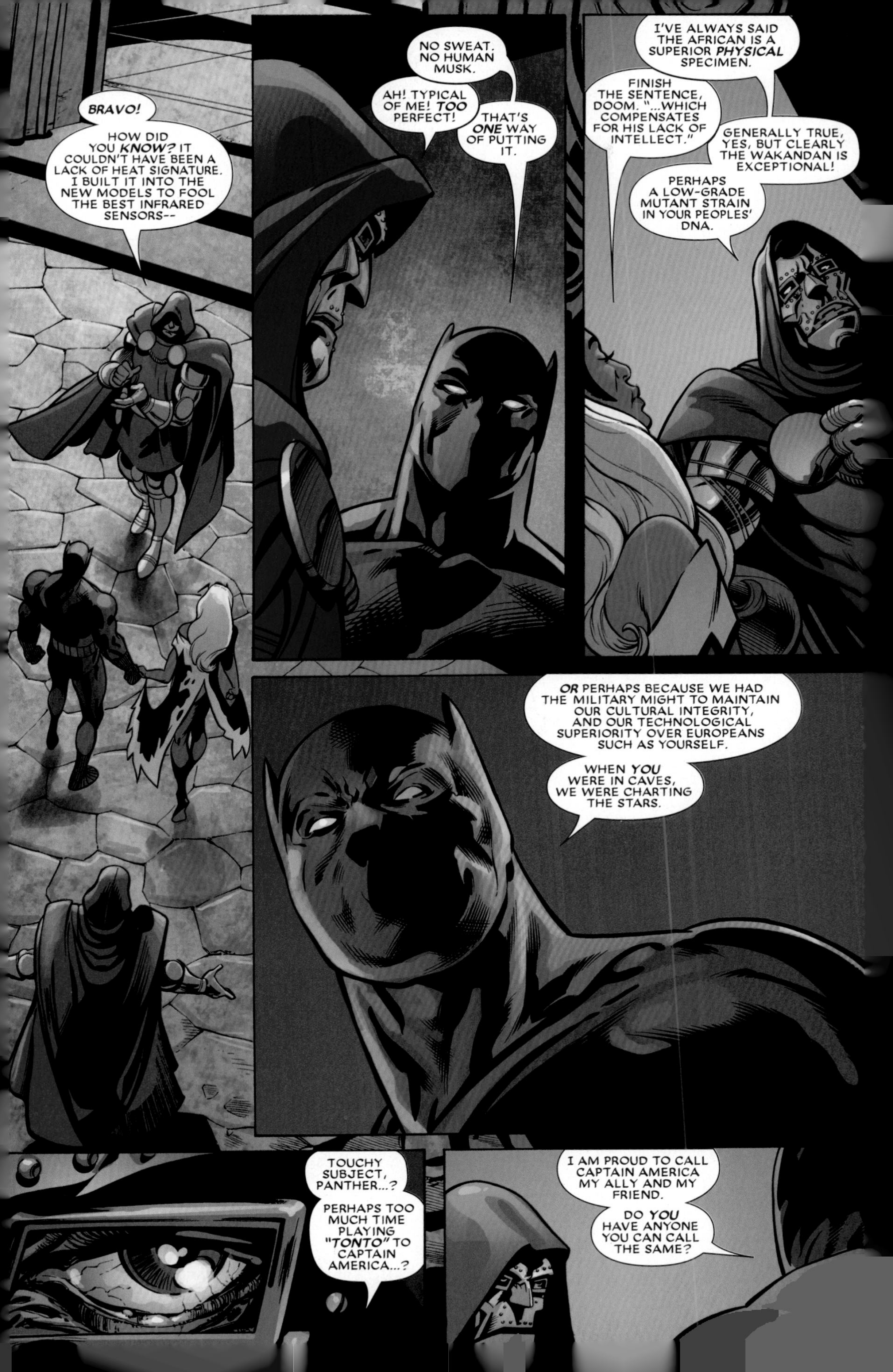

BRAVO!
HOW DID YOU KNOW? IT COULDN'T HAVE BEEN A LACK OF HEAT SIGNATURE. I BUILT IT INTO THE NEW MODELS TO FOOL THE BEST INFRARED SENSORS--
NO SWEAT. NO HUMAN MUSK.
AH! TYPICAL OF ME! TOO PERFECT!
THAT'S ONE WAY OF PUTTING IT.
I'VE ALWAYS SAID THE AFRICAN IS A SUPERIOR PHYSICAL SPECIMEN.
FINISH THE SENTENCE, DOOM. "...WHICH COMPENSATES FOR HIS LACK OF INTELLECT."
GENERALLY TRUE, YES, BUT CLEARLY THE WAKANDAN IS EXCEPTIONAL!
PERHAPS A LOW-GRADE MUTANT STRAIN IN YOUR PEOPLES' DNA.
OR PERHAPS BECAUSE WE HAD THE MILITARY MIGHT TO MAINTAIN OUR CULTURAL INTEGRITY, AND OUR TECHNOLOGICAL SUPERIORITY OVER EUROPEANS SUCH AS YOURSELF.
WHEN YOU WERE IN CAVES, WE WERE CHARTING THE STARS.
TOUCHY SUBJECT, PANTHER...?
PERHAPS TOO MUCH TIME PLAYING "TONTO" TO CAPTAIN AMERICA...?
I AM PROUD TO CALL CAPTAIN AMERICA MY ALLY AND MY FRIEND.
DO YOU HAVE ANYONE YOU CAN CALL THE SAME?

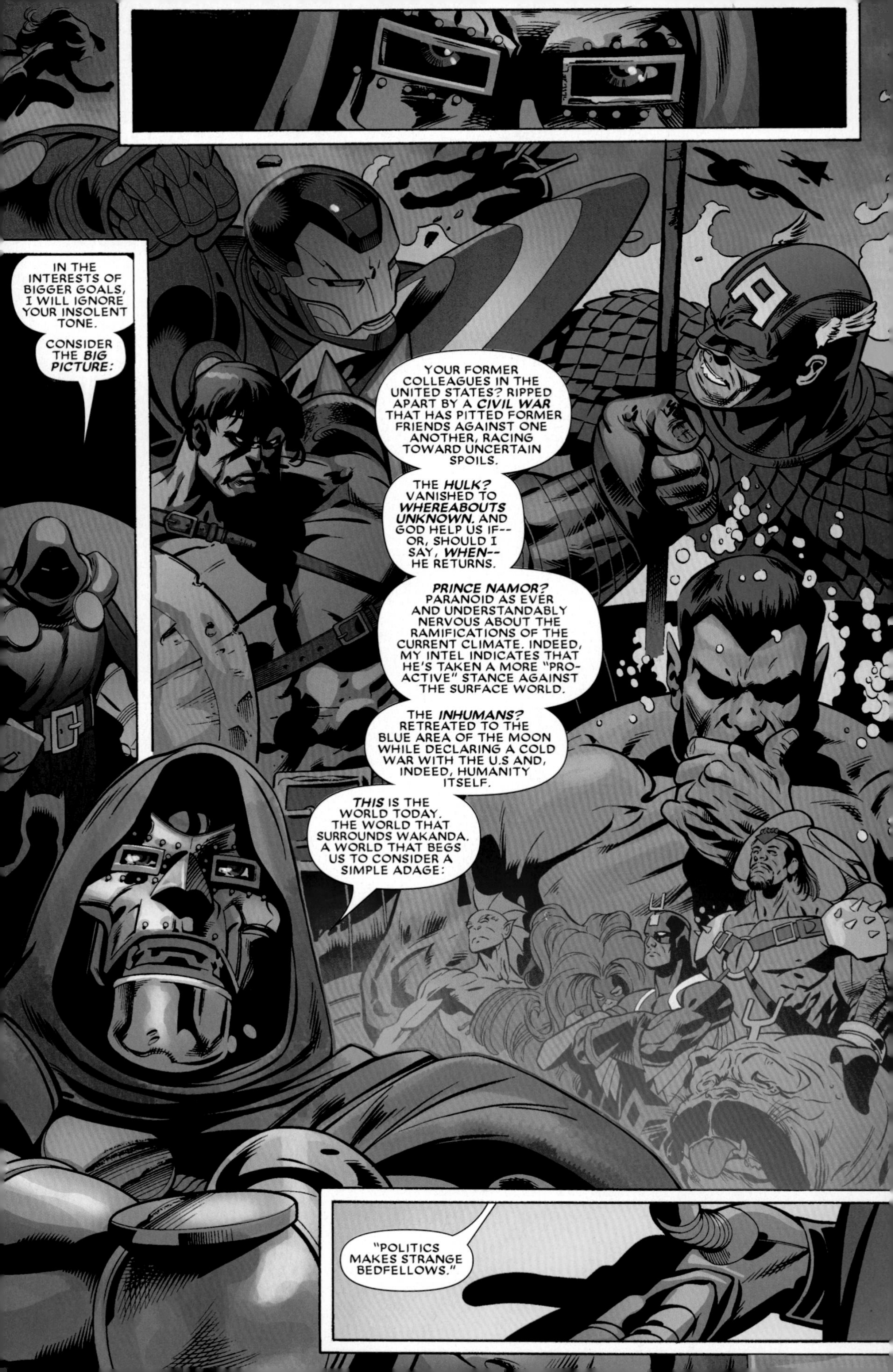
IN THE INTERESTS OF BIGGER GOALS, I WILL IGNORE YOUR INSOLENT TONE.
CONSIDER THE BIG PICTURE:
YOUR FORMER COLLEAGUES IN THE UNITED STATES? RIPPED APART BY A CIVIL WAR THAT HAS PITTED FORMER FRIENDS AGAINST ONE ANOTHER, RACING TOWARD UNCERTAIN SPOILS.
THE HULK? VANISHED TO WHEREABOUTS UNKNOWN. AND GOD HELP US IF-- OR, SHOULD I SAY, WHEN-- HE RETURNS.
PRINCE NAMOR? PARANOID AS EVER AND UNDERSTANDABLY NERVOUS ABOUT THE RAMIFICATIONS OF THE CURRENT CLIMATE. INDEED, MY INTEL INDICATES THAT HE'S TAKEN A MORE "PRO-ACTIVE" STANCE AGAINST THE SURFACE WORLD.
THE INHUMANS? RETREATED TO THE BLUE AREA OF THE MOON WHILE DECLARING A COLD WAR WITH THE U.S AND, INDEED, HUMANITY ITSELF.
THIS IS THE WORLD TODAY. THE WORLD THAT SURROUNDS WAKANDA. A WORLD THAT BEGS US TO CONSIDER A SIMPLE ADAGE:
"POLITICS MAKES STRANGE BEDFELLOWS."

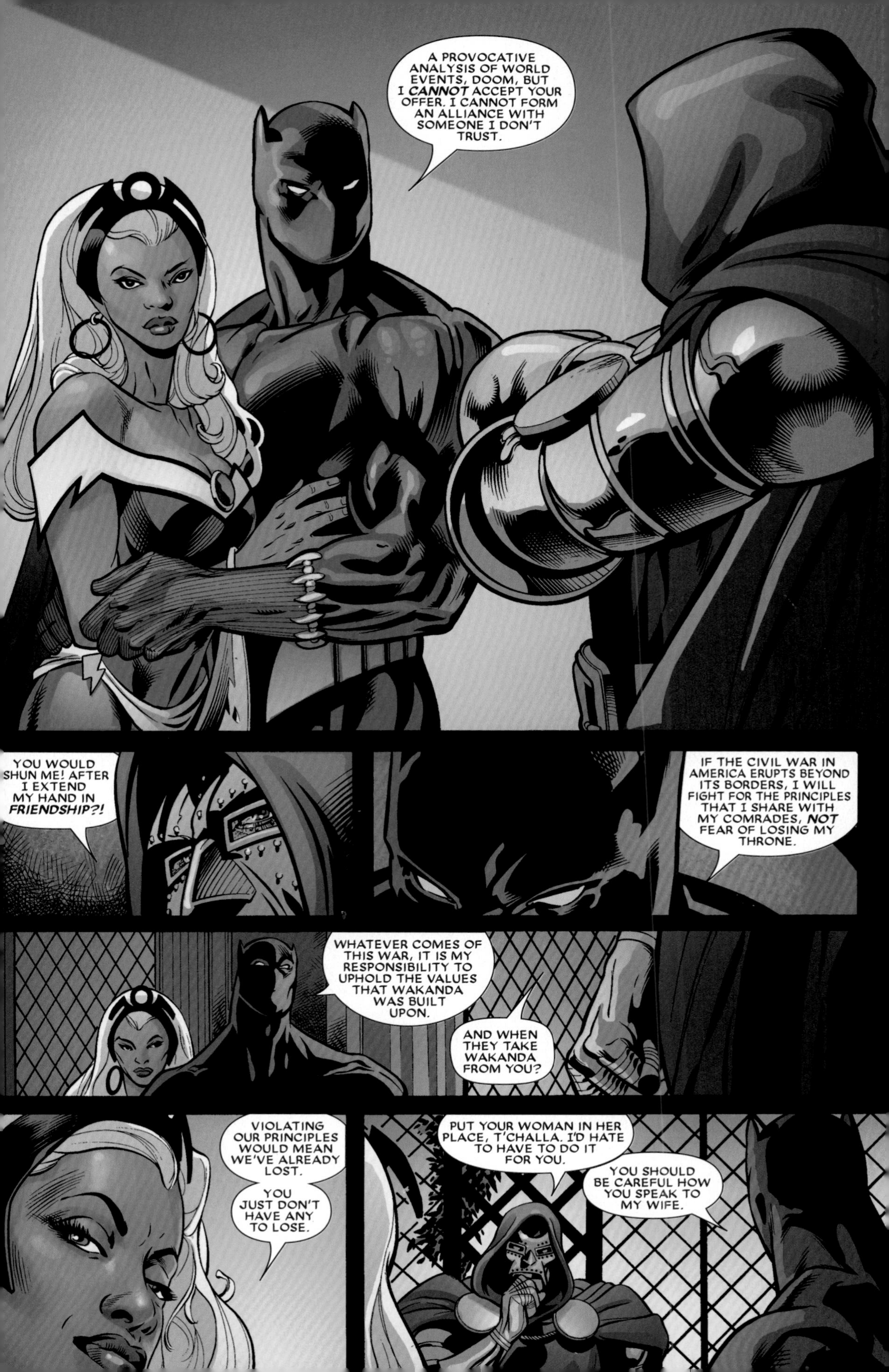
A PROVOCATIVE ANALYSIS OF WORLD EVENTS, DOOM, BUT I *CANNOT* ACCEPT YOUR OFFER. I CANNOT FORM AN ALLIANCE WITH SOMEONE I DON'T TRUST.
YOU WOULD SHUN ME! AFTER I EXTEND MY HAND IN *FRIENDSHIP?!*
IF THE CIVIL WAR IN AMERICA ERUPTS BEYOND ITS BORDERS, I WILL FIGHT FOR THE PRINCIPLES THAT I SHARE WITH MY COMRADES, *NOT* FEAR OF LOSING MY THRONE.
WHATEVER COMES OF THIS WAR, IT IS MY RESPONSIBILITY TO UPHOLD THE VALUES THAT WAKANDA WAS BUILT UPON.
AND WHEN THEY TAKE WAKANDA FROM YOU?
VIOLATING OUR PRINCIPLES WOULD MEAN WE'VE ALREADY LOST.
YOU JUST DON'T HAVE ANY TO LOSE.
PUT YOUR WOMAN IN HER PLACE, T'CHALLA. I'D HATE TO HAVE TO DO IT FOR YOU.
YOU SHOULD BE CAREFUL HOW YOU SPEAK TO MY WIFE.

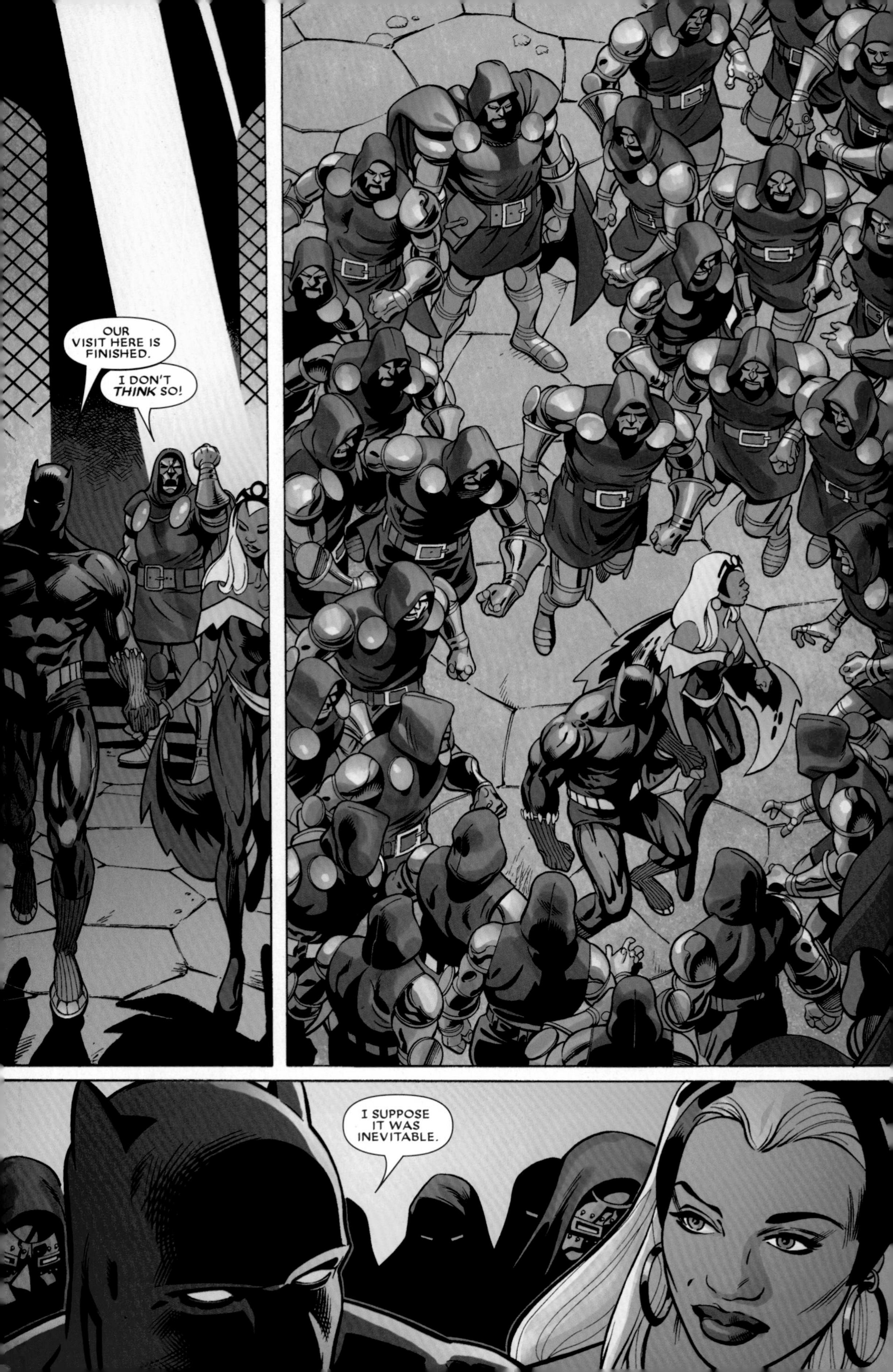
OUR VISIT HERE IS FINISHED.
I DON'T *THINK* SO!
I SUPPOSE IT WAS INEVITABLE.

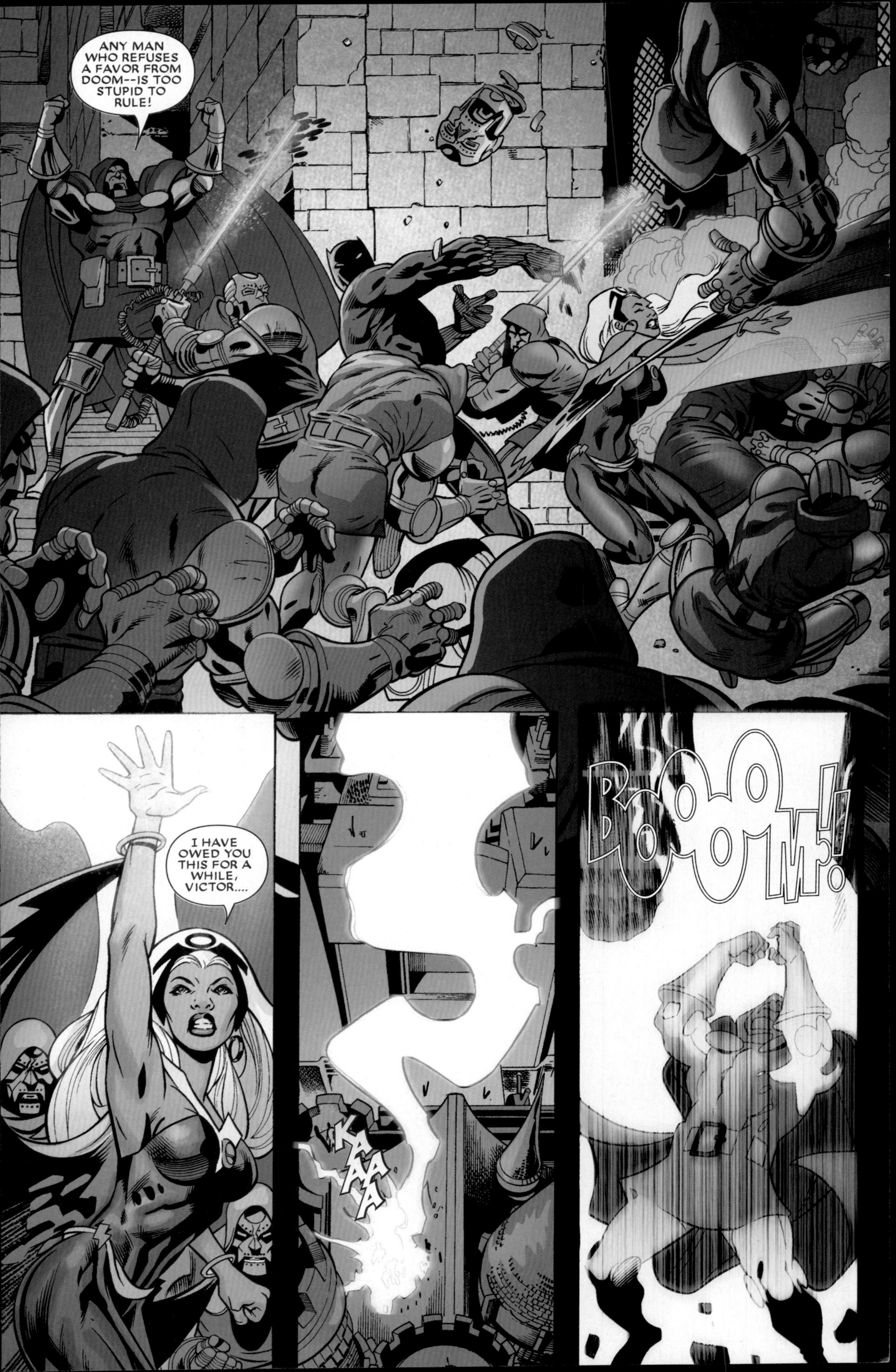
ANY MAN WHO REFUSES A FAVOR FROM DOOM--IS TOO STUPID TO RULE!
I HAVE OWED YOU THIS FOR A WHILE, VICTOR....
KAAAA

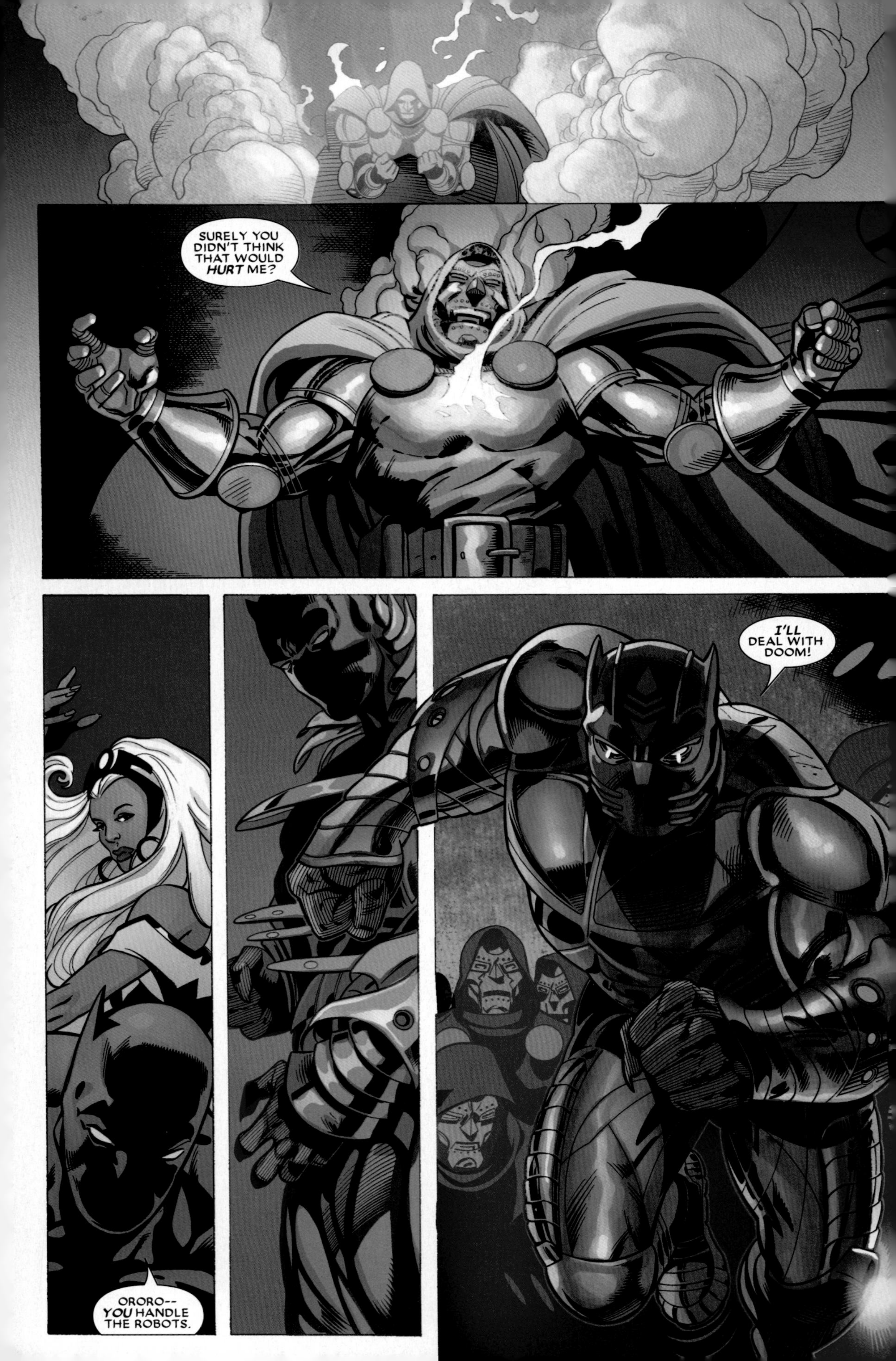
SURELY YOU DIDN'T THINK THAT WOULD *HURT* ME?
I'LL DEAL WITH DOOM!
ORORO-- *YOU* HANDLE THE ROBOTS.

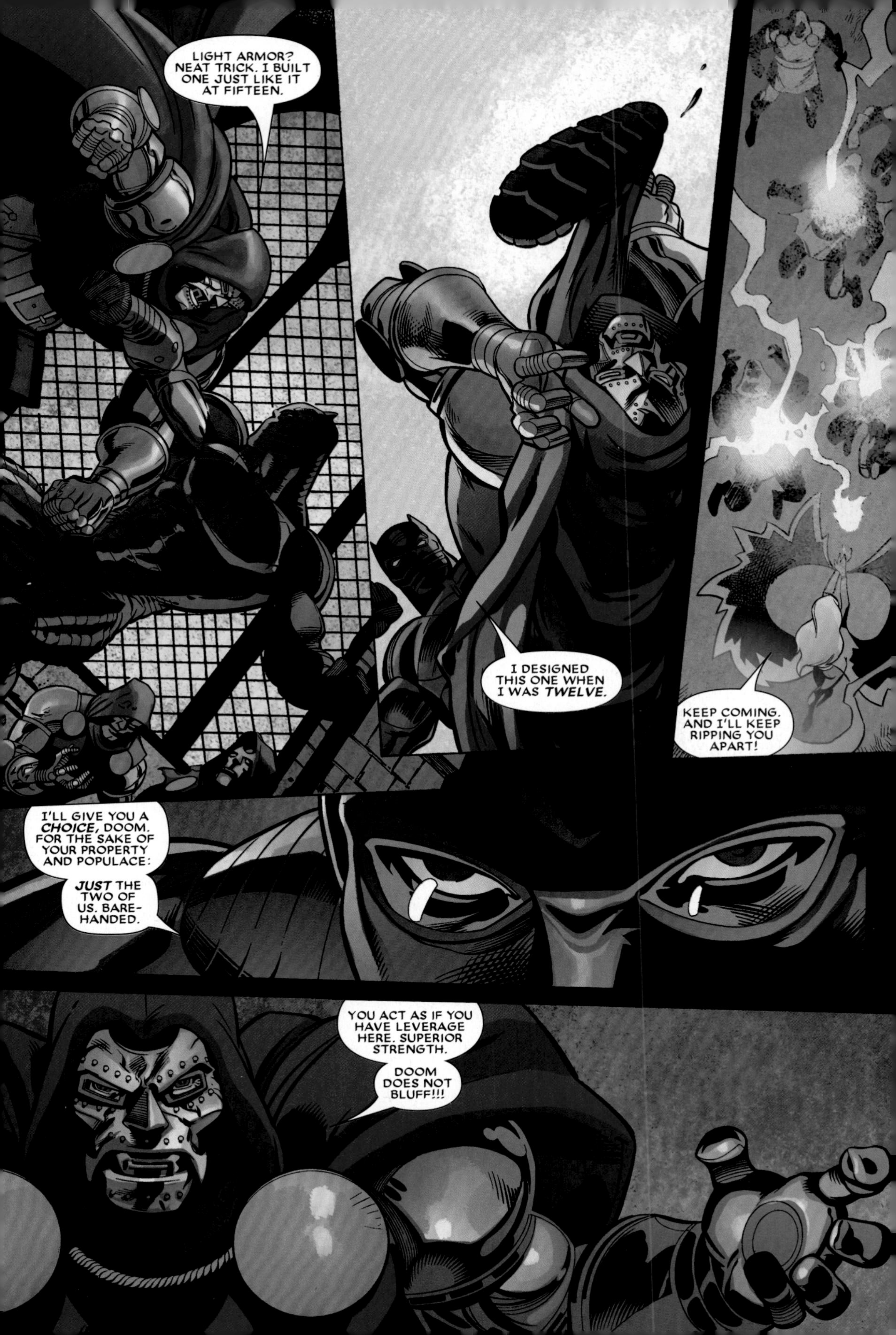
LIGHT ARMOR? NEAT TRICK. I BUILT ONE JUST LIKE IT AT FIFTEEN.
I DESIGNED THIS ONE WHEN I WAS *TWELVE.*
KEEP COMING. AND I'LL KEEP RIPPING YOU APART!
I'LL GIVE YOU A *CHOICE,* DOOM. FOR THE SAKE OF YOUR PROPERTY AND POPULACE:
JUST THE TWO OF US. BARE-HANDED.
YOU ACT AS IF YOU HAVE LEVERAGE HERE. SUPERIOR STRENGTH.
DOOM DOES NOT BLUFF!!!

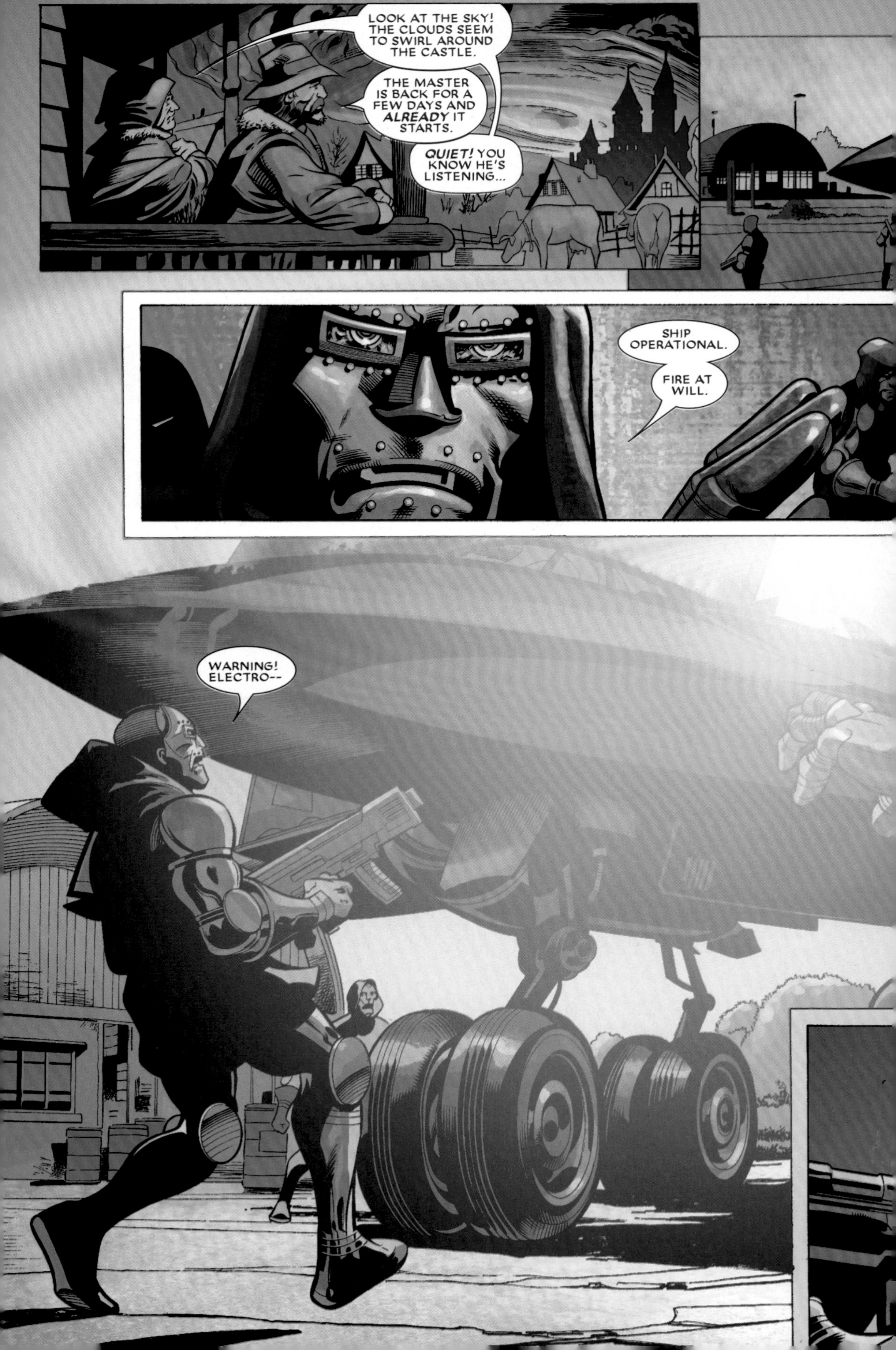
LOOK AT THE SKY! THE CLOUDS SEEM TO SWIRL AROUND THE CASTLE.
THE MASTER IS BACK FOR A FEW DAYS AND ALREADY IT STARTS.
QUIET! YOU KNOW HE'S LISTENING...
SHIP OPERATIONAL.
FIRE AT WILL.
WARNING! ELECTRO--

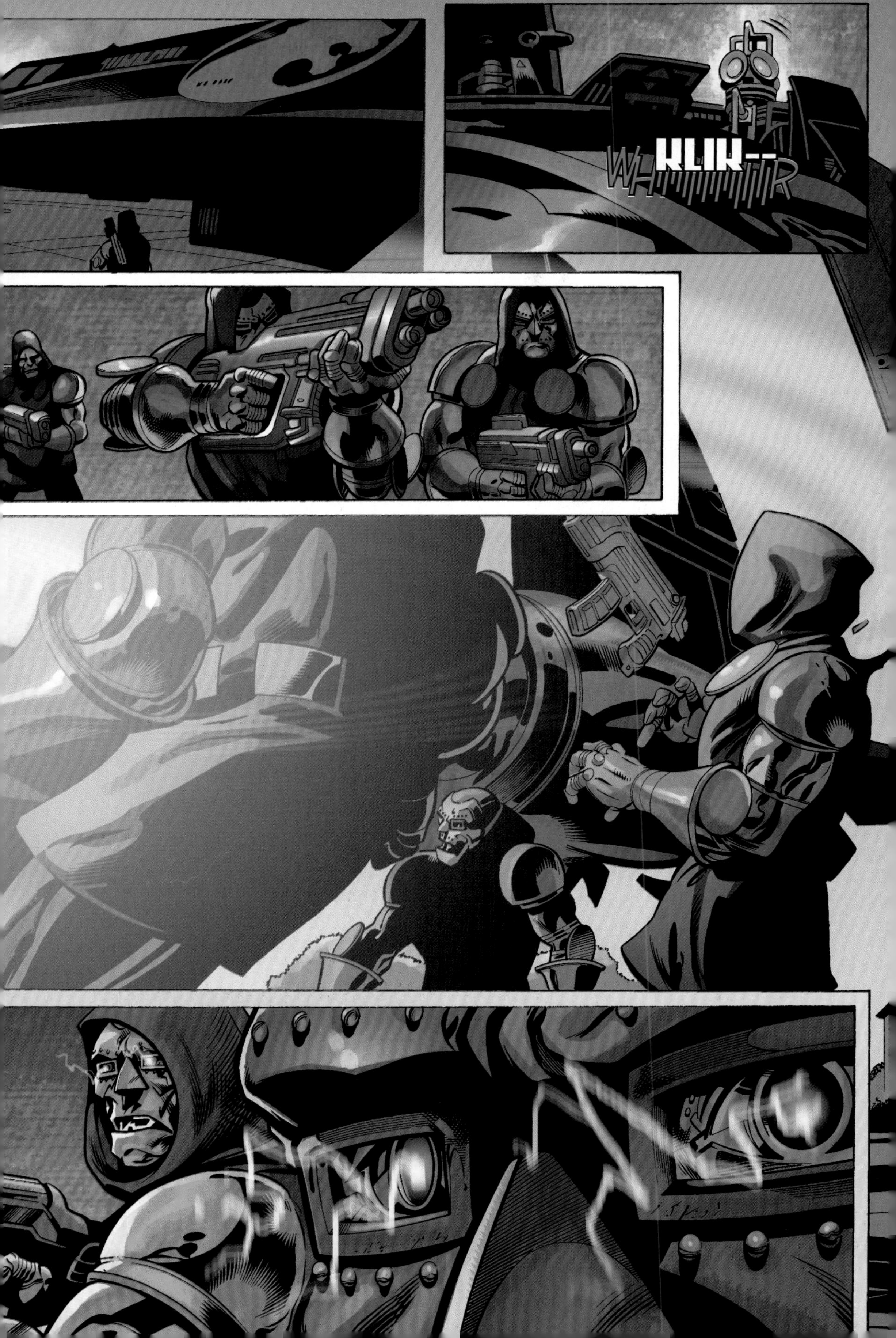
KLIK--

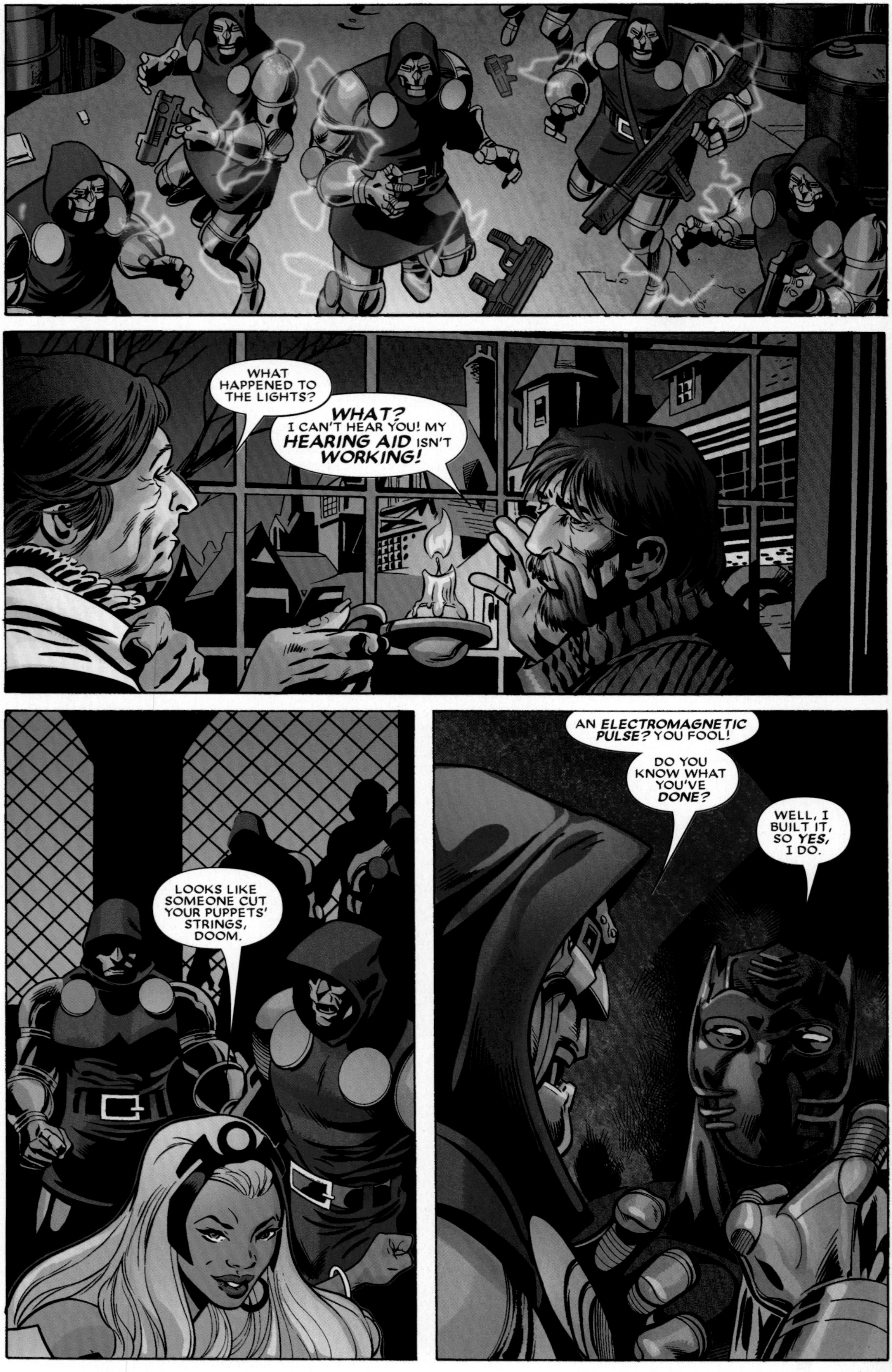
WHAT HAPPENED TO THE LIGHTS?
WHAT? I CAN'T HEAR YOU! MY HEARING AID ISN'T WORKING!
LOOKS LIKE SOMEONE CUT YOUR PUPPETS' STRINGS, DOOM.
AN ELECTROMAGNETIC PULSE? YOU FOOL!
DO YOU KNOW WHAT YOU'VE DONE?
WELL, I BUILT IT, SO YES, I DO.

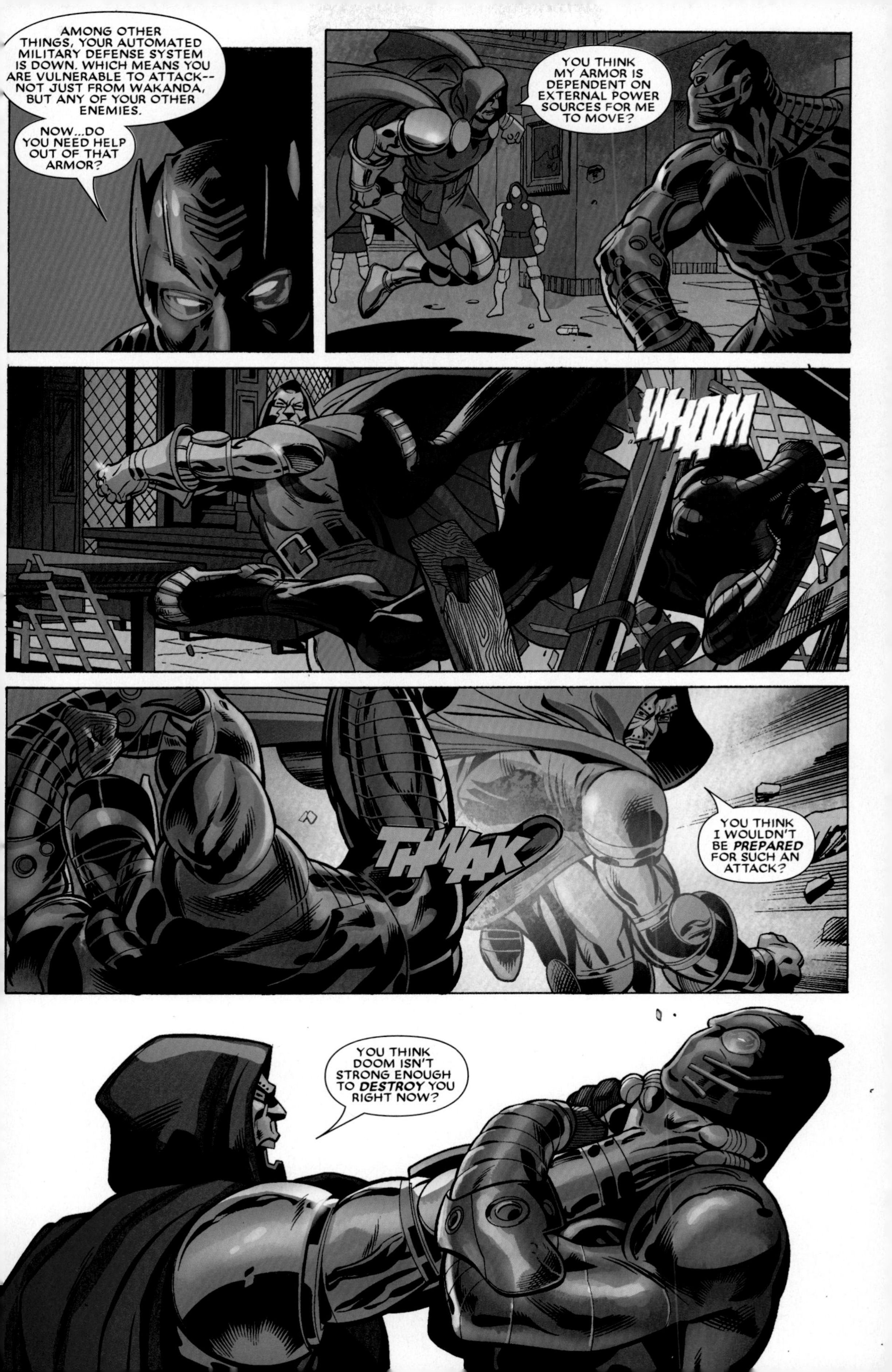

AMONG OTHER THINGS, YOUR AUTOMATED MILITARY DEFENSE SYSTEM IS DOWN. WHICH MEANS YOU ARE VULNERABLE TO ATTACK-- NOT JUST FROM WAKANDA, BUT ANY OF YOUR OTHER ENEMIES.
NOW...DO YOU NEED HELP OUT OF THAT ARMOR?
YOU THINK MY ARMOR IS DEPENDENT ON EXTERNAL POWER SOURCES FOR ME TO MOVE?
WHAM
THWAK
YOU THINK I WOULDN'T BE PREPARED FOR SUCH AN ATTACK?
YOU THINK DOOM ISN'T STRONG ENOUGH TO DESTROY YOU RIGHT NOW?

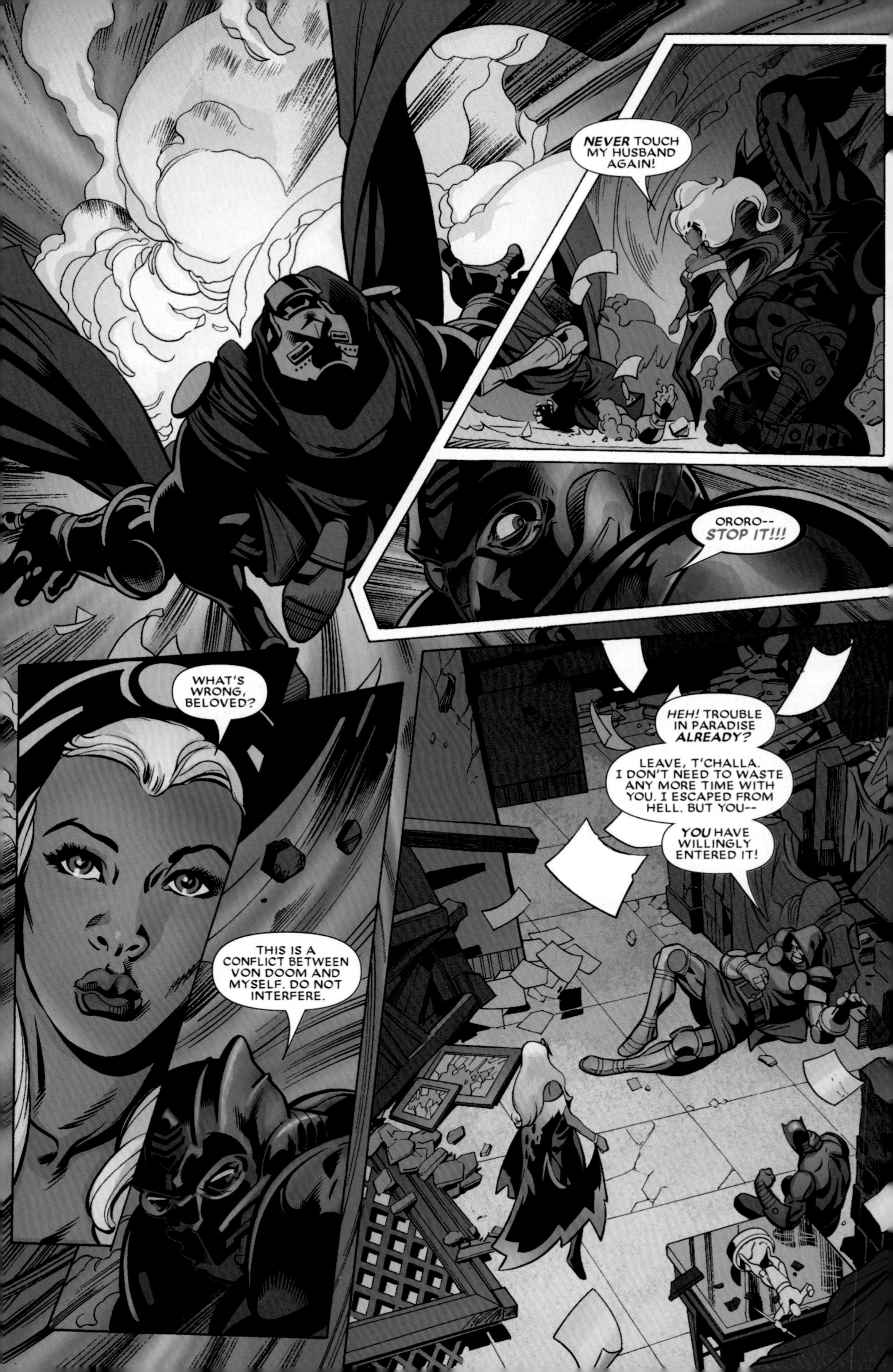

NEVER TOUCH MY HUSBAND AGAIN!
ORORO-- STOP IT!!!
WHAT'S WRONG, BELOVED?
THIS IS A CONFLICT BETWEEN VON DOOM AND MYSELF. DO NOT INTERFERE.
HEH! TROUBLE IN PARADISE ALREADY?
LEAVE, T'CHALLA. I DON'T NEED TO WASTE ANY MORE TIME WITH YOU. I ESCAPED FROM HELL. BUT YOU--
YOU HAVE WILLINGLY ENTERED IT!

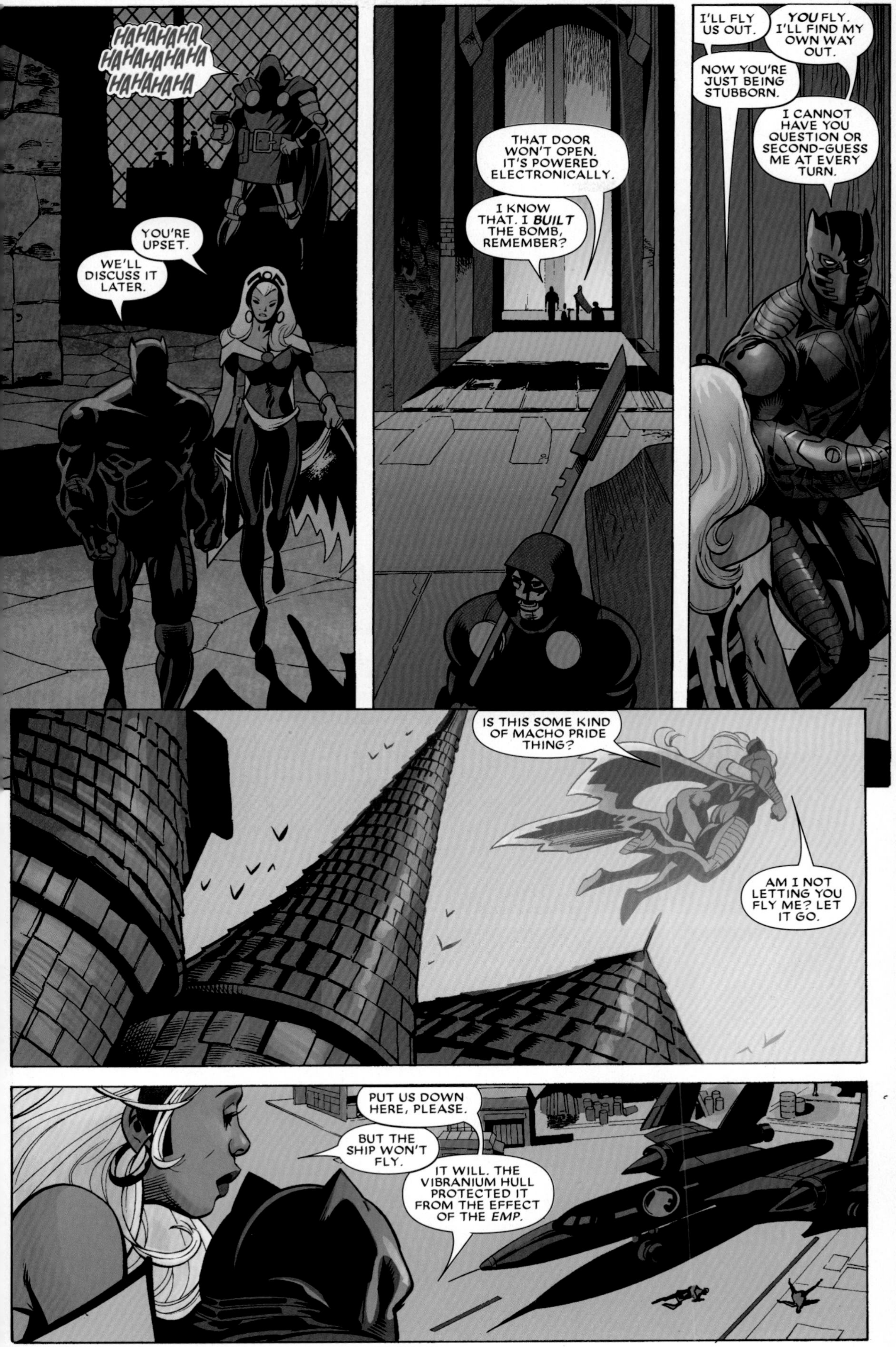
HAHAHAHA HAHAHAHAHA HAHAHAHA
YOU'RE UPSET.
WE'LL DISCUSS IT LATER.
THAT DOOR WON'T OPEN. IT'S POWERED ELECTRONICALLY.
I KNOW THAT. I BUILT THE BOMB, REMEMBER?
I'LL FLY US OUT.
YOU FLY. I'LL FIND MY OWN WAY OUT.
NOW YOU'RE JUST BEING STUBBORN.
I CANNOT HAVE YOU QUESTION OR SECOND-GUESS ME AT EVERY TURN.
IS THIS SOME KIND OF MACHO PRIDE THING?
AM I NOT LETTING YOU FLY ME? LET IT GO.
PUT US DOWN HERE, PLEASE.
BUT THE SHIP WON'T FLY.
IT WILL. THE VIBRANIUM HULL PROTECTED IT FROM THE EFFECT OF THE EMP.

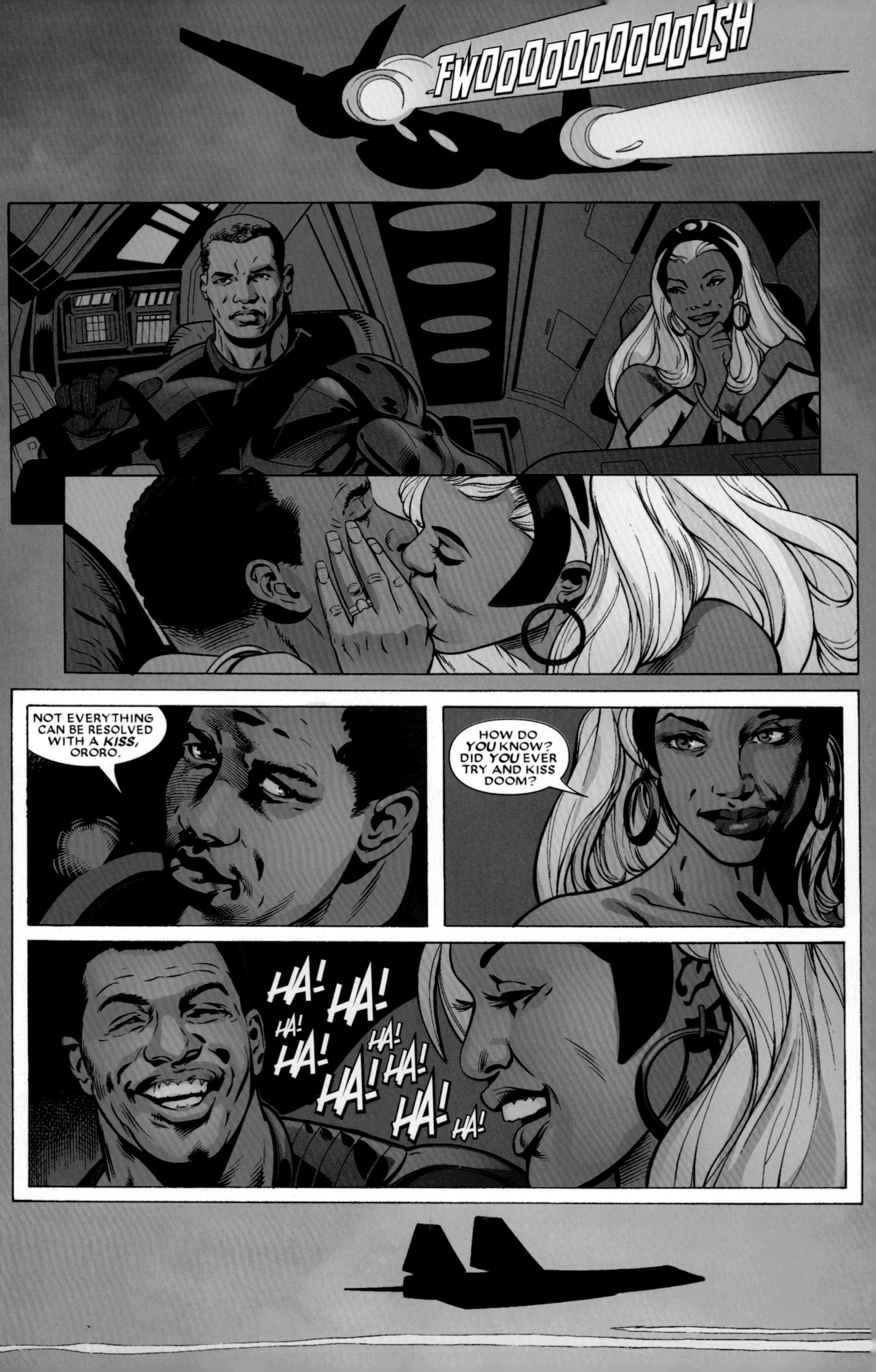
FWOOOOOOOOOOOOSH
NOT EVERYTHING CAN BE RESOLVED WITH A KISS, ORORO.
HOW DO YOU KNOW? DID YOU EVER TRY AND KISS DOOM?
HA! HA! HA! HA! HA! HA! HA! HA! HA!

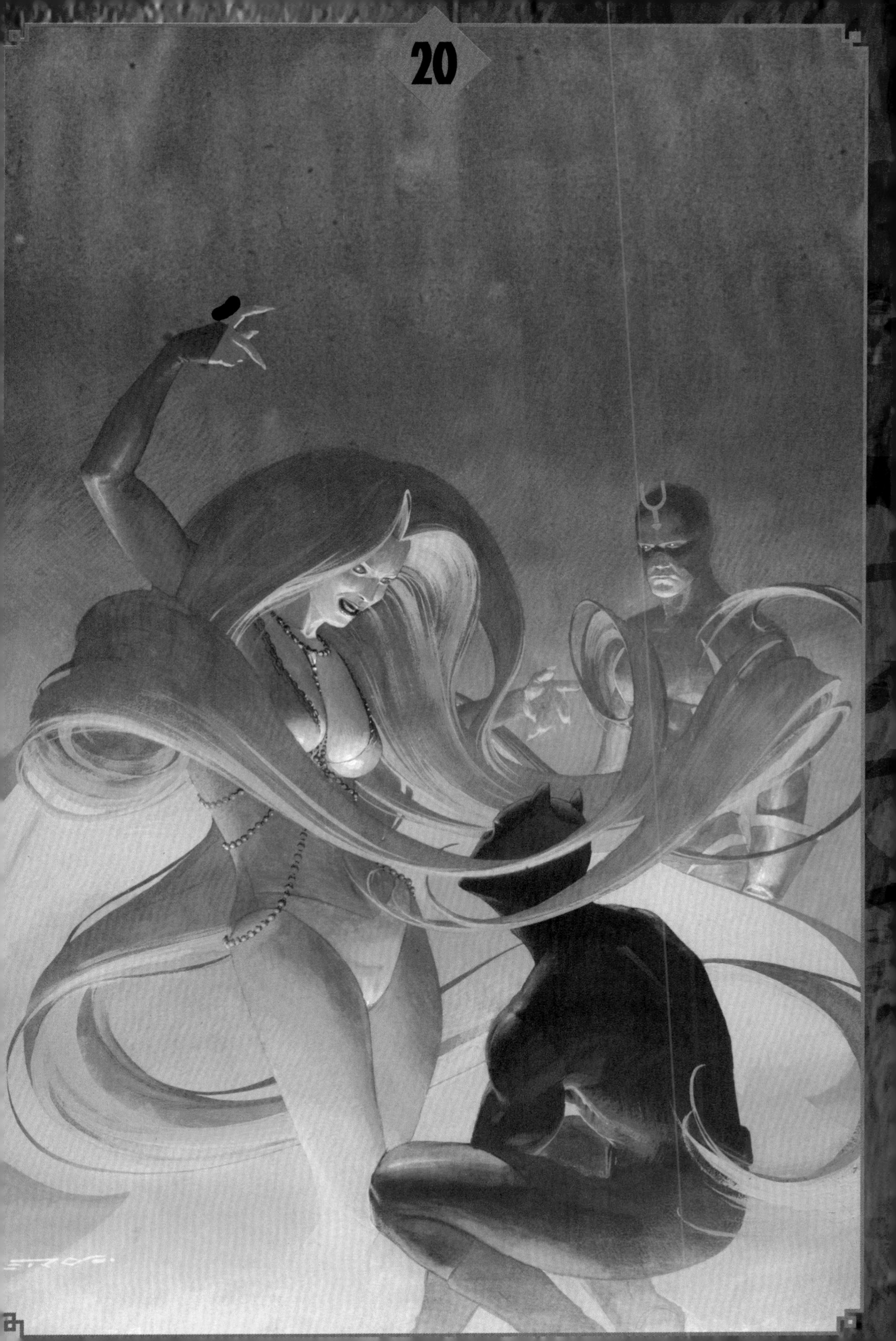
20

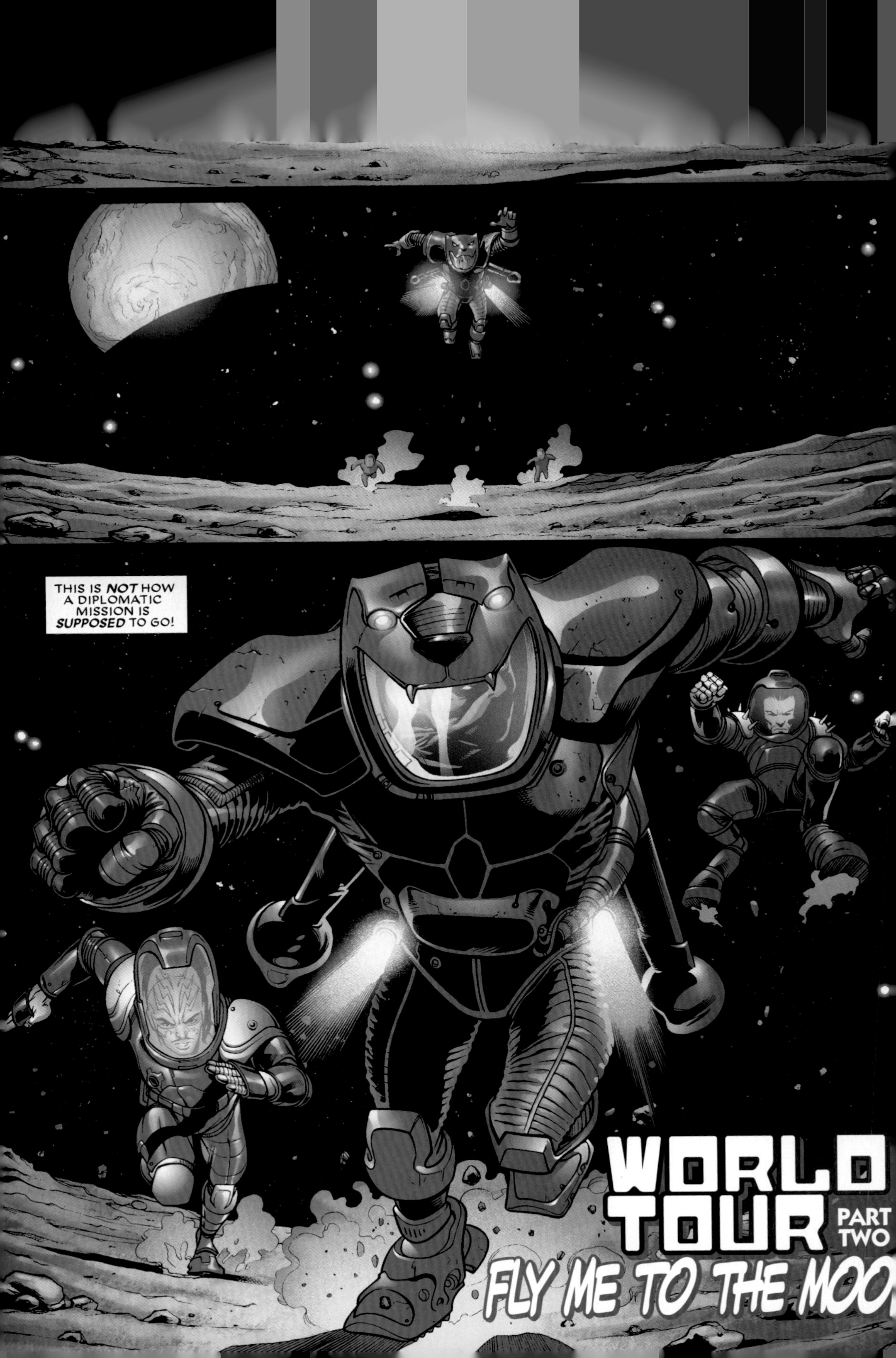
THIS IS NOT HOW A DIPLOMATIC MISSION IS SUPPOSED TO GO!
WORLD TOUR PART TWO
FLY ME TO THE MOO

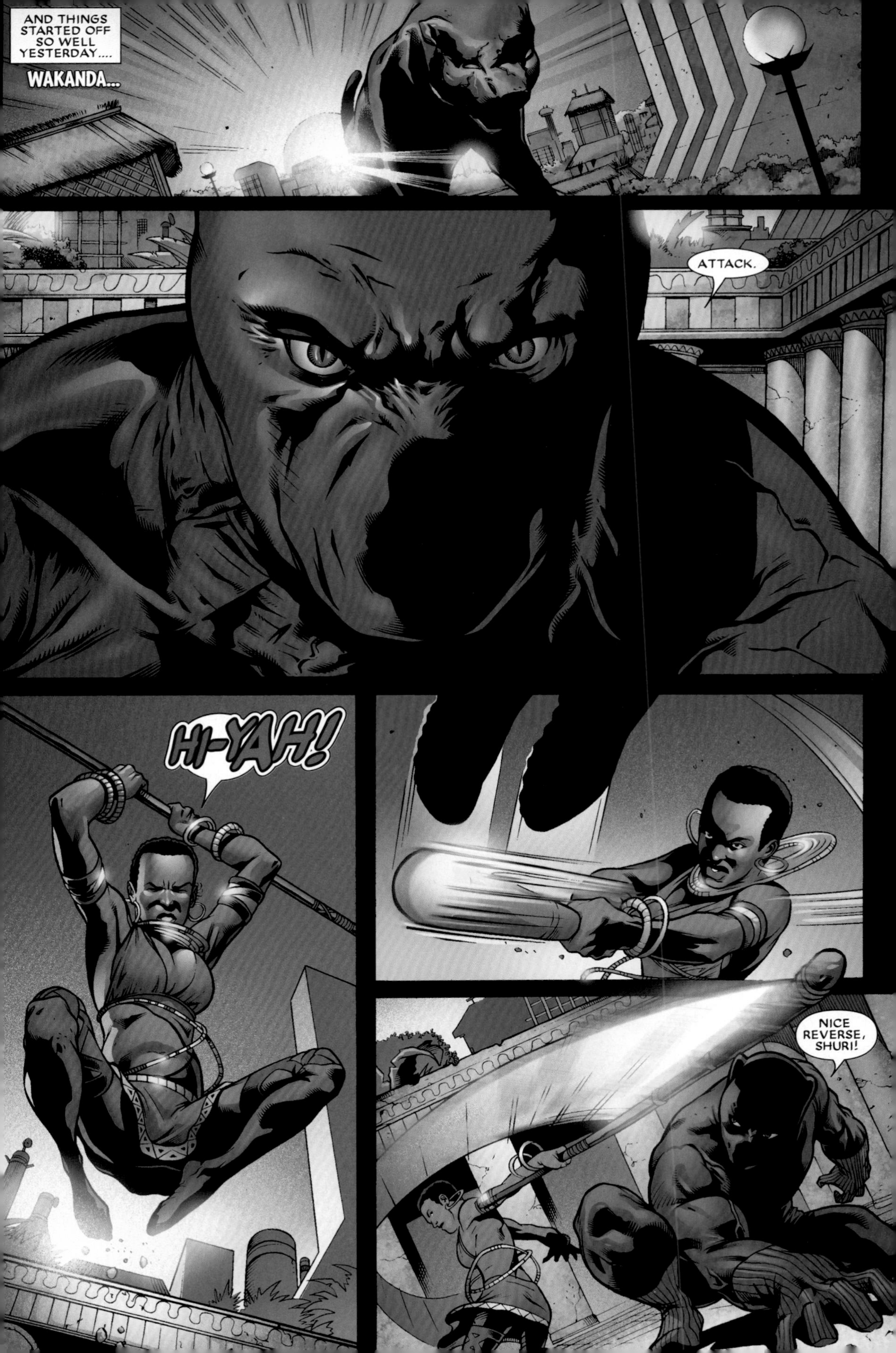
AND THINGS STARTED OFF SO WELL YESTERDAY....
WAKANDA...
ATTACK.
HI-YAH!
NICE REVERSE, SHURI!

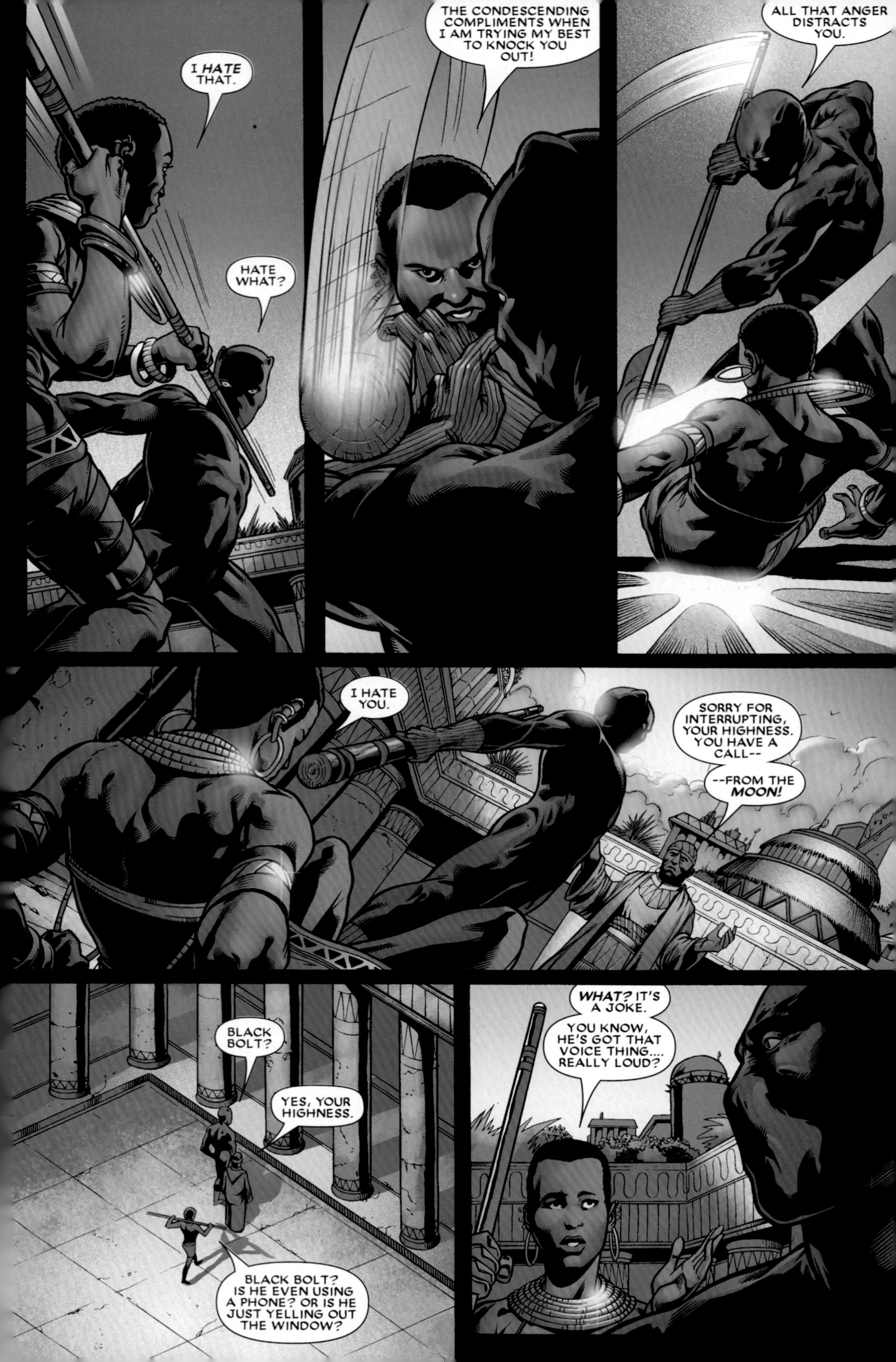
I HATE THAT.
HATE WHAT?
THE CONDESCENDING COMPLIMENTS WHEN I AM TRYING MY BEST TO KNOCK YOU OUT!
ALL THAT ANGER DISTRACTS YOU.
I HATE YOU.
SORRY FOR INTERRUPTING, YOUR HIGHNESS. YOU HAVE A CALL--
--FROM THE MOON!
BLACK BOLT?
YES, YOUR HIGHNESS.
BLACK BOLT? IS HE EVEN USING A PHONE? OR IS HE JUST YELLING OUT THE WINDOW?
WHAT? IT'S A JOKE.
YOU KNOW, HE'S GOT THAT VOICE THING.... REALLY LOUD?

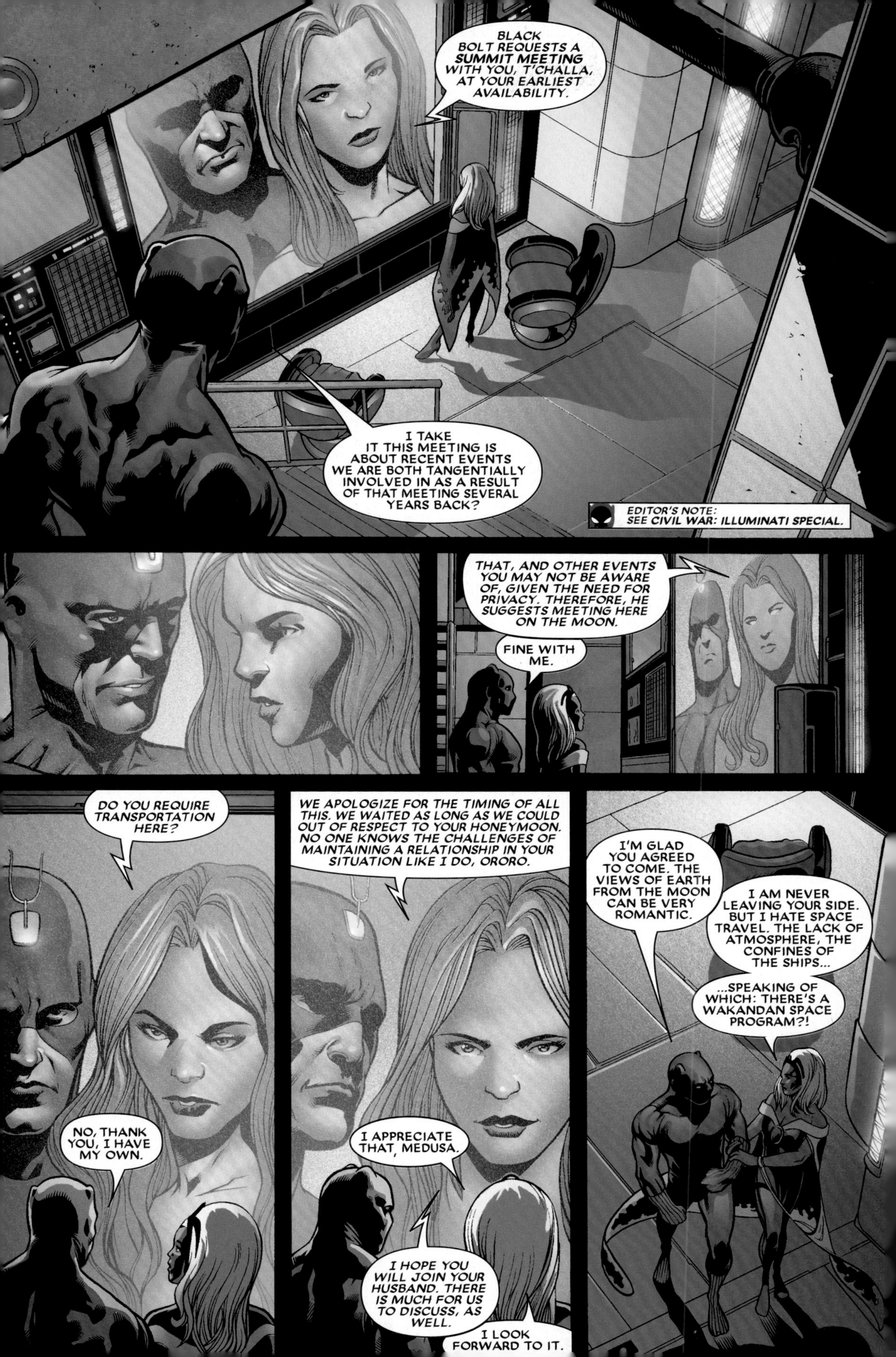
BLACK BOLT REQUESTS A SUMMIT MEETING WITH YOU, T'CHALLA, AT YOUR EARLIEST AVAILABILITY.
I TAKE IT THIS MEETING IS ABOUT RECENT EVENTS WE ARE BOTH TANGENTIALLY INVOLVED IN AS A RESULT OF THAT MEETING SEVERAL YEARS BACK?
EDITOR'S NOTE: SEE CIVIL WAR: ILLUMINATI SPECIAL.
THAT, AND OTHER EVENTS YOU MAY NOT BE AWARE OF, GIVEN THE NEED FOR PRIVACY. THEREFORE, HE SUGGESTS MEETING HERE ON THE MOON.
FINE WITH ME.
DO YOU REQUIRE TRANSPORTATION HERE?
NO, THANK YOU, I HAVE MY OWN.
WE APOLOGIZE FOR THE TIMING OF ALL THIS. WE WAITED AS LONG AS WE COULD OUT OF RESPECT TO YOUR HONEYMOON. NO ONE KNOWS THE CHALLENGES OF MAINTAINING A RELATIONSHIP IN YOUR SITUATION LIKE I DO, ORORO.
I APPRECIATE THAT, MEDUSA.
I HOPE YOU WILL JOIN YOUR HUSBAND. THERE IS MUCH FOR US TO DISCUSS, AS WELL.
I LOOK FORWARD TO IT.
I'M GLAD YOU AGREED TO COME. THE VIEWS OF EARTH FROM THE MOON CAN BE VERY ROMANTIC.
I AM NEVER LEAVING YOUR SIDE. BUT I HATE SPACE TRAVEL. THE LACK OF ATMOSPHERE, THE CONFINES OF THE SHIPS...
...SPEAKING OF WHICH: THERE'S A WAKANDAN SPACE PROGRAM?!

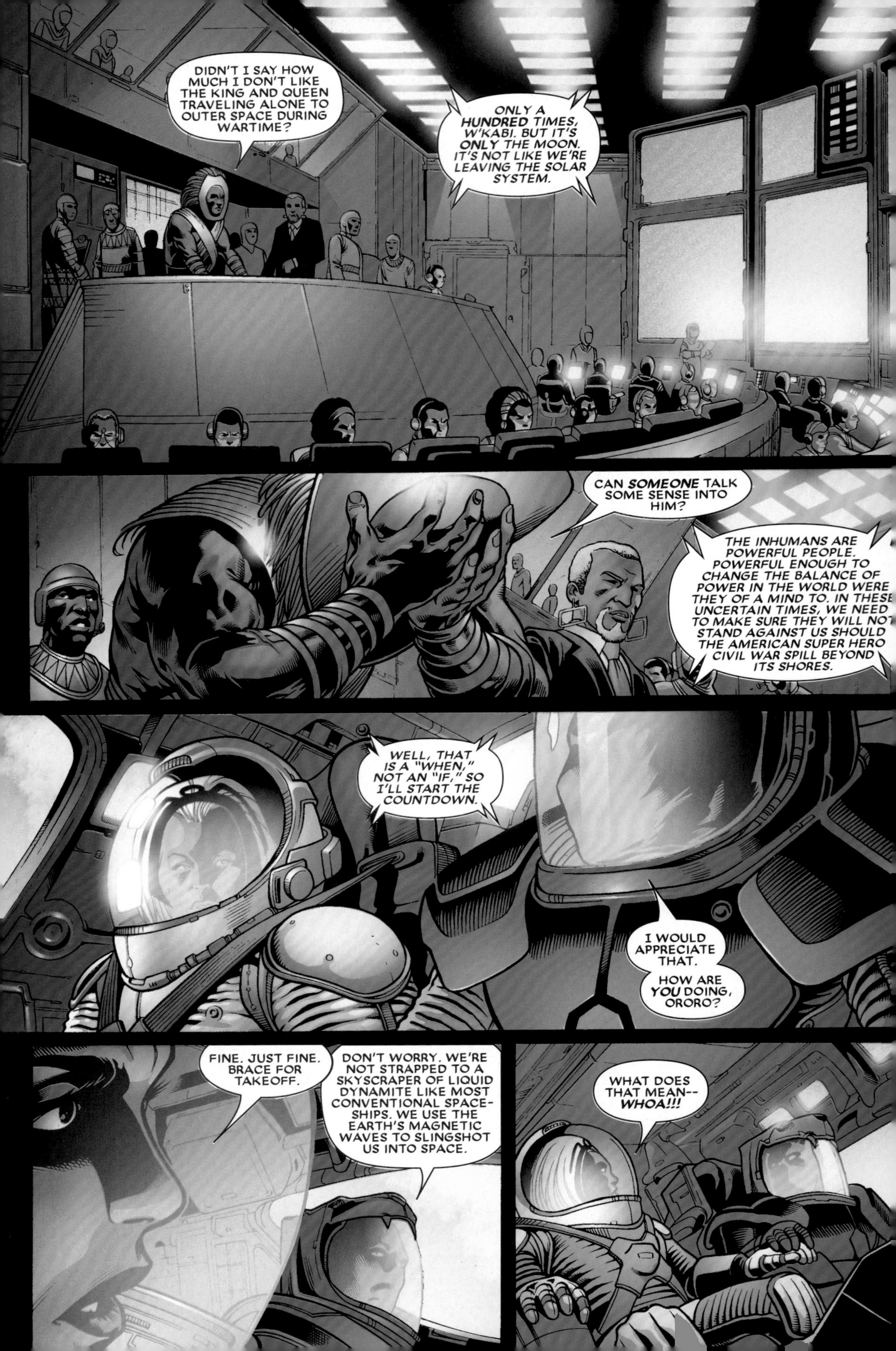
DIDN'T I SAY HOW MUCH I DON'T LIKE THE KING AND QUEEN TRAVELING ALONE TO OUTER SPACE DURING WARTIME?
ONLY A HUNDRED TIMES, W'KABI. BUT IT'S ONLY THE MOON. IT'S NOT LIKE WE'RE LEAVING THE SOLAR SYSTEM.
CAN SOMEONE TALK SOME SENSE INTO HIM?
THE INHUMANS ARE POWERFUL PEOPLE. POWERFUL ENOUGH TO CHANGE THE BALANCE OF POWER IN THE WORLD WERE THEY OF A MIND TO. IN THESE UNCERTAIN TIMES, WE NEED TO MAKE SURE THEY WILL NOT STAND AGAINST US SHOULD THE AMERICAN SUPER HERO CIVIL WAR SPILL BEYOND ITS SHORES.
WELL, THAT IS A "WHEN," NOT AN "IF," SO I'LL START THE COUNTDOWN.
I WOULD APPRECIATE THAT.
HOW ARE YOU DOING, ORORO?
FINE. JUST FINE. BRACE FOR TAKEOFF.
DON'T WORRY. WE'RE NOT STRAPPED TO A SKYSCRAPER OF LIQUID DYNAMITE LIKE MOST CONVENTIONAL SPACE-SHIPS. WE USE THE EARTH'S MAGNETIC WAVES TO SLINGSHOT US INTO SPACE.
WHAT DOES THAT MEAN-- WHOA!!!

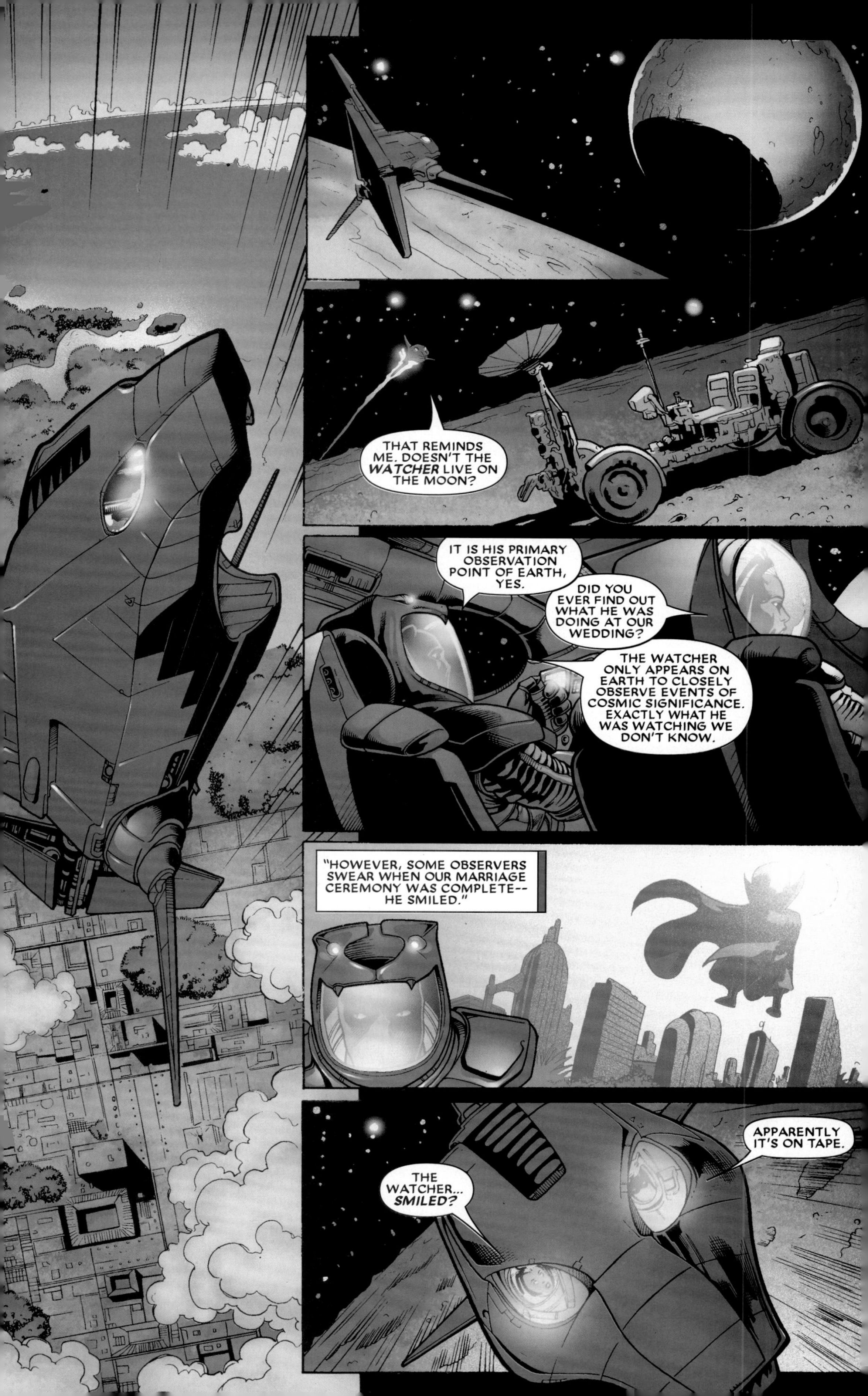
THAT REMINDS ME. DOESN'T THE *WATCHER* LIVE ON THE MOON?
IT IS HIS PRIMARY OBSERVATION POINT OF EARTH, YES.
DID YOU EVER FIND OUT WHAT HE WAS DOING AT OUR WEDDING?
THE WATCHER ONLY APPEARS ON EARTH TO CLOSELY OBSERVE EVENTS OF COSMIC SIGNIFICANCE. EXACTLY WHAT HE WAS WATCHING WE DON'T KNOW.
"HOWEVER, SOME OBSERVERS SWEAR WHEN OUR MARRIAGE CEREMONY WAS COMPLETE--HE SMILED."
APPARENTLY IT'S ON TAPE.
THE WATCHER... *SMILED?*

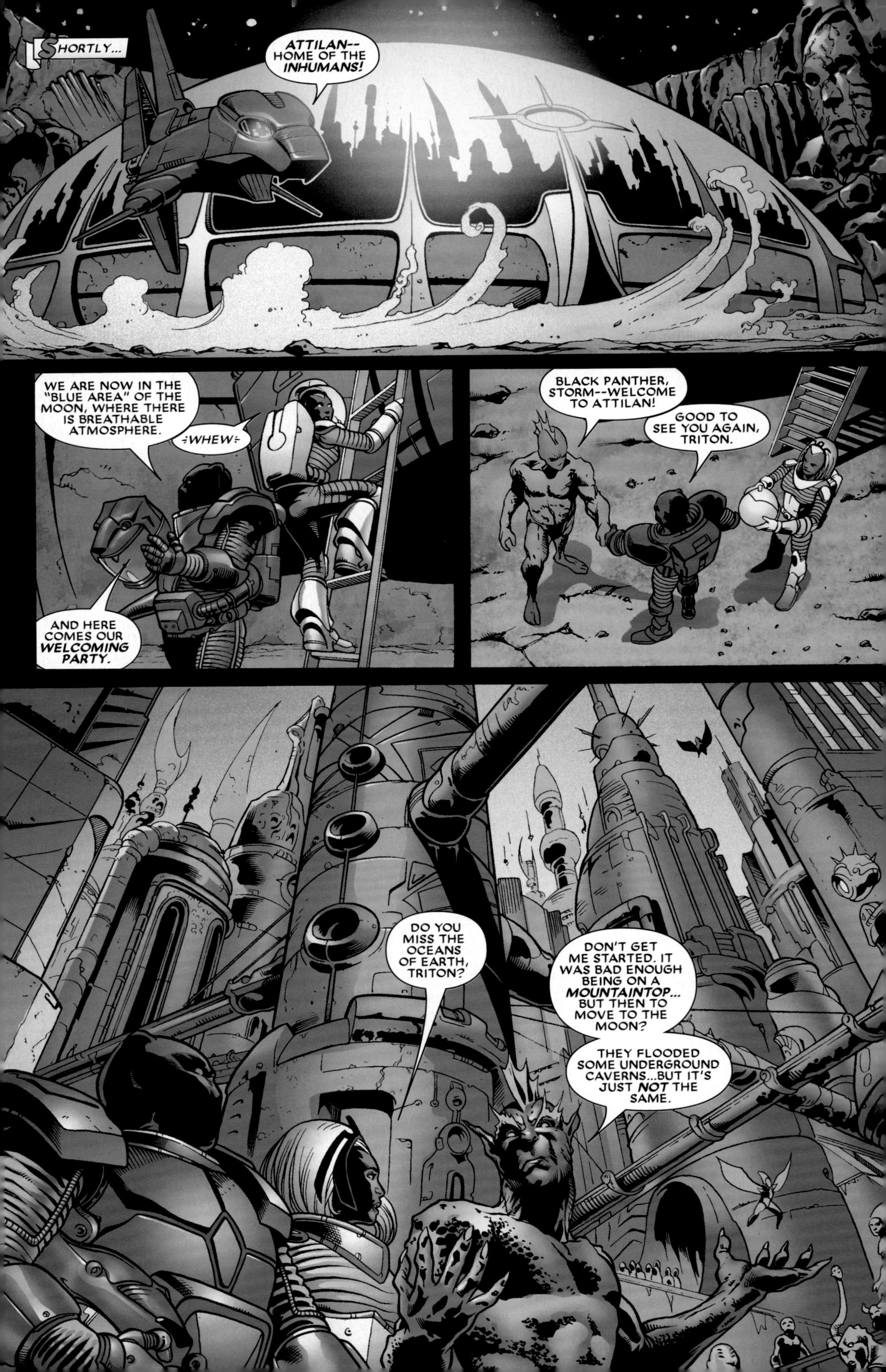
SHORTLY...
ATTILAN-- HOME OF THE INHUMANS!
WE ARE NOW IN THE "BLUE AREA" OF THE MOON, WHERE THERE IS BREATHABLE ATMOSPHERE.
WHEW
AND HERE COMES OUR WELCOMING PARTY.
BLACK PANTHER, STORM--WELCOME TO ATTILAN!
GOOD TO SEE YOU AGAIN, TRITON.
DO YOU MISS THE OCEANS OF EARTH, TRITON?
DON'T GET ME STARTED. IT WAS BAD ENOUGH BEING ON A MOUNTAINTOP... BUT THEN TO MOVE TO THE MOON?
THEY FLOODED SOME UNDERGROUND CAVERNS...BUT IT'S JUST NOT THE SAME.

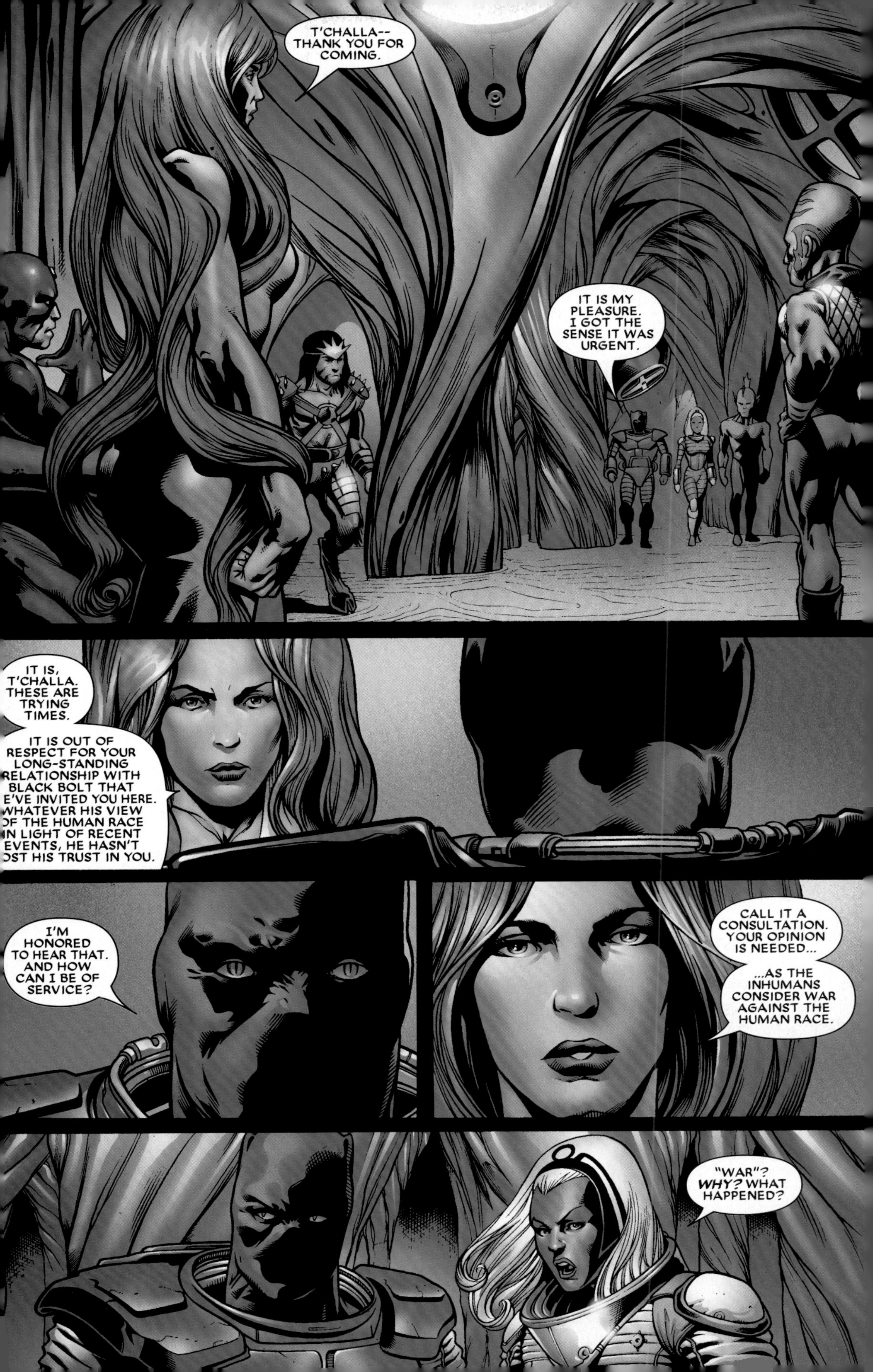

T'CHALLA--
THANK YOU FOR COMING.
IT IS MY PLEASURE. I GOT THE SENSE IT WAS URGENT.
IT IS, T'CHALLA. THESE ARE TRYING TIMES.
IT IS OUT OF RESPECT FOR YOUR LONG-STANDING RELATIONSHIP WITH BLACK BOLT THAT E'VE INVITED YOU HERE. WHATEVER HIS VIEW OF THE HUMAN RACE IN LIGHT OF RECENT EVENTS, HE HASN'T OST HIS TRUST IN YOU.
I'M HONORED TO HEAR THAT. AND HOW CAN I BE OF SERVICE?
CALL IT A CONSULTATION. YOUR OPINION IS NEEDED...
...AS THE INHUMANS CONSIDER WAR AGAINST THE HUMAN RACE.
"WAR"? WHY? WHAT HAPPENED?

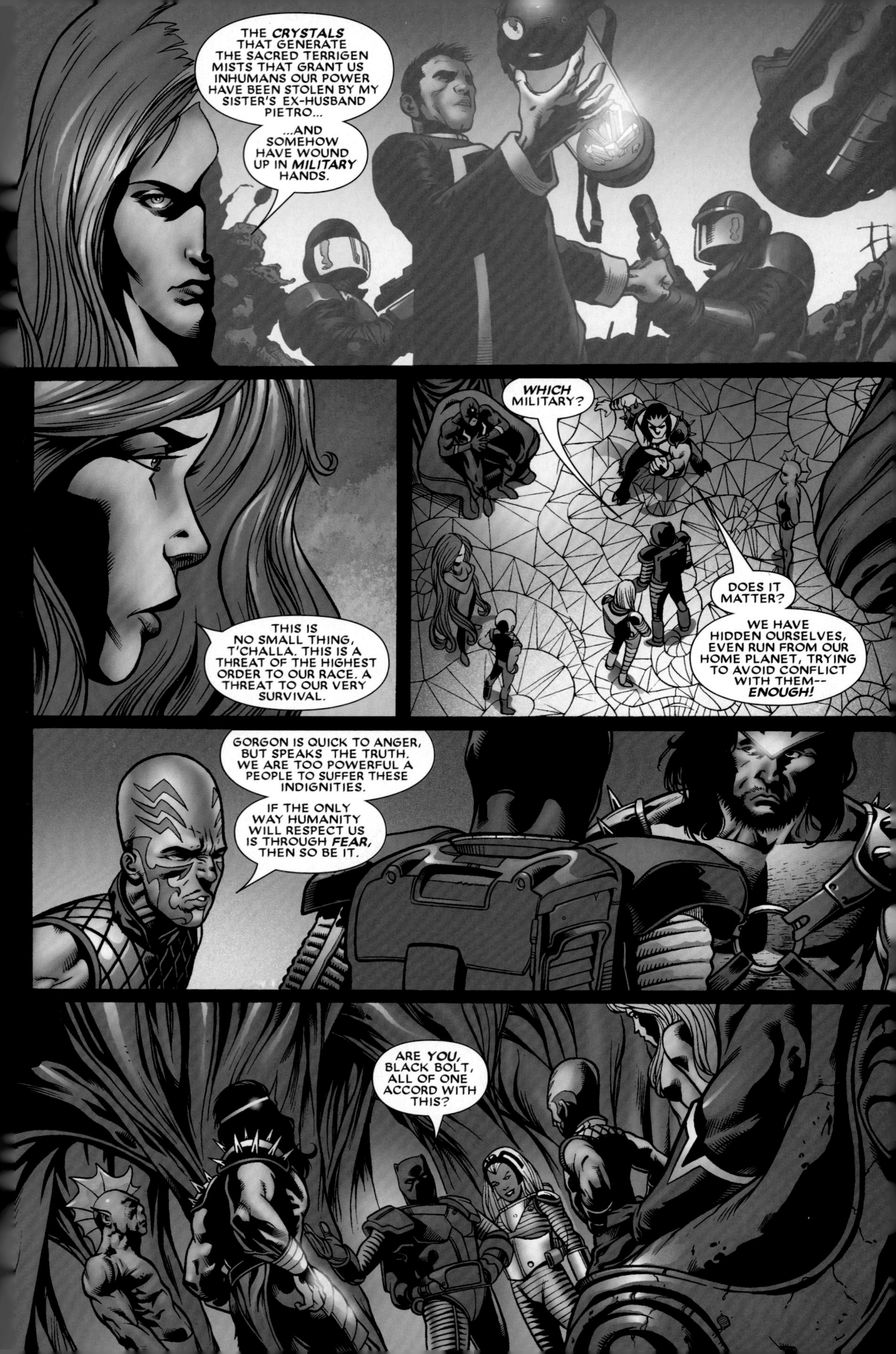
THE CRYSTALS THAT GENERATE THE SACRED TERRIGEN MISTS THAT GRANT US INHUMANS OUR POWER HAVE BEEN STOLEN BY MY SISTER'S EX-HUSBAND PIETRO...
...AND SOMEHOW HAVE WOUND UP IN MILITARY HANDS.
THIS IS NO SMALL THING, T'CHALLA. THIS IS A THREAT OF THE HIGHEST ORDER TO OUR RACE. A THREAT TO OUR VERY SURVIVAL.
WHICH MILITARY?
DOES IT MATTER?
WE HAVE HIDDEN OURSELVES, EVEN RUN FROM OUR HOME PLANET, TRYING TO AVOID CONFLICT WITH THEM-- ENOUGH!
GORGON IS QUICK TO ANGER, BUT SPEAKS THE TRUTH. WE ARE TOO POWERFUL A PEOPLE TO SUFFER THESE INDIGNITIES.
IF THE ONLY WAY HUMANITY WILL RESPECT US IS THROUGH FEAR, THEN SO BE IT.
ARE YOU, BLACK BOLT, ALL OF ONE ACCORD WITH THIS?

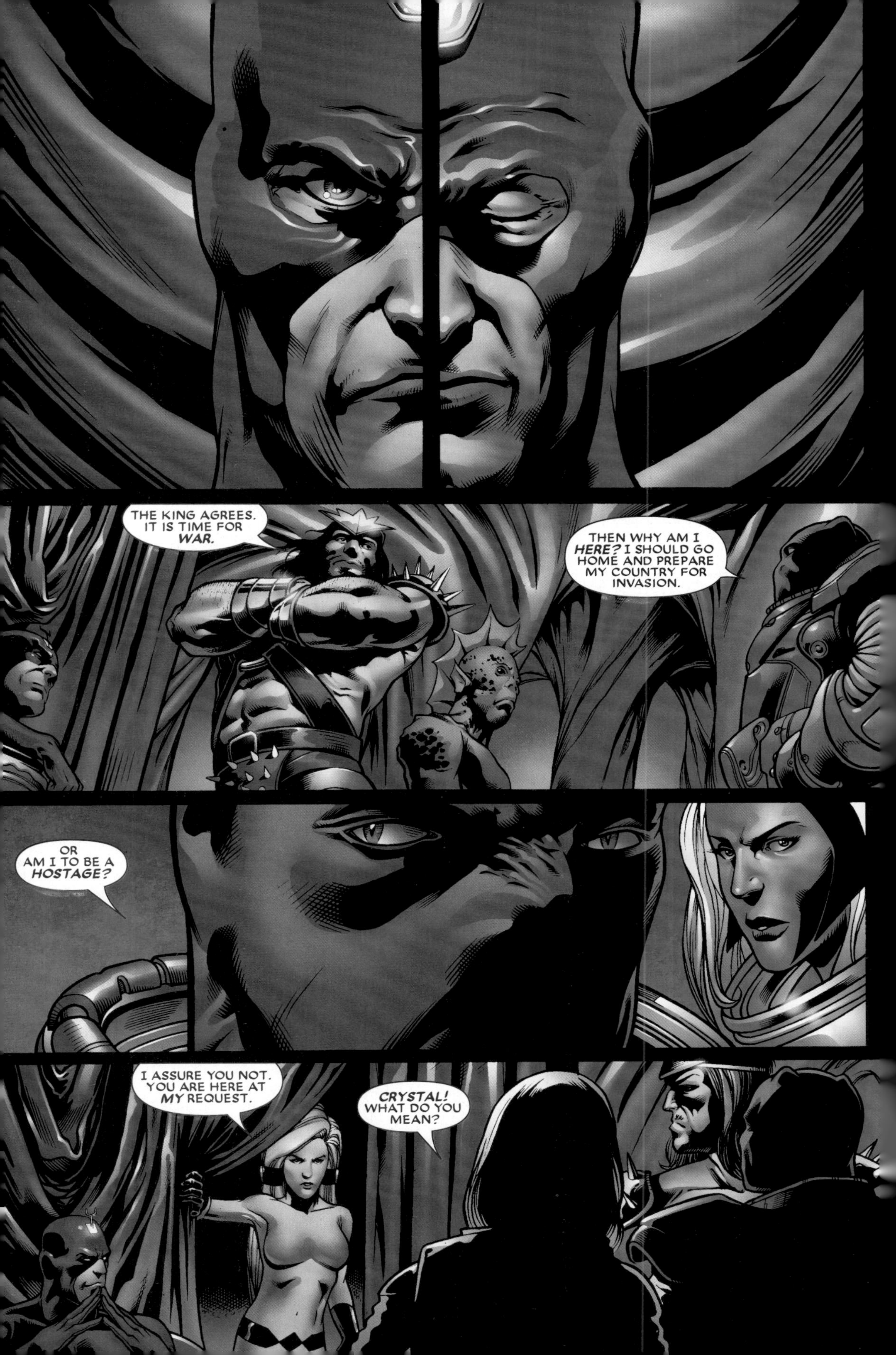
THE KING AGREES. IT IS TIME FOR WAR.
THEN WHY AM I HERE? I SHOULD GO HOME AND PREPARE MY COUNTRY FOR INVASION.
OR AM I TO BE A HOSTAGE?
I ASSURE YOU NOT. YOU ARE HERE AT MY REQUEST.
CRYSTAL! WHAT DO YOU MEAN?

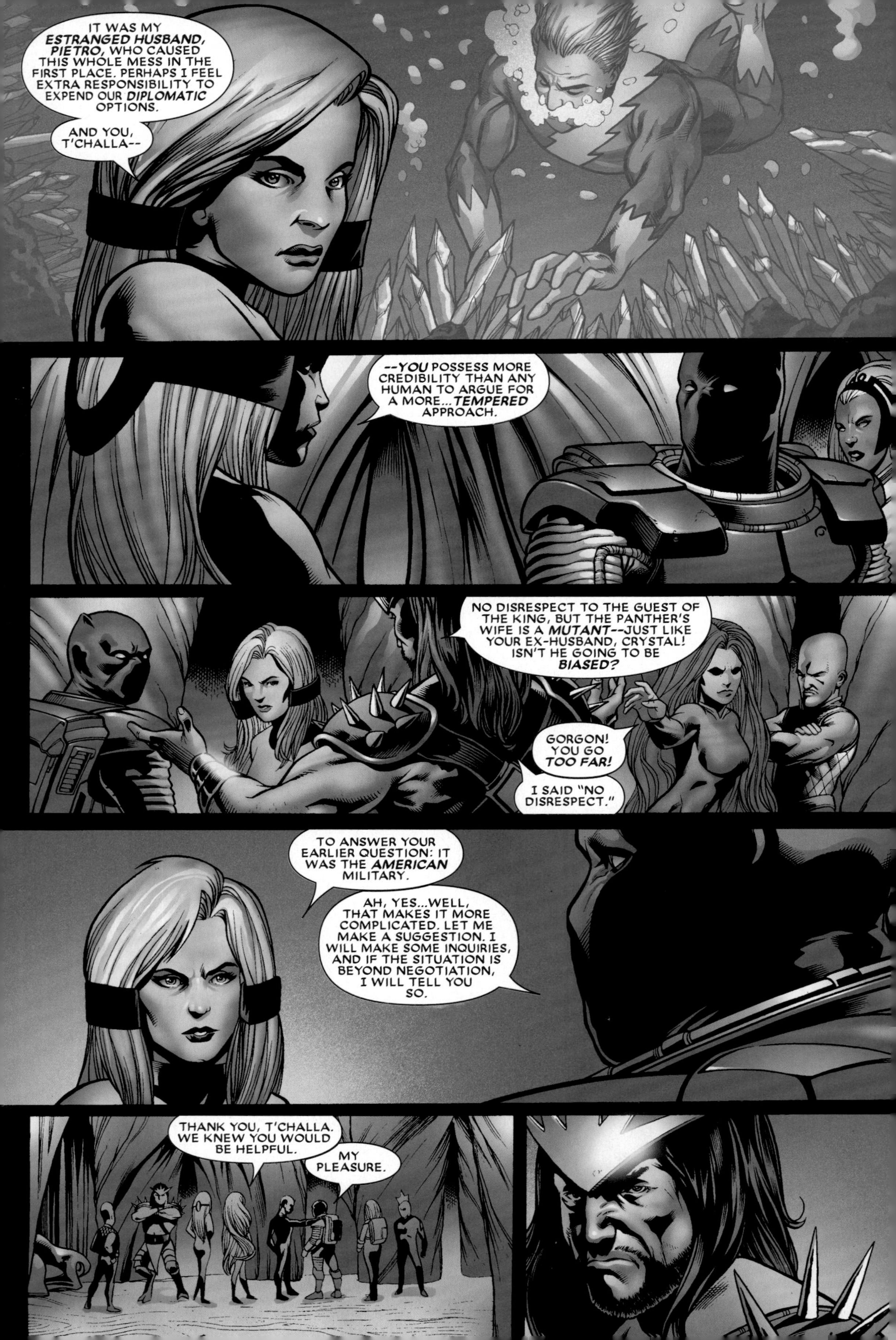
IT WAS MY ESTRANGED HUSBAND, PIETRO, WHO CAUSED THIS WHOLE MESS IN THE FIRST PLACE. PERHAPS I FEEL EXTRA RESPONSIBILITY TO EXPEND OUR DIPLOMATIC OPTIONS.
AND YOU, T'CHALLA--
--YOU POSSESS MORE CREDIBILITY THAN ANY HUMAN TO ARGUE FOR A MORE...TEMPERED APPROACH.
NO DISRESPECT TO THE GUEST OF THE KING, BUT THE PANTHER'S WIFE IS A MUTANT--JUST LIKE YOUR EX-HUSBAND, CRYSTAL! ISN'T HE GOING TO BE BIASED?
GORGON! YOU GO TOO FAR!
I SAID "NO DISRESPECT."
TO ANSWER YOUR EARLIER QUESTION: IT WAS THE AMERICAN MILITARY.
AH, YES...WELL, THAT MAKES IT MORE COMPLICATED. LET ME MAKE A SUGGESTION. I WILL MAKE SOME INQUIRIES, AND IF THE SITUATION IS BEYOND NEGOTIATION, I WILL TELL YOU SO.
THANK YOU, T'CHALLA. WE KNEW YOU WOULD BE HELPFUL.
MY PLEASURE.

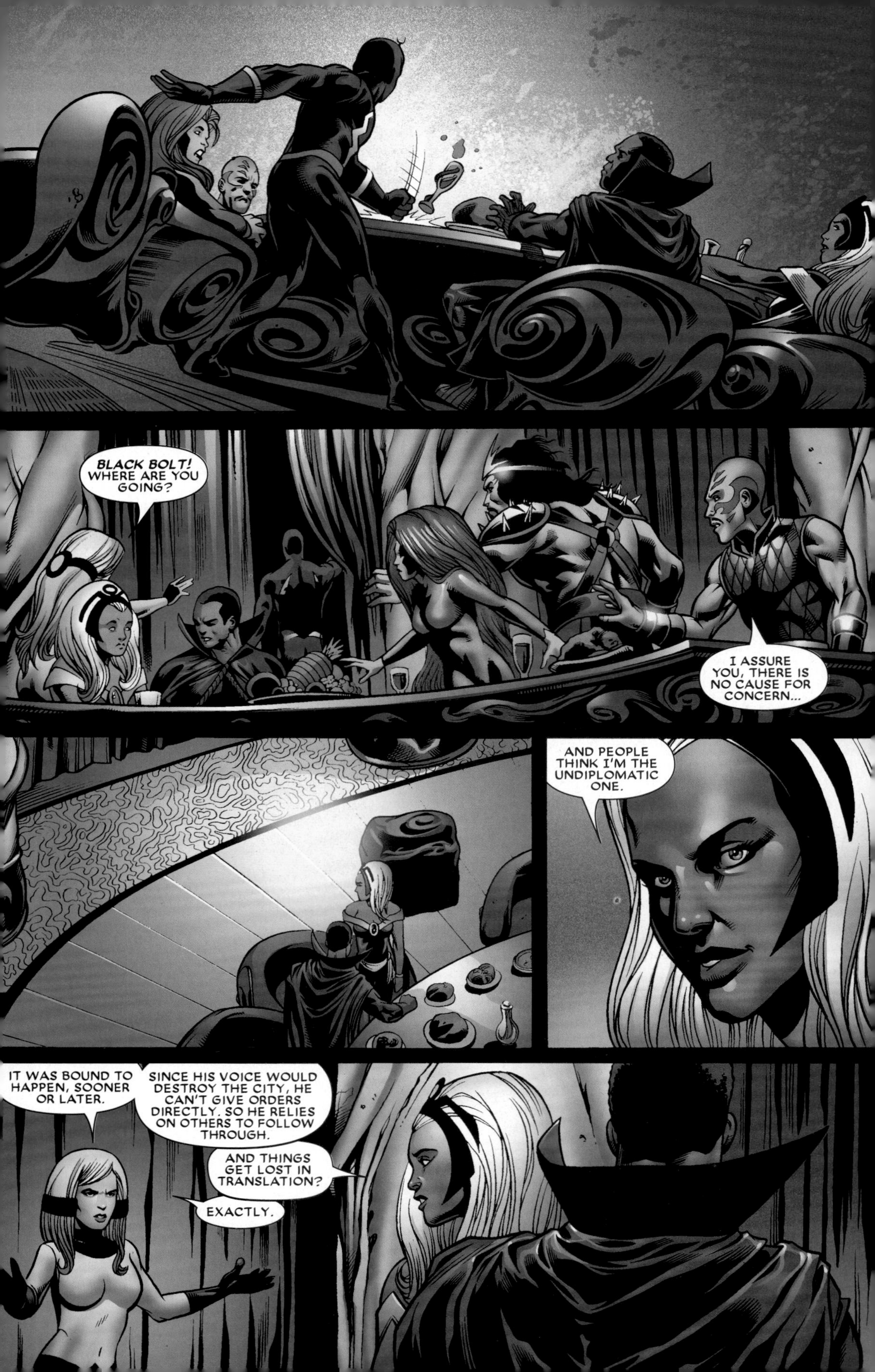
BLACK BOLT! WHERE ARE YOU GOING?
I ASSURE YOU, THERE IS NO CAUSE FOR CONCERN...
AND PEOPLE THINK I'M THE UNDIPLOMATIC ONE.
IT WAS BOUND TO HAPPEN, SOONER OR LATER.
SINCE HIS VOICE WOULD DESTROY THE CITY, HE CAN'T GIVE ORDERS DIRECTLY. SO HE RELIES ON OTHERS TO FOLLOW THROUGH.
AND THINGS GET LOST IN TRANSLATION?
EXACTLY.

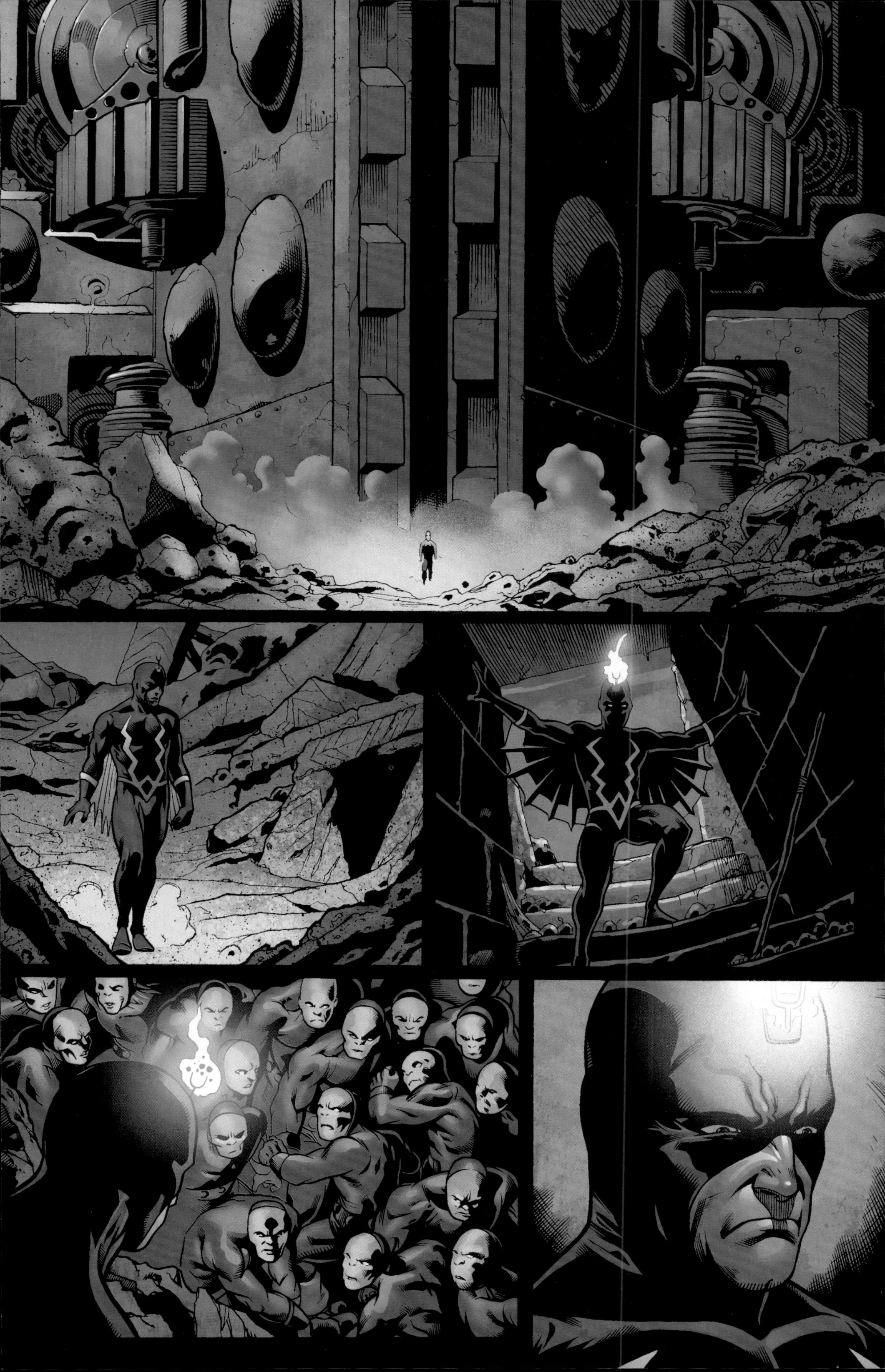

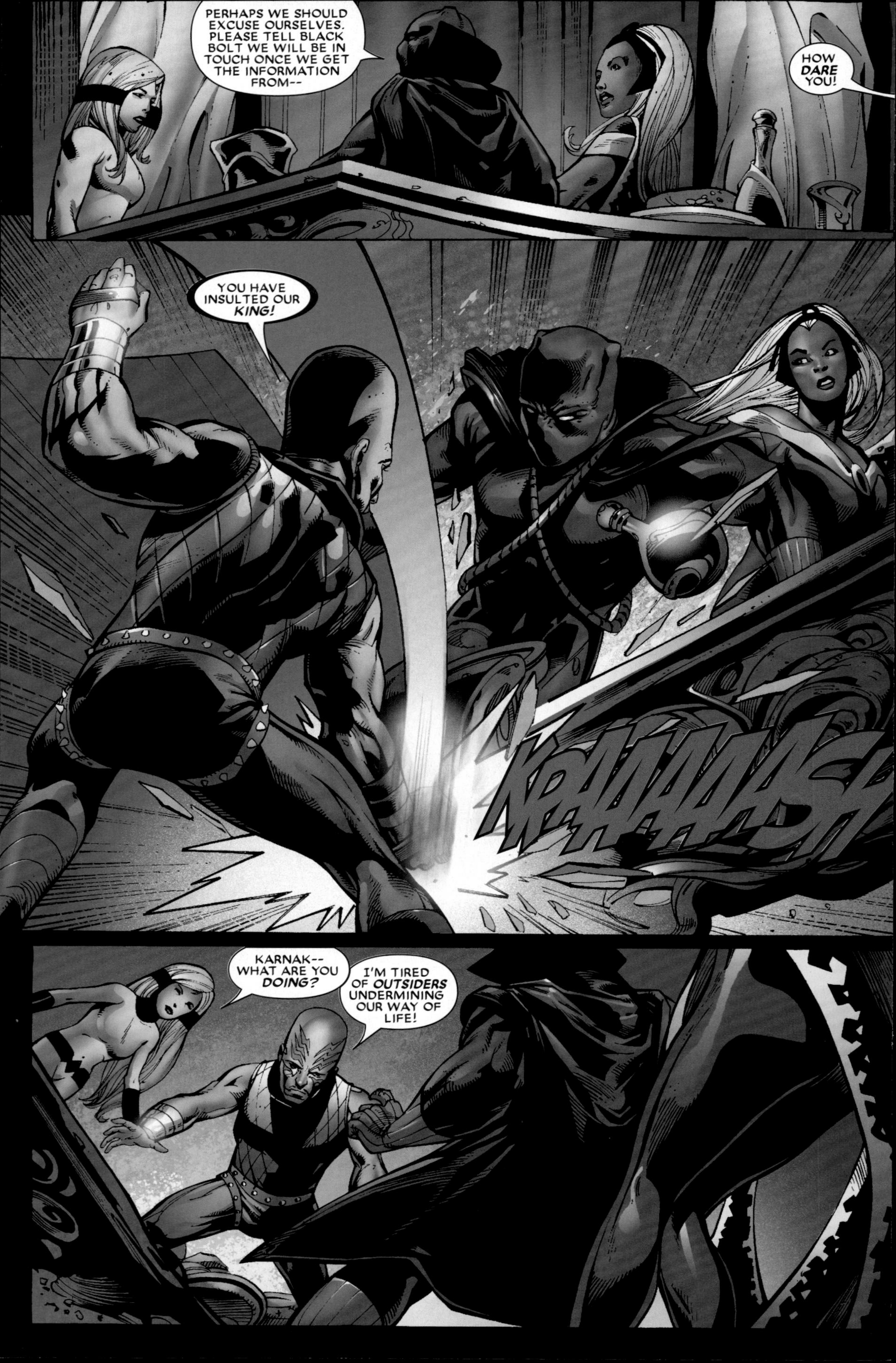
PERHAPS WE SHOULD EXCUSE OURSELVES. PLEASE TELL BLACK BOLT WE WILL BE IN TOUCH ONCE WE GET THE INFORMATION FROM--
HOW *DARE* YOU!
YOU HAVE INSULTED OUR *KING!*
KRAAAAASH
KARNAK-- WHAT ARE YOU *DOING?*
I'M TIRED OF *OUTSIDERS* UNDERMINING OUR WAY OF LIFE!

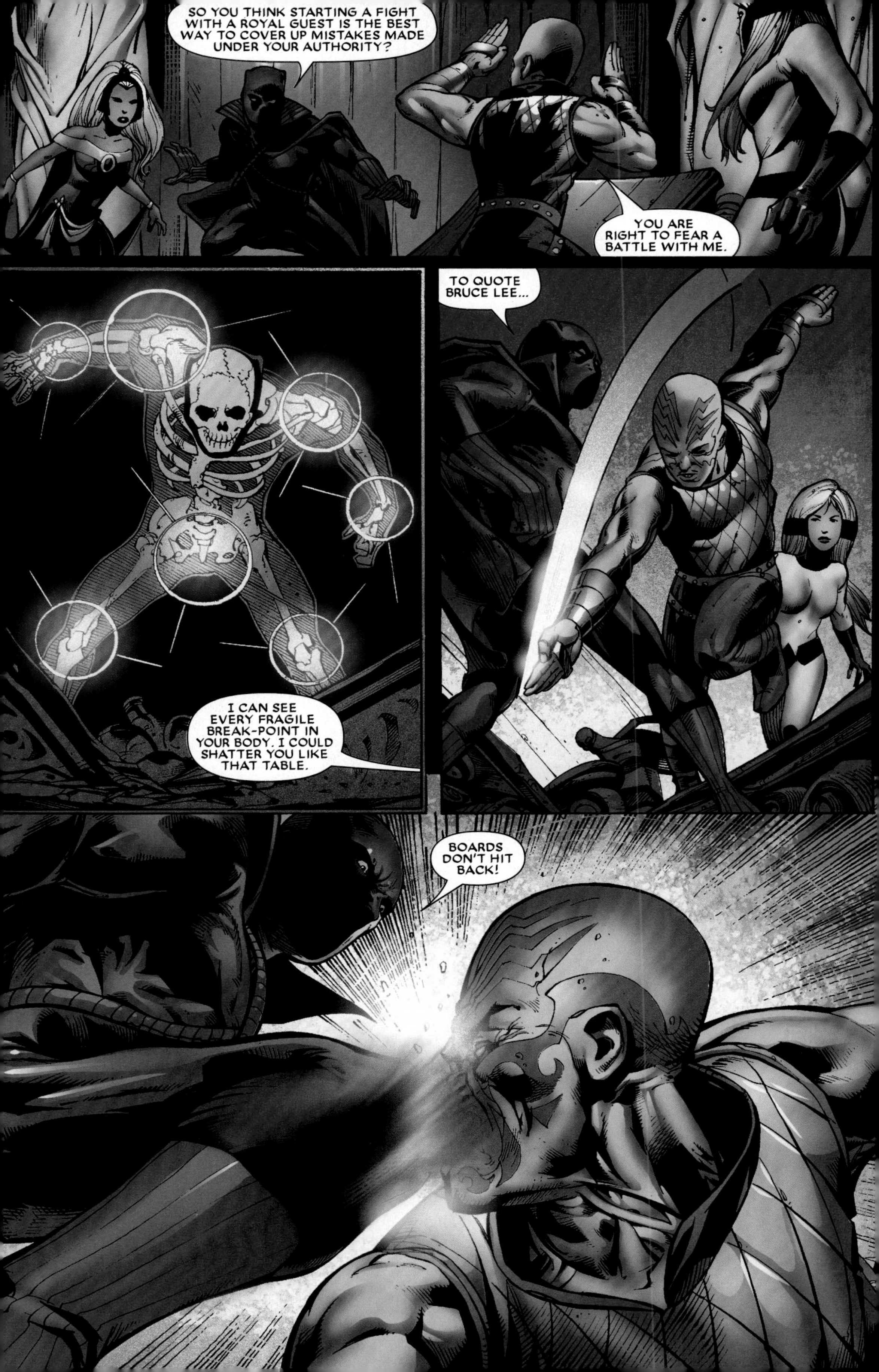

SO YOU THINK STARTING A FIGHT WITH A ROYAL GUEST IS THE BEST WAY TO COVER UP MISTAKES MADE UNDER YOUR AUTHORITY?
YOU ARE RIGHT TO FEAR A BATTLE WITH ME.
I CAN SEE EVERY FRAGILE BREAK-POINT IN YOUR BODY. I COULD SHATTER YOU LIKE THAT TABLE.
TO QUOTE BRUCE LEE...
BOARDS DON'T HIT BACK!

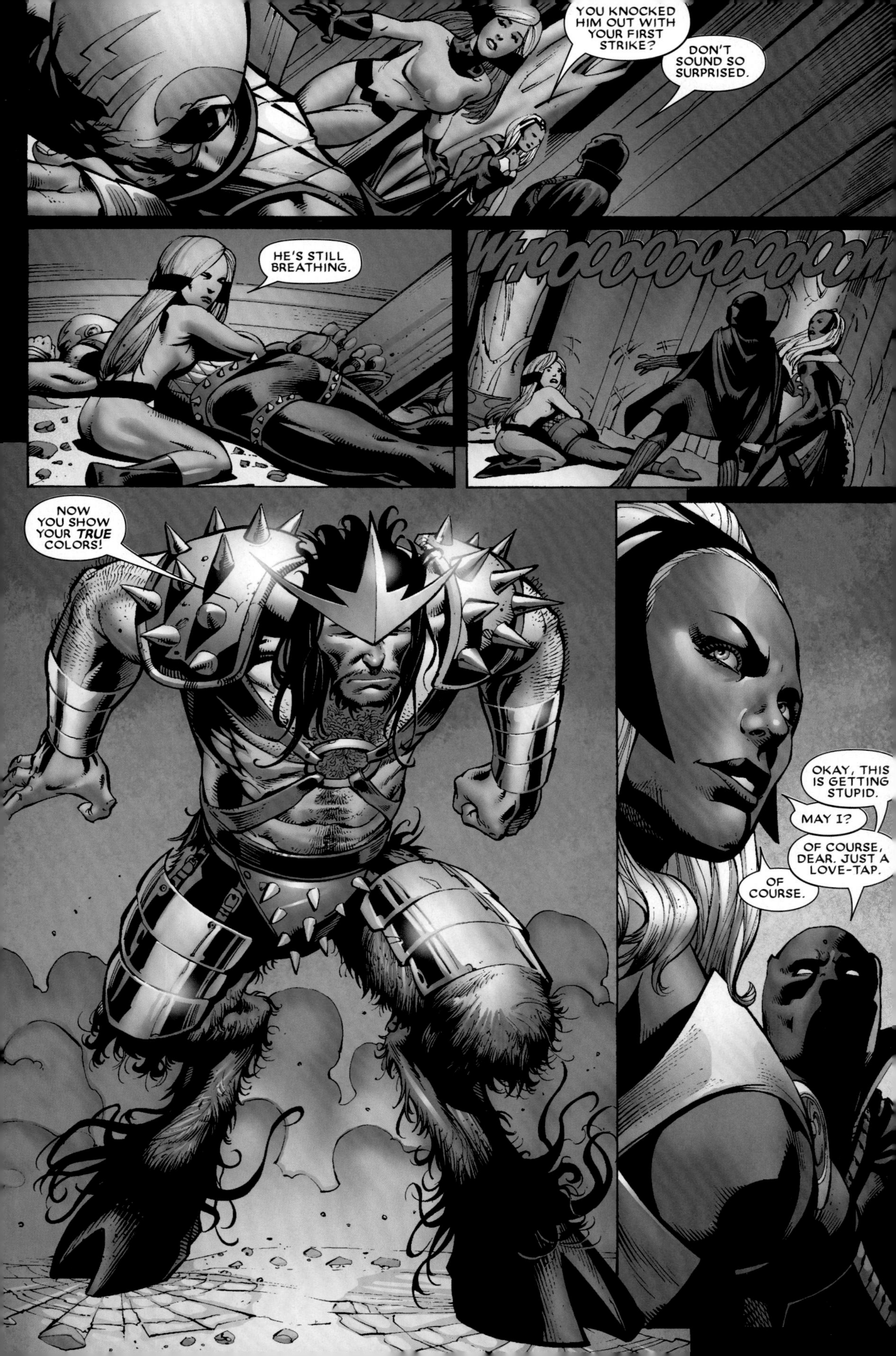
YOU KNOCKED HIM OUT WITH YOUR FIRST STRIKE?
DON'T SOUND SO SURPRISED.
HE'S STILL BREATHING.
WHOOOOOOOOOOOOM
NOW YOU SHOW YOUR *TRUE* COLORS!
OKAY, THIS IS GETTING STUPID.
MAY I?
OF COURSE, DEAR. JUST A LOVE-TAP.
OF COURSE.

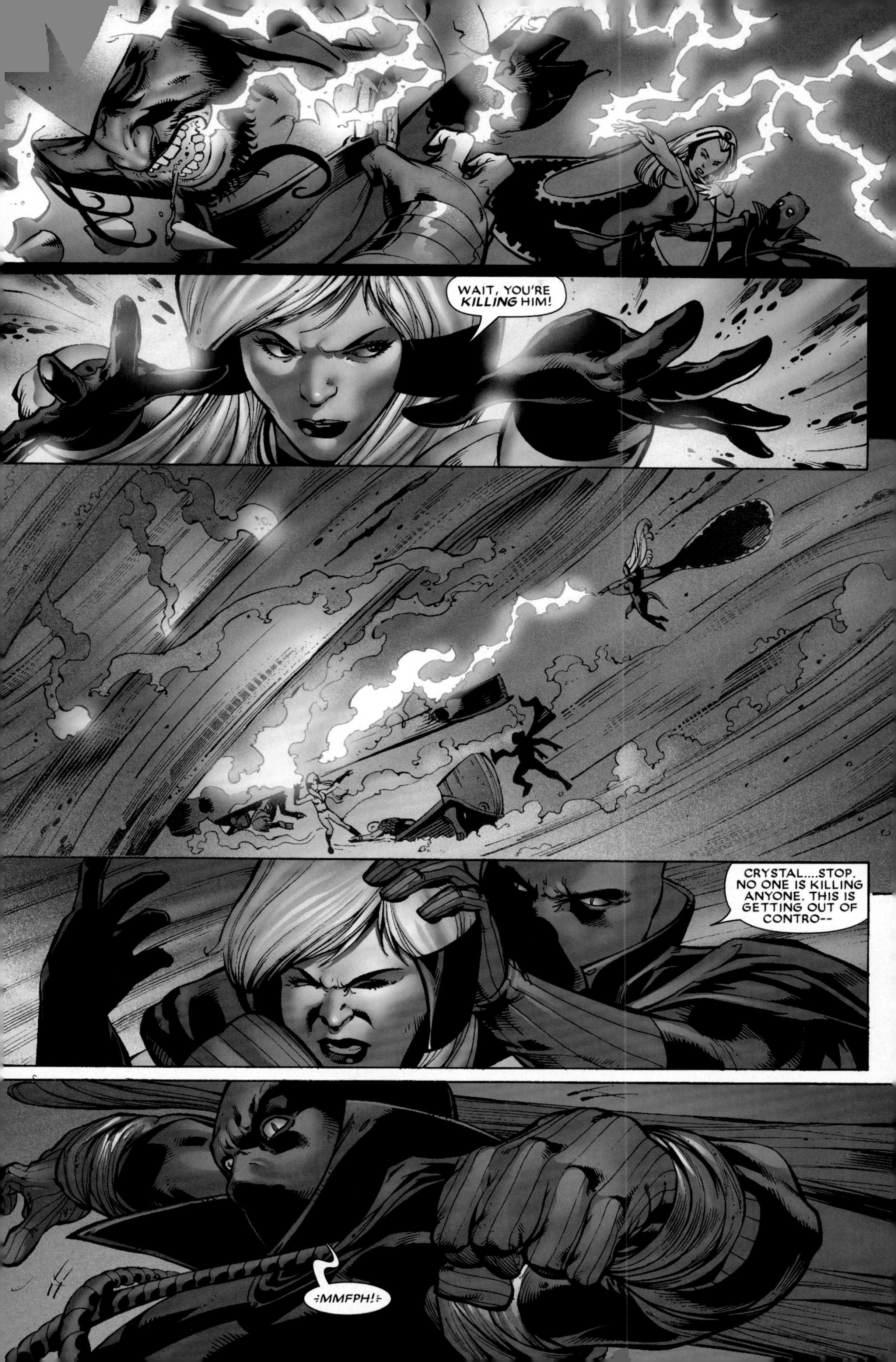
WAIT, YOU'RE KILLING HIM!
CRYSTAL....STOP. NO ONE IS KILLING ANYONE. THIS IS GETTING OUT OF CONTRO--
MMFPH!

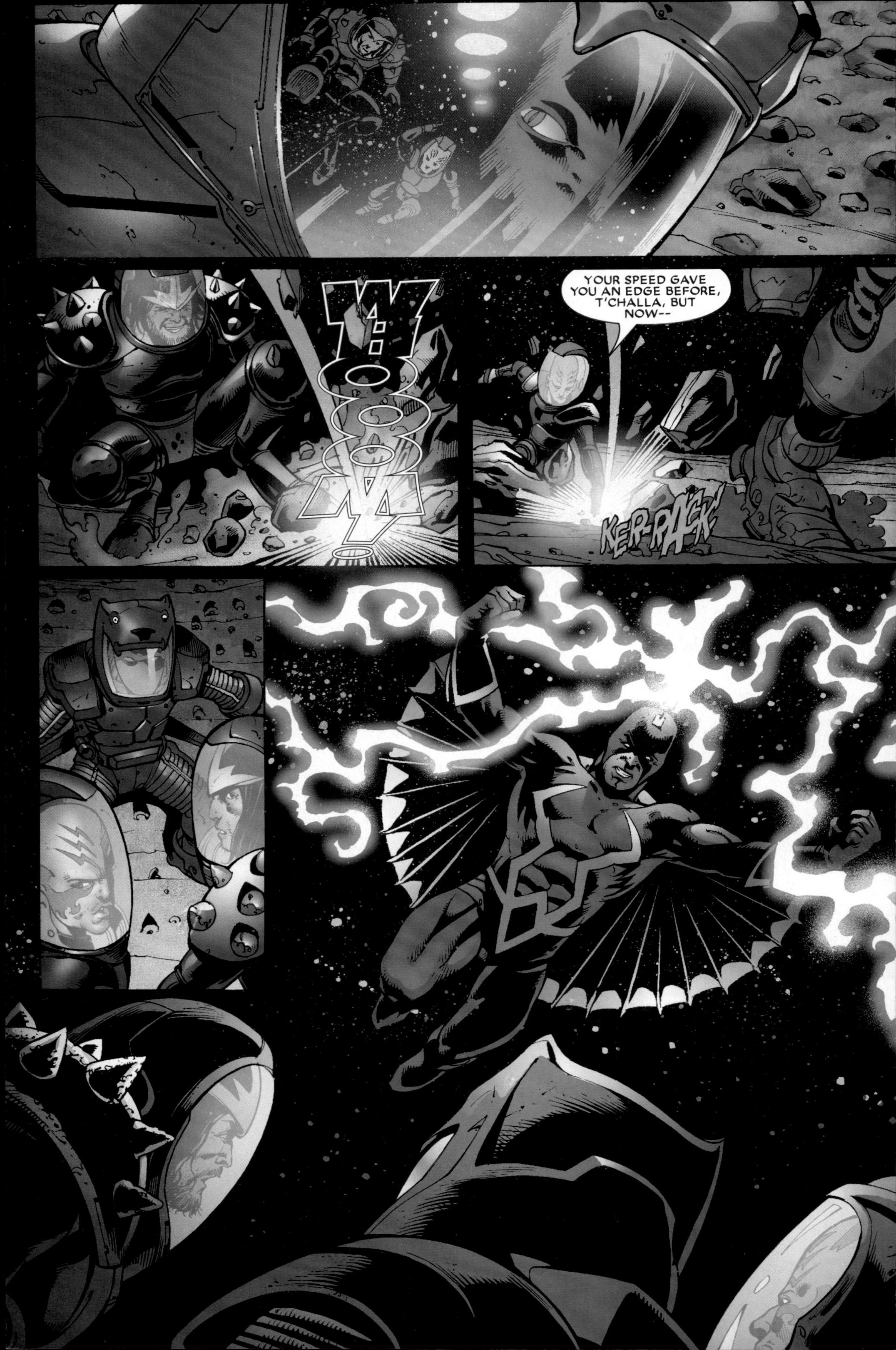
WOOOM!
YOUR SPEED GAVE YOU AN EDGE BEFORE, T'CHALLA, BUT NOW--
KER-RACK!

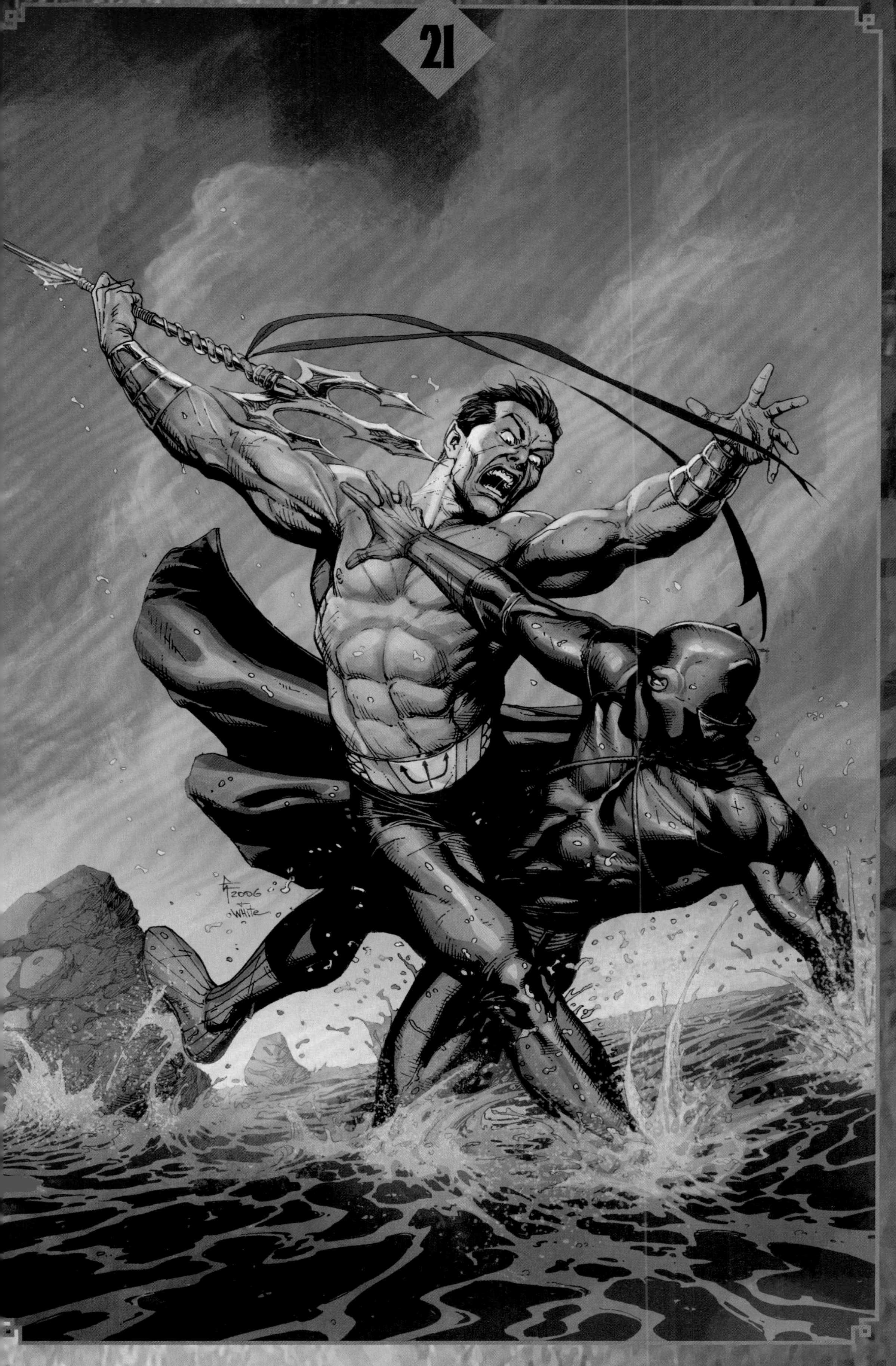
21

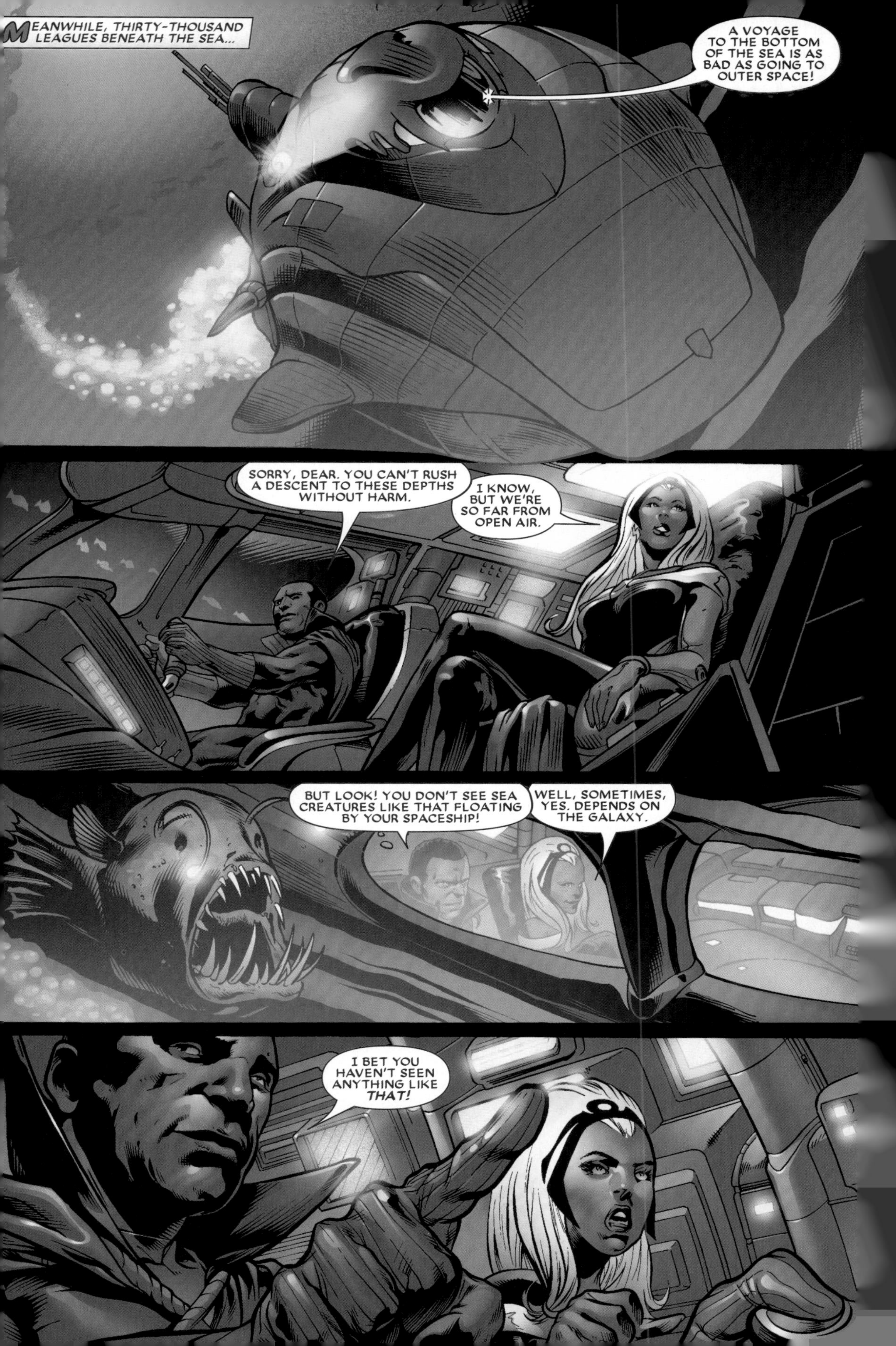
MEANWHILE, THIRTY-THOUSAND LEAGUES BENEATH THE SEA...
A VOYAGE TO THE BOTTOM OF THE SEA IS AS BAD AS GOING TO OUTER SPACE!
SORRY, DEAR. YOU CAN'T RUSH A DESCENT TO THESE DEPTHS WITHOUT HARM.
I KNOW, BUT WE'RE SO FAR FROM OPEN AIR.
BUT LOOK! YOU DON'T SEE SEA CREATURES LIKE THAT FLOATING BY YOUR SPACESHIP!
WELL, SOMETIMES, YES. DEPENDS ON THE GALAXY.
I BET YOU HAVEN'T SEEN ANYTHING LIKE *THAT!*

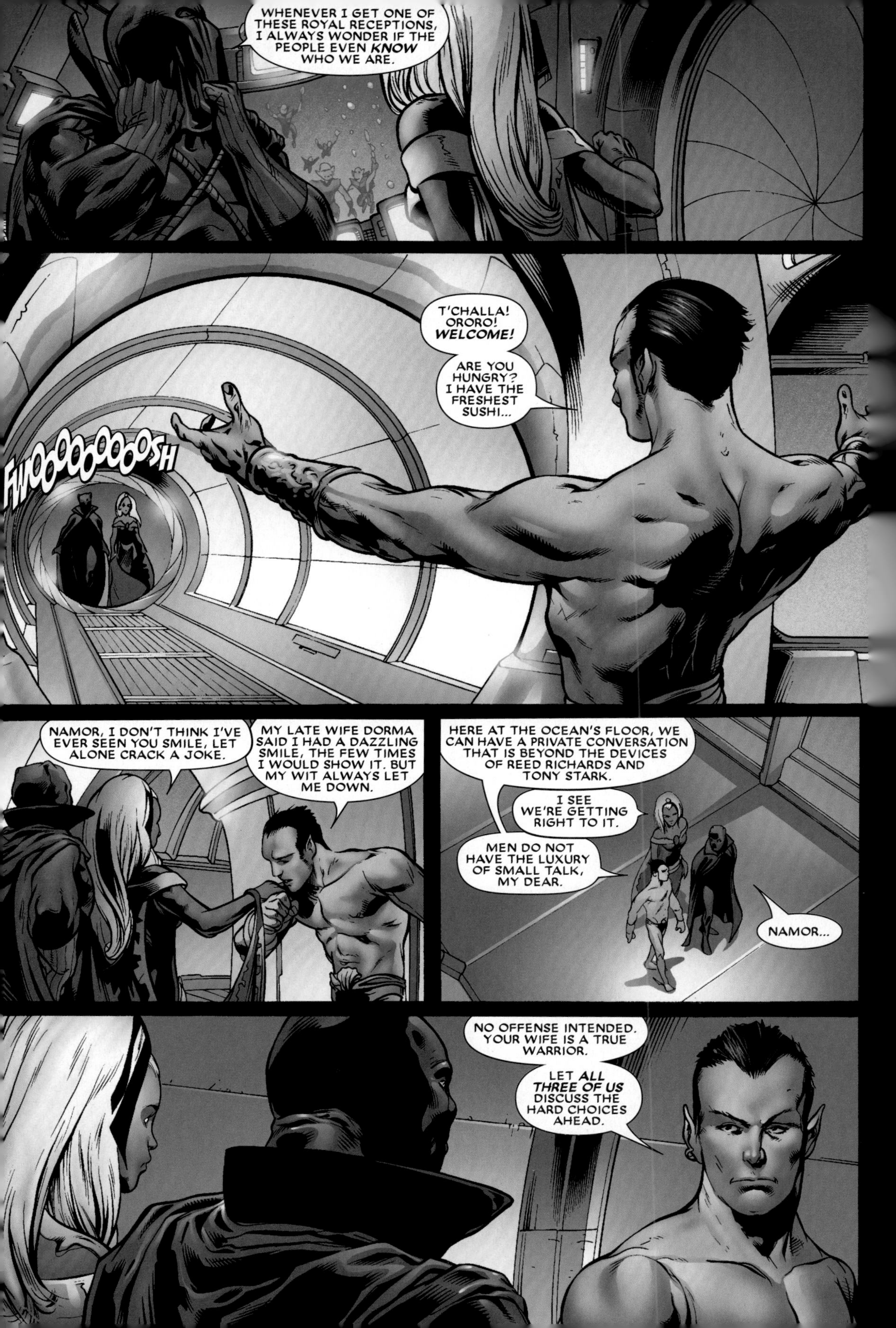

WHENEVER I GET ONE OF THESE ROYAL RECEPTIONS, I ALWAYS WONDER IF THE PEOPLE EVEN *KNOW* WHO WE ARE.
T'CHALLA! ORORO! ***WELCOME!***
ARE YOU HUNGRY? I HAVE THE FRESHEST SUSHI...
FWOOOOOOOOOOSH
NAMOR, I DON'T THINK I'VE EVER SEEN YOU SMILE, LET ALONE CRACK A JOKE.
MY LATE WIFE DORMA SAID I HAD A DAZZLING SMILE, THE FEW TIMES I WOULD SHOW IT. BUT MY WIT ALWAYS LET ME DOWN.
HERE AT THE OCEAN'S FLOOR, WE CAN HAVE A PRIVATE CONVERSATION THAT IS BEYOND THE DEVICES OF REED RICHARDS AND TONY STARK.
I SEE WE'RE GETTING RIGHT TO IT.
MEN DO NOT HAVE THE LUXURY OF SMALL TALK, MY DEAR.
NAMOR...
NO OFFENSE INTENDED. YOUR WIFE IS A TRUE WARRIOR.
LET ***ALL THREE OF US*** DISCUSS THE HARD CHOICES AHEAD.

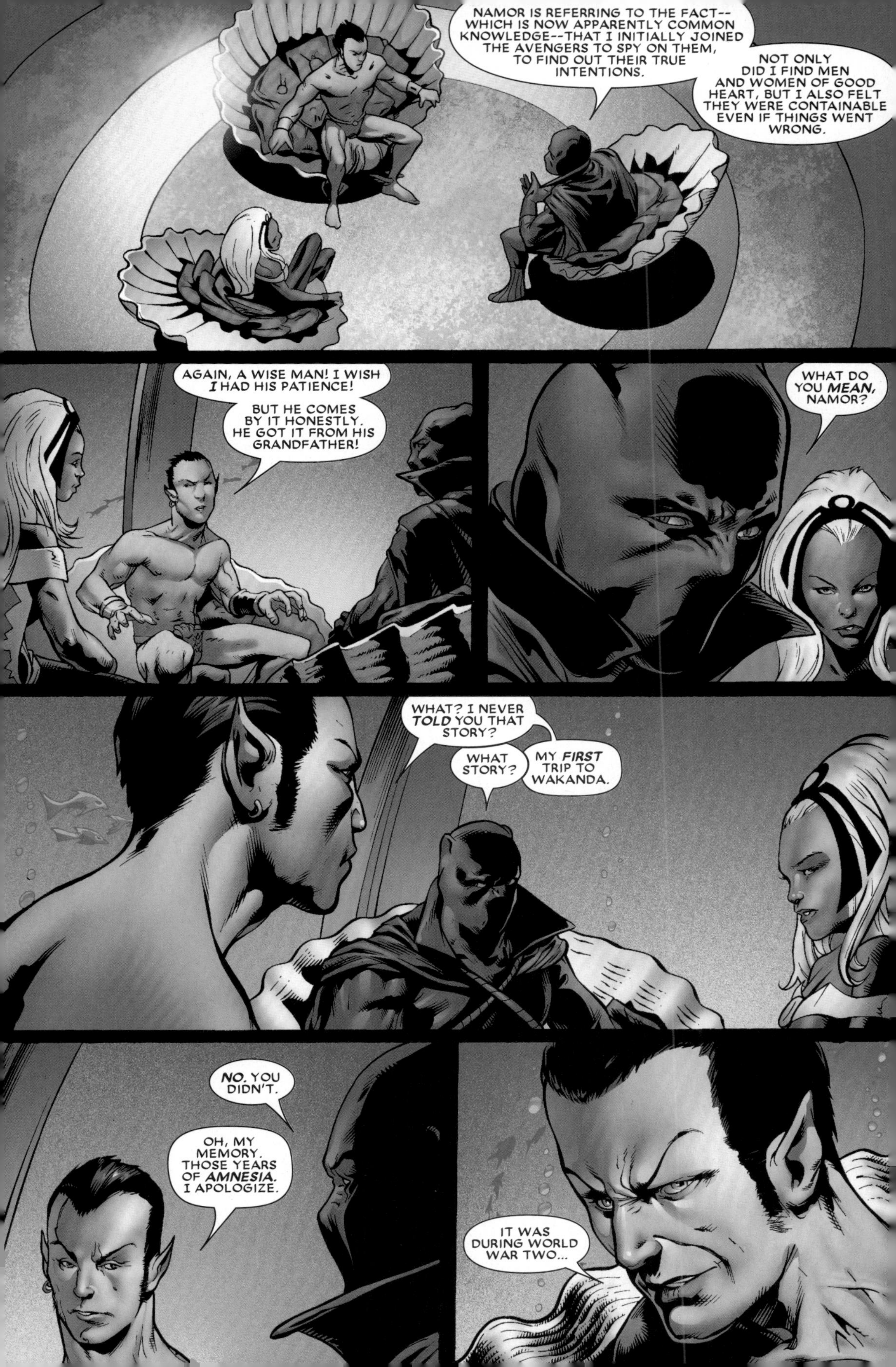
NAMOR IS REFERRING TO THE FACT--WHICH IS NOW APPARENTLY COMMON KNOWLEDGE--THAT I INITIALLY JOINED THE AVENGERS TO SPY ON THEM, TO FIND OUT THEIR TRUE INTENTIONS.
NOT ONLY DID I FIND MEN AND WOMEN OF GOOD HEART, BUT I ALSO FELT THEY WERE CONTAINABLE EVEN IF THINGS WENT WRONG.
AGAIN, A WISE MAN! I WISH *I* HAD HIS PATIENCE!
BUT HE COMES BY IT HONESTLY. HE GOT IT FROM HIS GRANDFATHER!
WHAT DO YOU *MEAN,* NAMOR?
WHAT? I NEVER *TOLD* YOU THAT STORY?
WHAT STORY?
MY *FIRST* TRIP TO WAKANDA.
NO. YOU DIDN'T.
OH, MY MEMORY. THOSE YEARS OF *AMNESIA.* I APOLOGIZE.
IT WAS DURING WORLD WAR TWO...

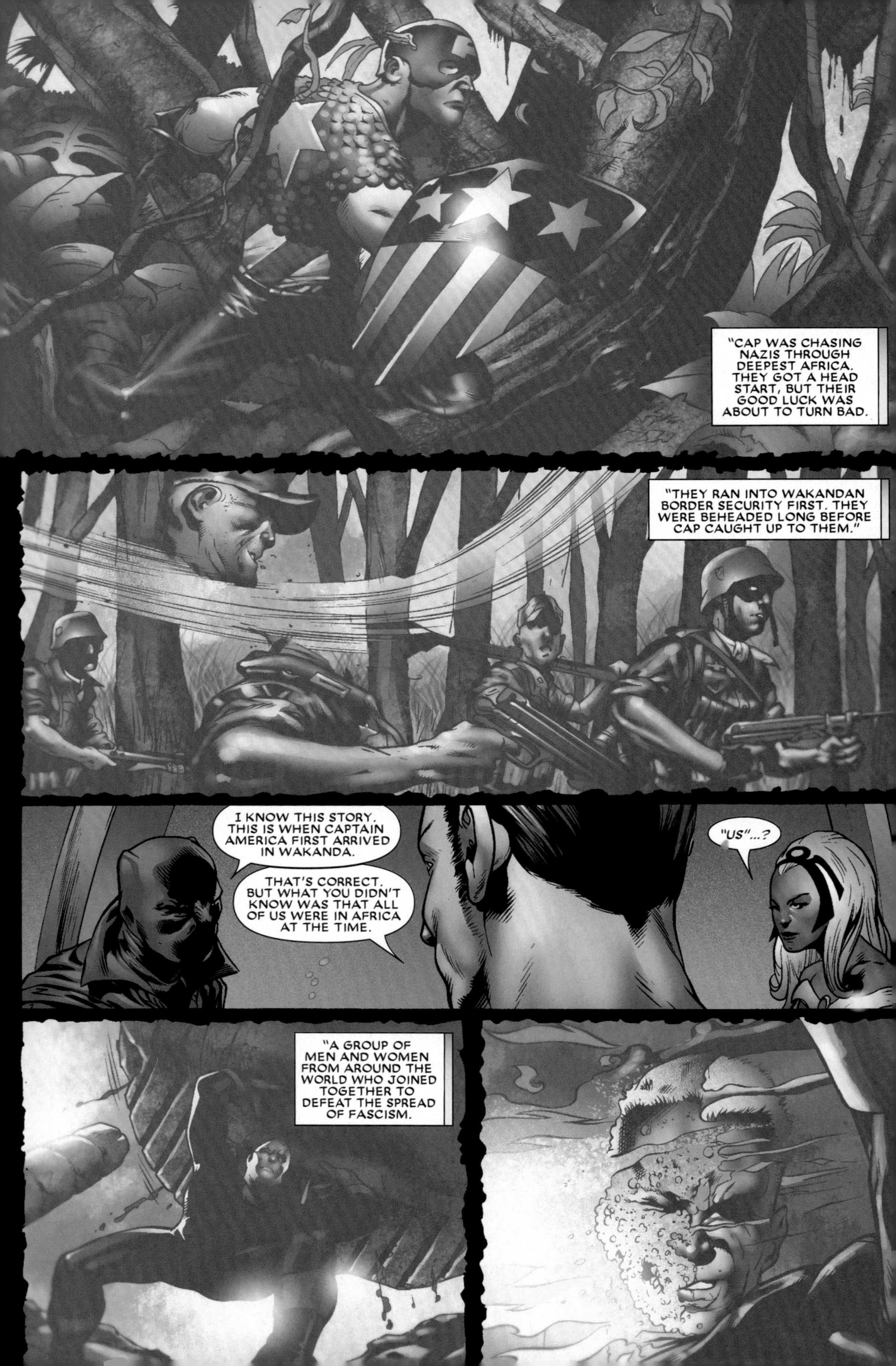
"CAP WAS CHASING NAZIS THROUGH DEEPEST AFRICA. THEY GOT A HEAD START, BUT THEIR GOOD LUCK WAS ABOUT TO TURN BAD.
"THEY RAN INTO WAKANDAN BORDER SECURITY FIRST. THEY WERE BEHEADED LONG BEFORE CAP CAUGHT UP TO THEM."
I KNOW THIS STORY. THIS IS WHEN CAPTAIN AMERICA FIRST ARRIVED IN WAKANDA.
THAT'S CORRECT. BUT WHAT YOU DIDN'T KNOW WAS THAT ALL OF US WERE IN AFRICA AT THE TIME.
"US"...?
"A GROUP OF MEN AND WOMEN FROM AROUND THE WORLD WHO JOINED TOGETHER TO DEFEAT THE SPREAD OF FASCISM.

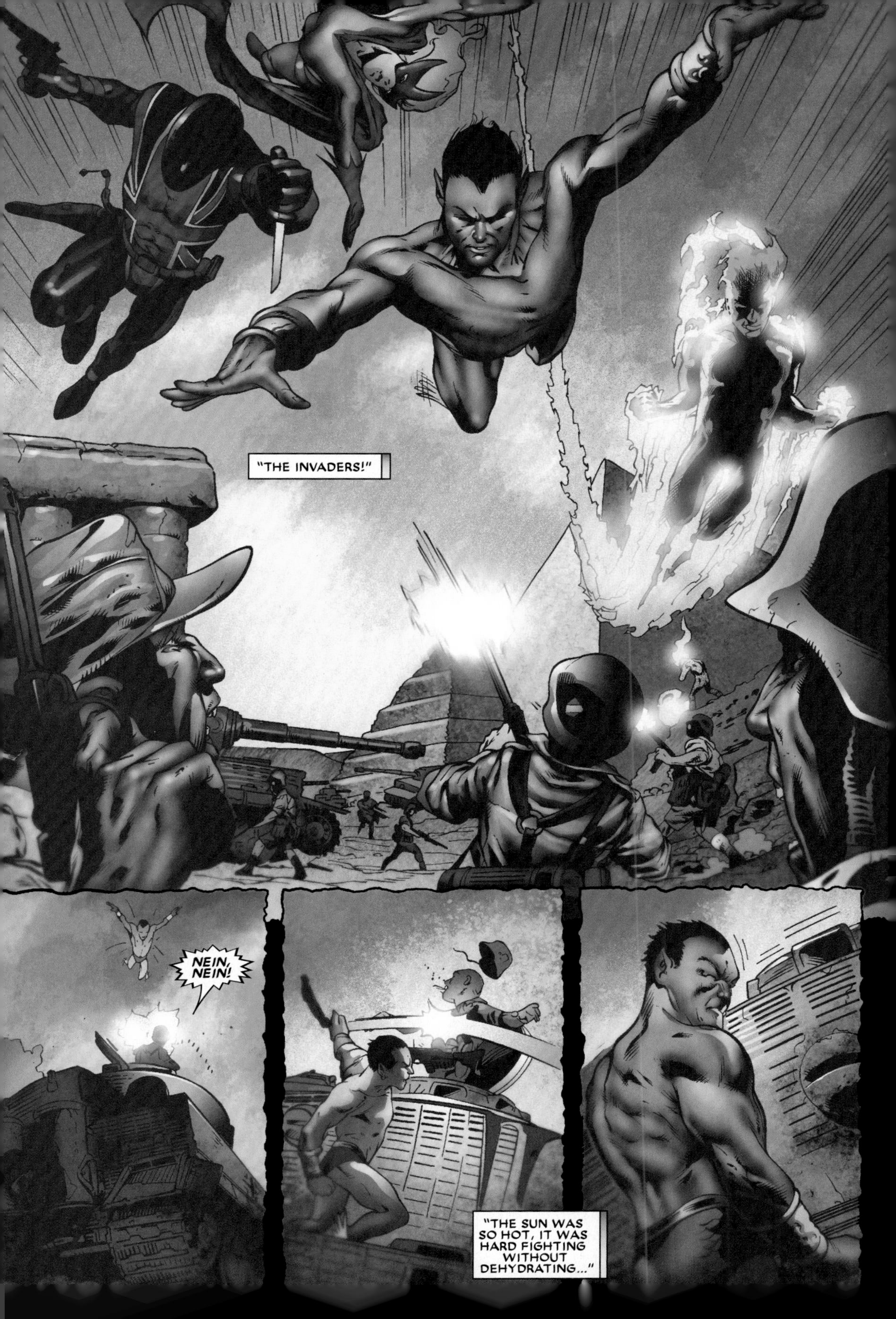
"THE INVADERS!"
NEIN, NEIN!
"THE SUN WAS SO HOT, IT WAS HARD FIGHTING WITHOUT DEHYDRATING..."

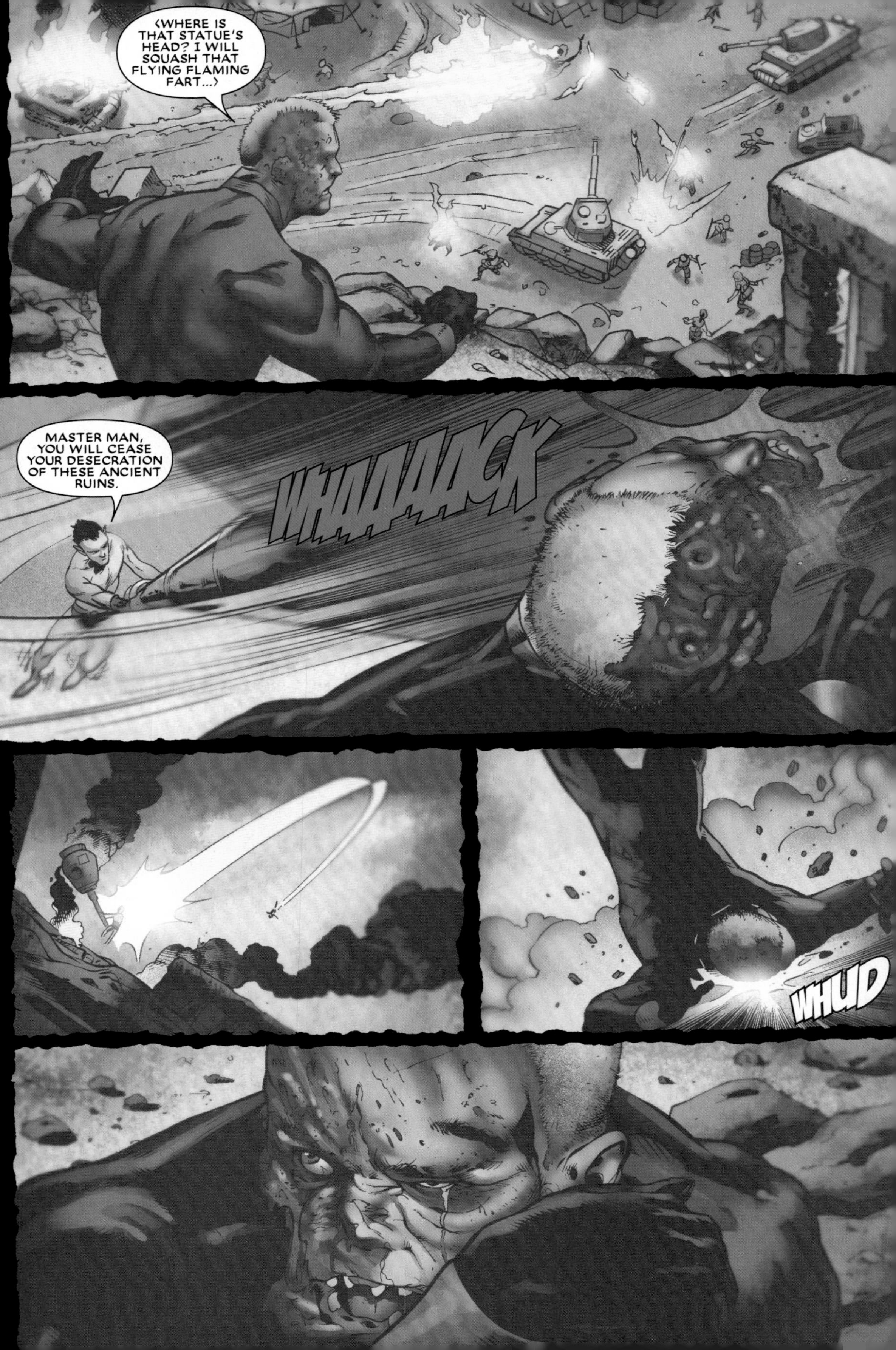
‹WHERE IS THAT STATUE'S HEAD? I WILL SQUASH THAT FLYING FLAMING FART...›
MASTER MAN, YOU WILL CEASE YOUR DESECRATION OF THESE ANCIENT RUINS.
WHAAAACK
WHUD

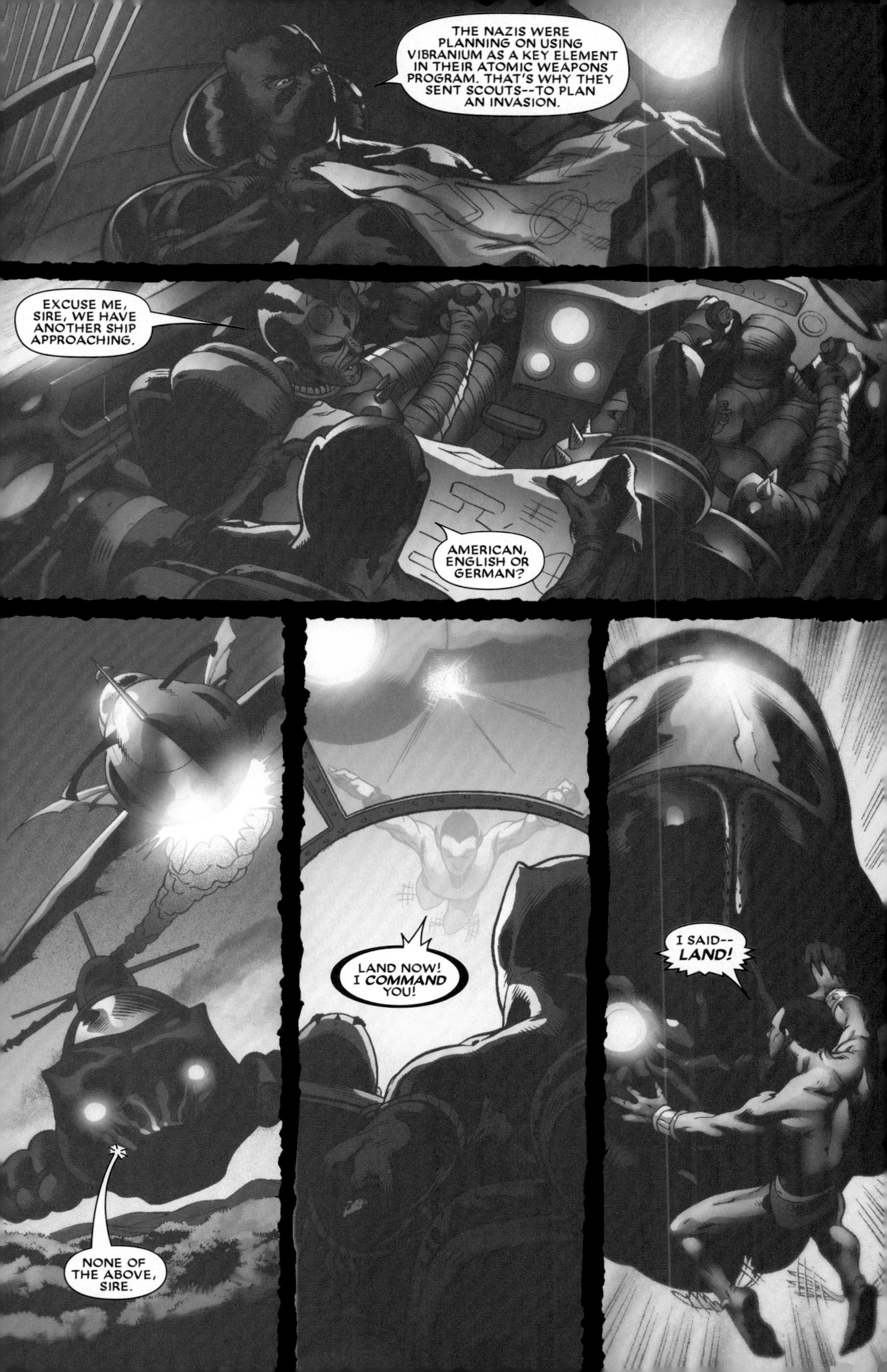
THE NAZIS WERE PLANNING ON USING VIBRANIUM AS A KEY ELEMENT IN THEIR ATOMIC WEAPONS PROGRAM. THAT'S WHY THEY SENT SCOUTS--TO PLAN AN INVASION.
EXCUSE ME, SIRE, WE HAVE ANOTHER SHIP APPROACHING.
AMERICAN, ENGLISH OR GERMAN?
NONE OF THE ABOVE, SIRE.
LAND NOW! I **COMMAND** YOU!
I SAID-- ***LAND!***

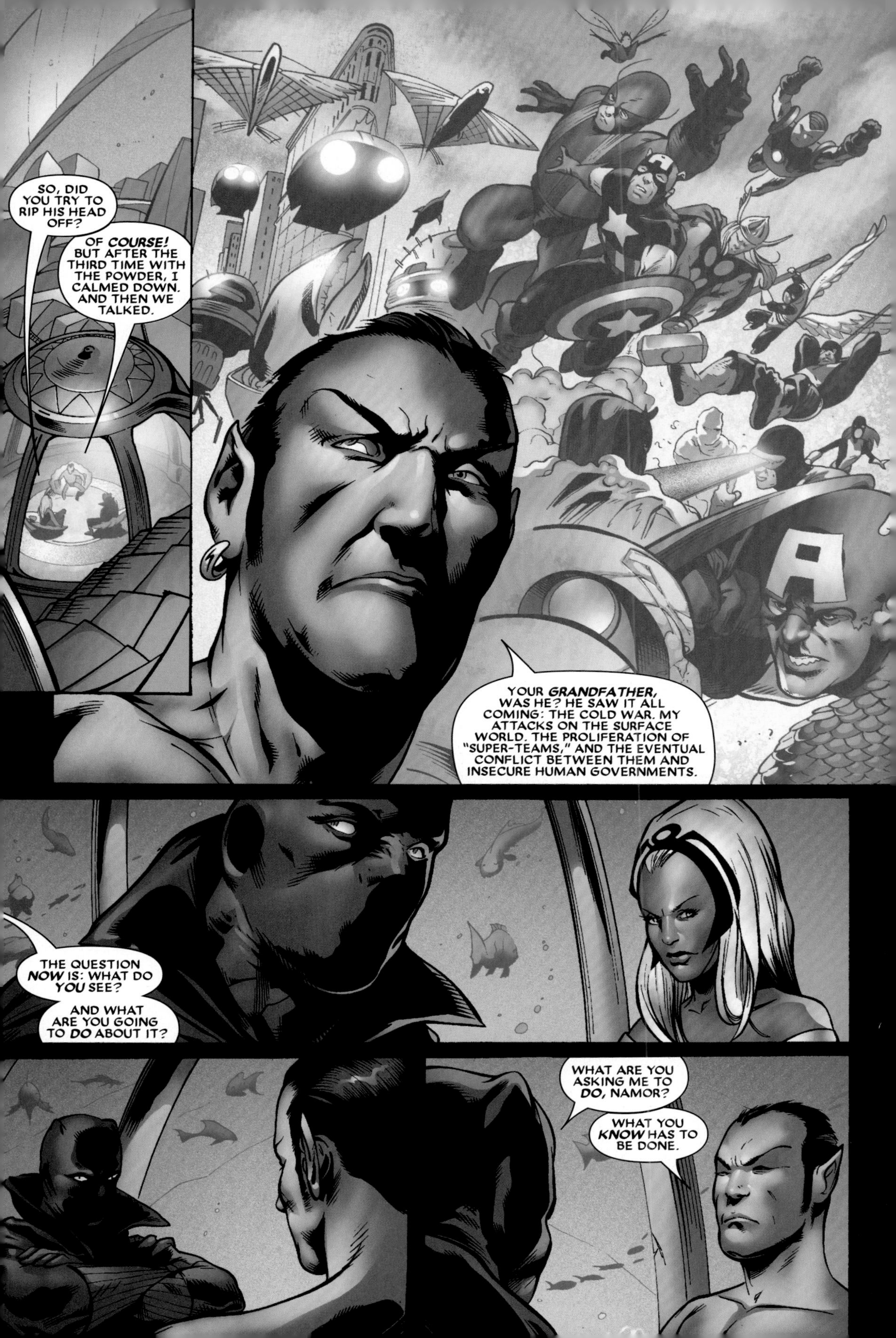
SO, DID YOU TRY TO RIP HIS HEAD OFF?
OF *COURSE!* BUT AFTER THE THIRD TIME WITH THE POWDER, I CALMED DOWN. AND THEN WE TALKED.
YOUR *GRANDFATHER,* WAS HE? HE SAW IT ALL COMING: THE COLD WAR. MY ATTACKS ON THE SURFACE WORLD. THE PROLIFERATION OF "SUPER-TEAMS," AND THE EVENTUAL CONFLICT BETWEEN THEM AND INSECURE HUMAN GOVERNMENTS.
THE QUESTION *NOW* IS: WHAT DO *YOU* SEE?
AND WHAT ARE YOU GOING TO *DO* ABOUT IT?
WHAT ARE YOU ASKING ME TO *DO,* NAMOR?
WHAT YOU *KNOW* HAS TO BE DONE.

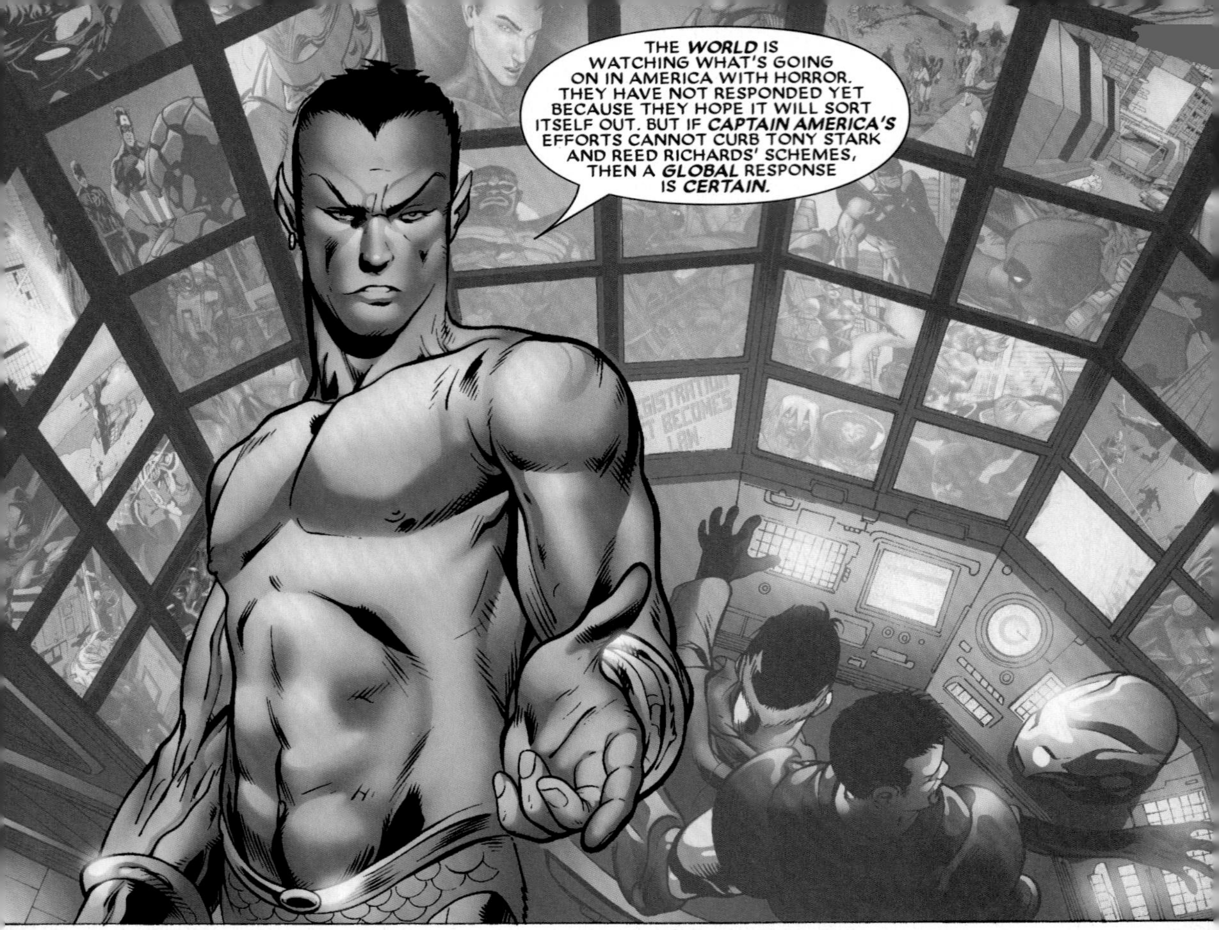
THE WORLD IS WATCHING WHAT'S GOING ON IN AMERICA WITH HORROR. THEY HAVE NOT RESPONDED YET BECAUSE THEY HOPE IT WILL SORT ITSELF OUT. BUT IF CAPTAIN AMERICA'S EFFORTS CANNOT CURB TONY STARK AND REED RICHARDS' SCHEMES, THEN A GLOBAL RESPONSE IS CERTAIN.

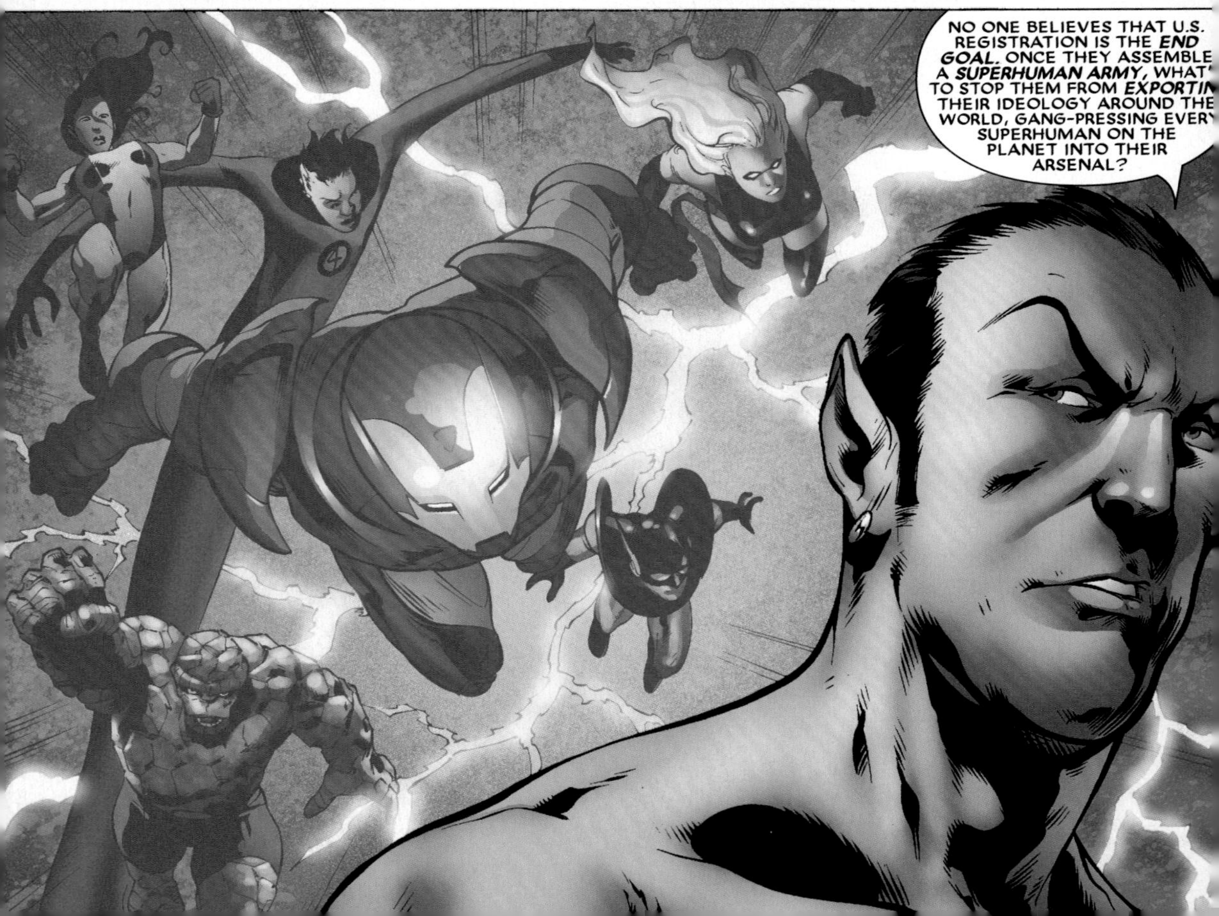
NO ONE BELIEVES THAT U.S. REGISTRATION IS THE END GOAL. ONCE THEY ASSEMBLE A SUPERHUMAN ARMY, WHAT' TO STOP THEM FROM EXPORTIN THEIR IDEOLOGY AROUND THE WORLD, GANG-PRESSING EVERY SUPERHUMAN ON THE PLANET INTO THEIR ARSENAL?

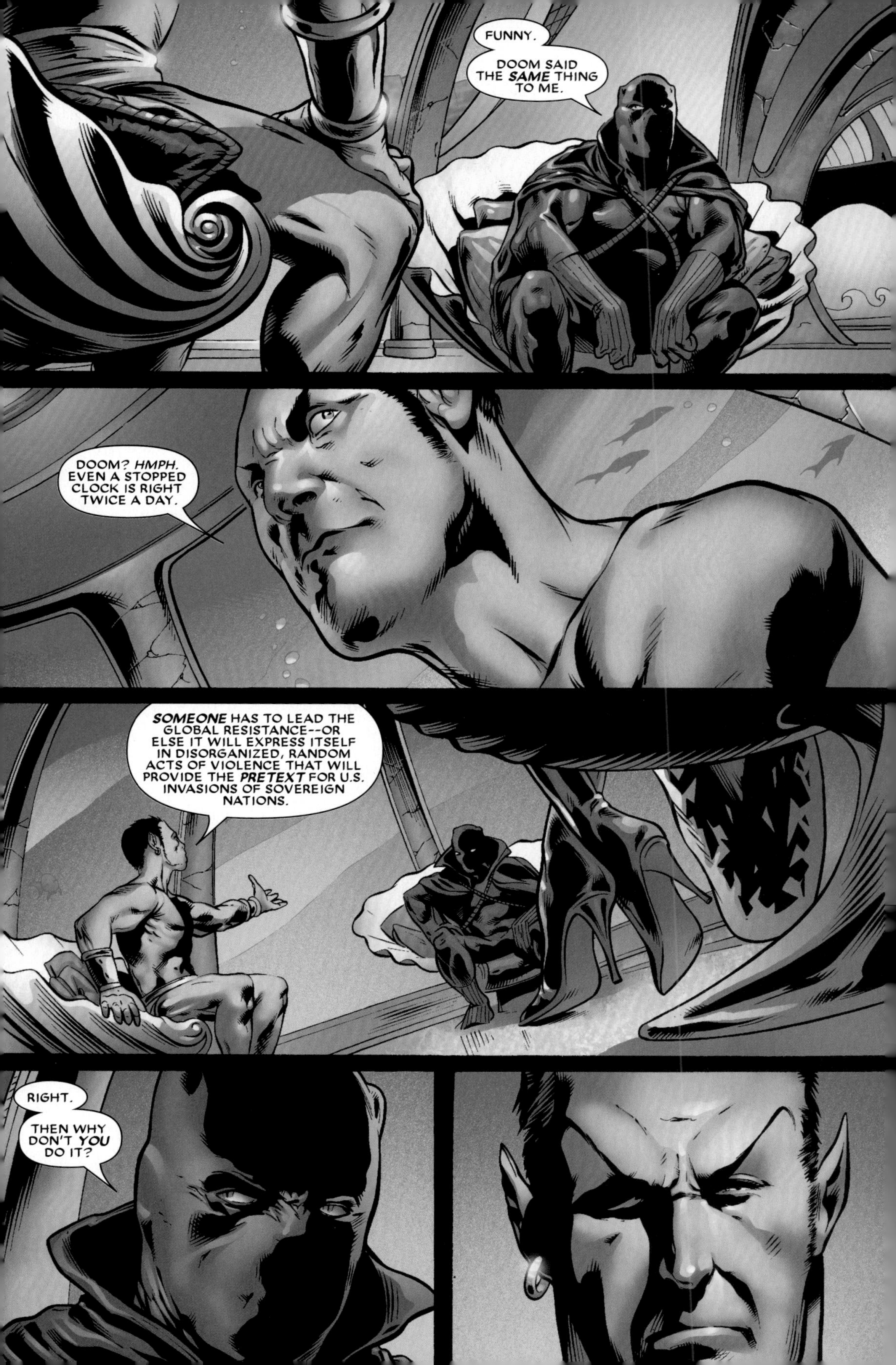

FUNNY.
DOOM SAID THE *SAME* THING TO ME.
DOOM? *HMPH.* EVEN A STOPPED CLOCK IS RIGHT TWICE A DAY.
SOMEONE HAS TO LEAD THE GLOBAL RESISTANCE--OR ELSE IT WILL EXPRESS ITSELF IN DISORGANIZED, RANDOM ACTS OF VIOLENCE THAT WILL PROVIDE THE *PRETEXT* FOR U.S. INVASIONS OF SOVEREIGN NATIONS.
RIGHT.
THEN WHY DON'T *YOU* DO IT?

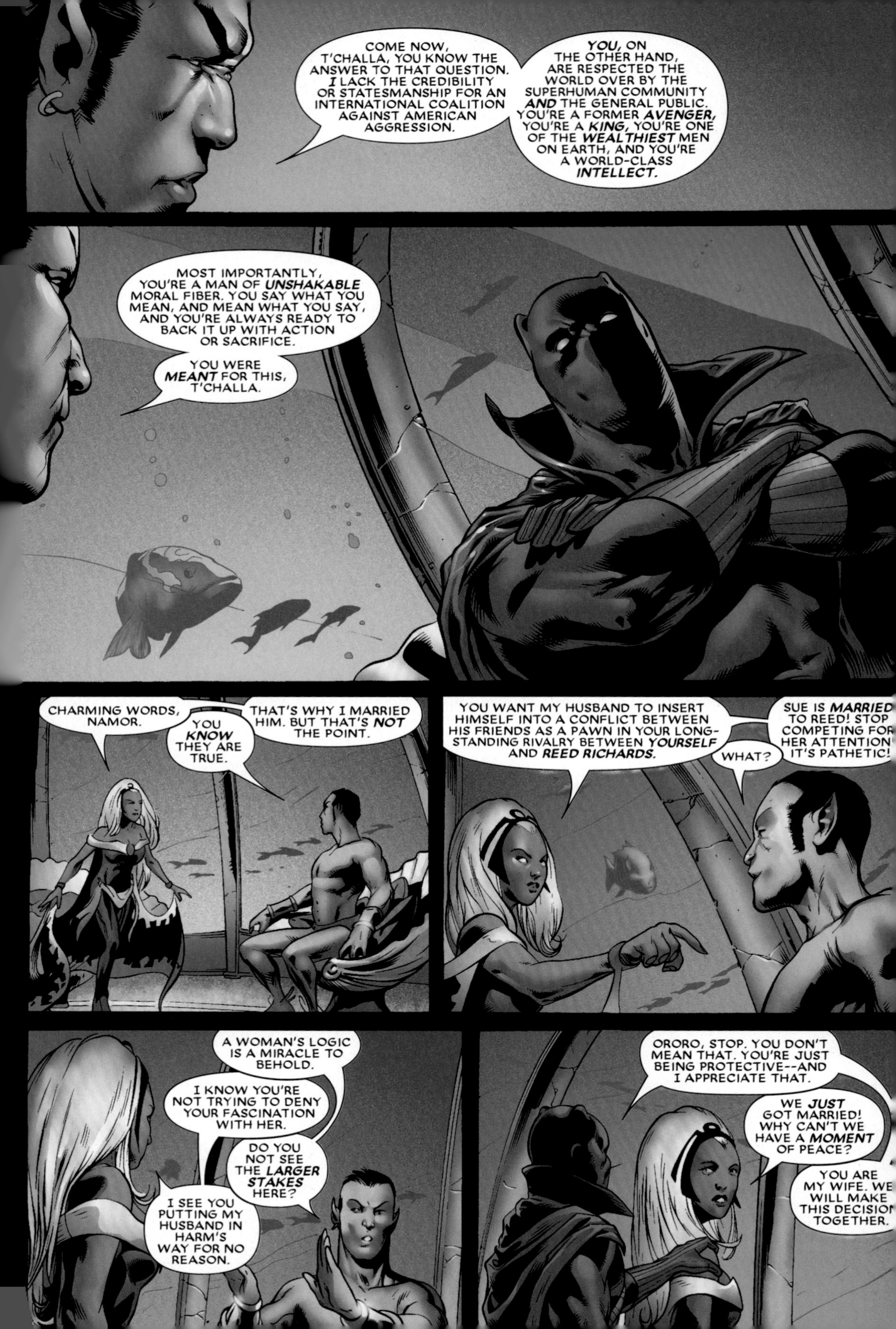

COME NOW, T'CHALLA, YOU KNOW THE ANSWER TO THAT QUESTION. I LACK THE CREDIBILITY OR STATESMANSHIP FOR AN INTERNATIONAL COALITION AGAINST AMERICAN AGGRESSION.
YOU, ON THE OTHER HAND, ARE RESPECTED THE WORLD OVER BY THE SUPERHUMAN COMMUNITY AND THE GENERAL PUBLIC. YOU'RE A FORMER AVENGER, YOU'RE A KING, YOU'RE ONE OF THE WEALTHIEST MEN ON EARTH, AND YOU'RE A WORLD-CLASS INTELLECT.
MOST IMPORTANTLY, YOU'RE A MAN OF UNSHAKABLE MORAL FIBER. YOU SAY WHAT YOU MEAN, AND MEAN WHAT YOU SAY, AND YOU'RE ALWAYS READY TO BACK IT UP WITH ACTION OR SACRIFICE.
YOU WERE MEANT FOR THIS, T'CHALLA.
CHARMING WORDS, NAMOR.
YOU KNOW THEY ARE TRUE.
THAT'S WHY I MARRIED HIM. BUT THAT'S NOT THE POINT.
YOU WANT MY HUSBAND TO INSERT HIMSELF INTO A CONFLICT BETWEEN HIS FRIENDS AS A PAWN IN YOUR LONG-STANDING RIVALRY BETWEEN YOURSELF AND REED RICHARDS.
WHAT?
SUE IS MARRIED TO REED! STOP COMPETING FOR HER ATTENTION! IT'S PATHETIC!
A WOMAN'S LOGIC IS A MIRACLE TO BEHOLD.
I KNOW YOU'RE NOT TRYING TO DENY YOUR FASCINATION WITH HER.
DO YOU NOT SEE THE LARGER STAKES HERE?
I SEE YOU PUTTING MY HUSBAND IN HARM'S WAY FOR NO REASON.
ORORO, STOP. YOU DON'T MEAN THAT. YOU'RE JUST BEING PROTECTIVE--AND I APPRECIATE THAT.
WE JUST GOT MARRIED! WHY CAN'T WE HAVE A MOMENT OF PEACE?
YOU ARE MY WIFE. WE WILL MAKE THIS DECISION TOGETHER.

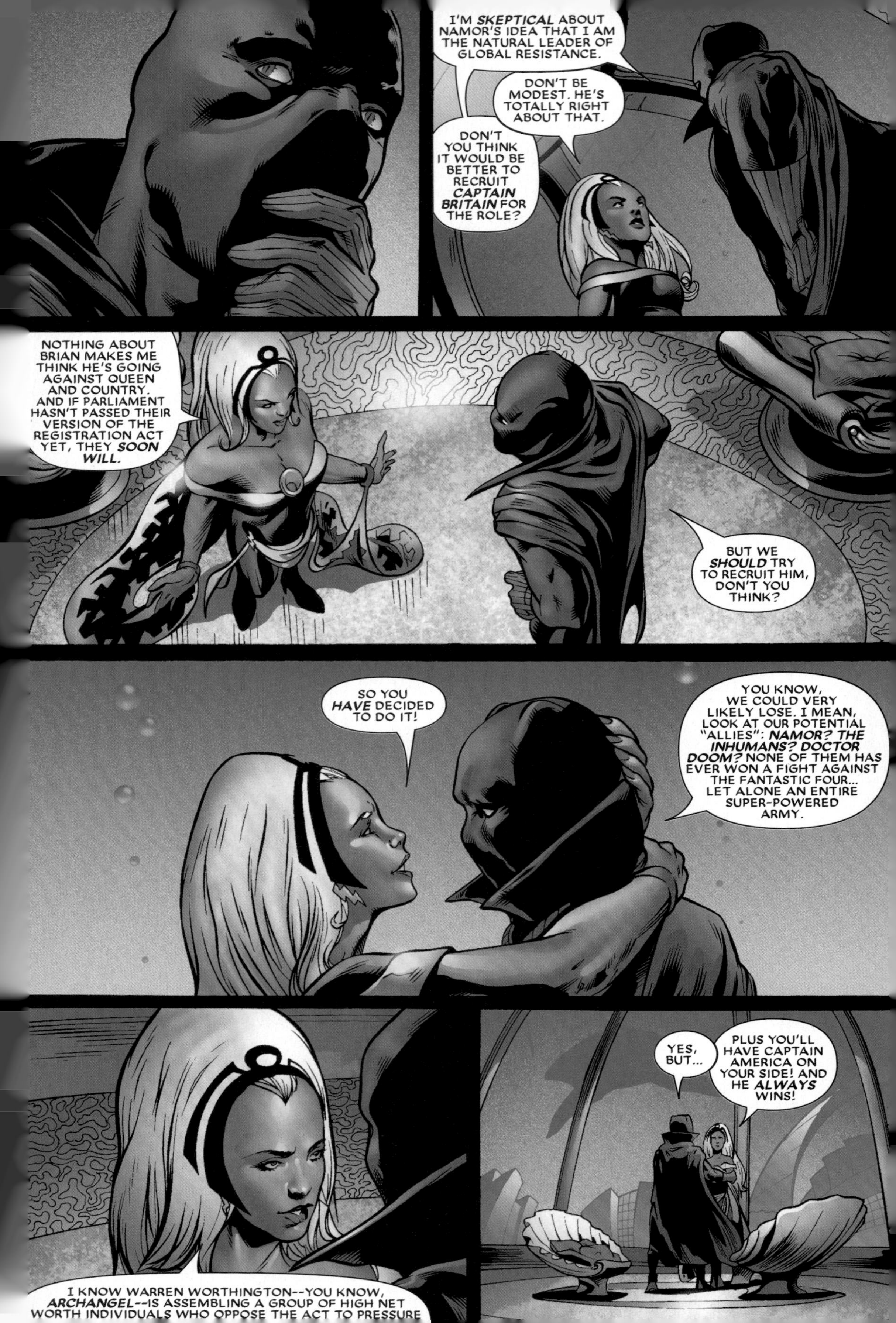

I'M SKEPTICAL ABOUT NAMOR'S IDEA THAT I AM THE NATURAL LEADER OF GLOBAL RESISTANCE.
DON'T BE MODEST. HE'S TOTALLY RIGHT ABOUT THAT.
DON'T YOU THINK IT WOULD BE BETTER TO RECRUIT CAPTAIN BRITAIN FOR THE ROLE?
NOTHING ABOUT BRIAN MAKES ME THINK HE'S GOING AGAINST QUEEN AND COUNTRY. AND IF PARLIAMENT HASN'T PASSED THEIR VERSION OF THE REGISTRATION ACT YET, THEY SOON WILL.
BUT WE SHOULD TRY TO RECRUIT HIM, DON'T YOU THINK?
SO YOU HAVE DECIDED TO DO IT!
YOU KNOW, WE COULD VERY LIKELY LOSE. I MEAN, LOOK AT OUR POTENTIAL "ALLIES": NAMOR? THE INHUMANS? DOCTOR DOOM? NONE OF THEM HAS EVER WON A FIGHT AGAINST THE FANTASTIC FOUR... LET ALONE AN ENTIRE SUPER-POWERED ARMY.
YES, BUT...
PLUS YOU'LL HAVE CAPTAIN AMERICA ON YOUR SIDE! AND HE ALWAYS WINS!
I KNOW WARREN WORTHINGTON--YOU KNOW, ARCHANGEL--IS ASSEMBLING A GROUP OF HIGH NET WORTH INDIVIDUALS WHO OPPOSE THE ACT TO PRESSURE

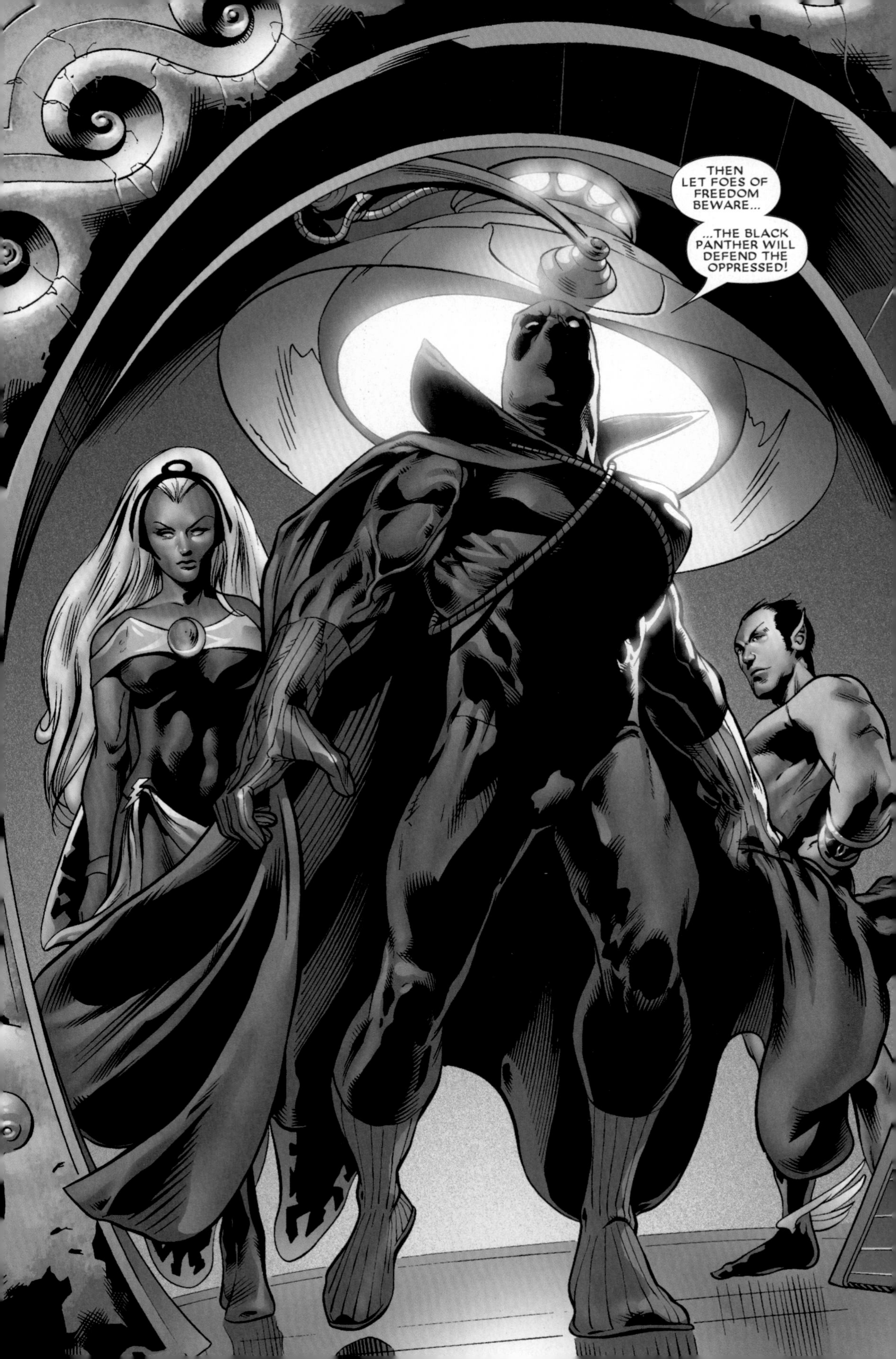
THEN LET FOES OF FREEDOM BEWARE...
...THE BLACK PANTHER WILL DEFEND THE OPPRESSED!

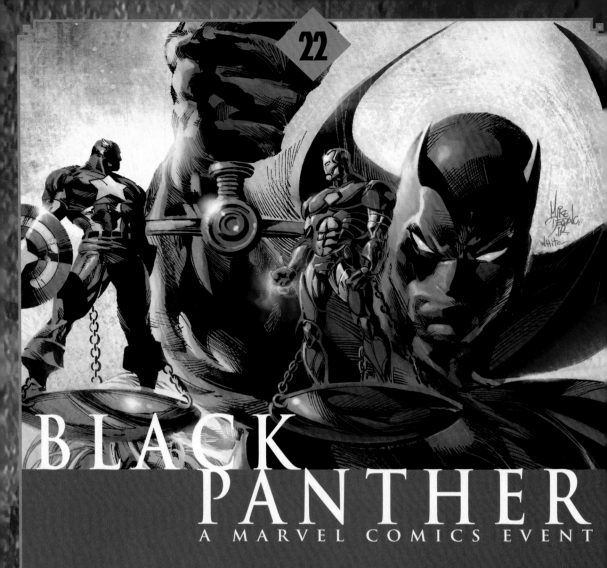

BLACK PANTHER

A MARVEL COMICS EVENT

CIVIL WAR

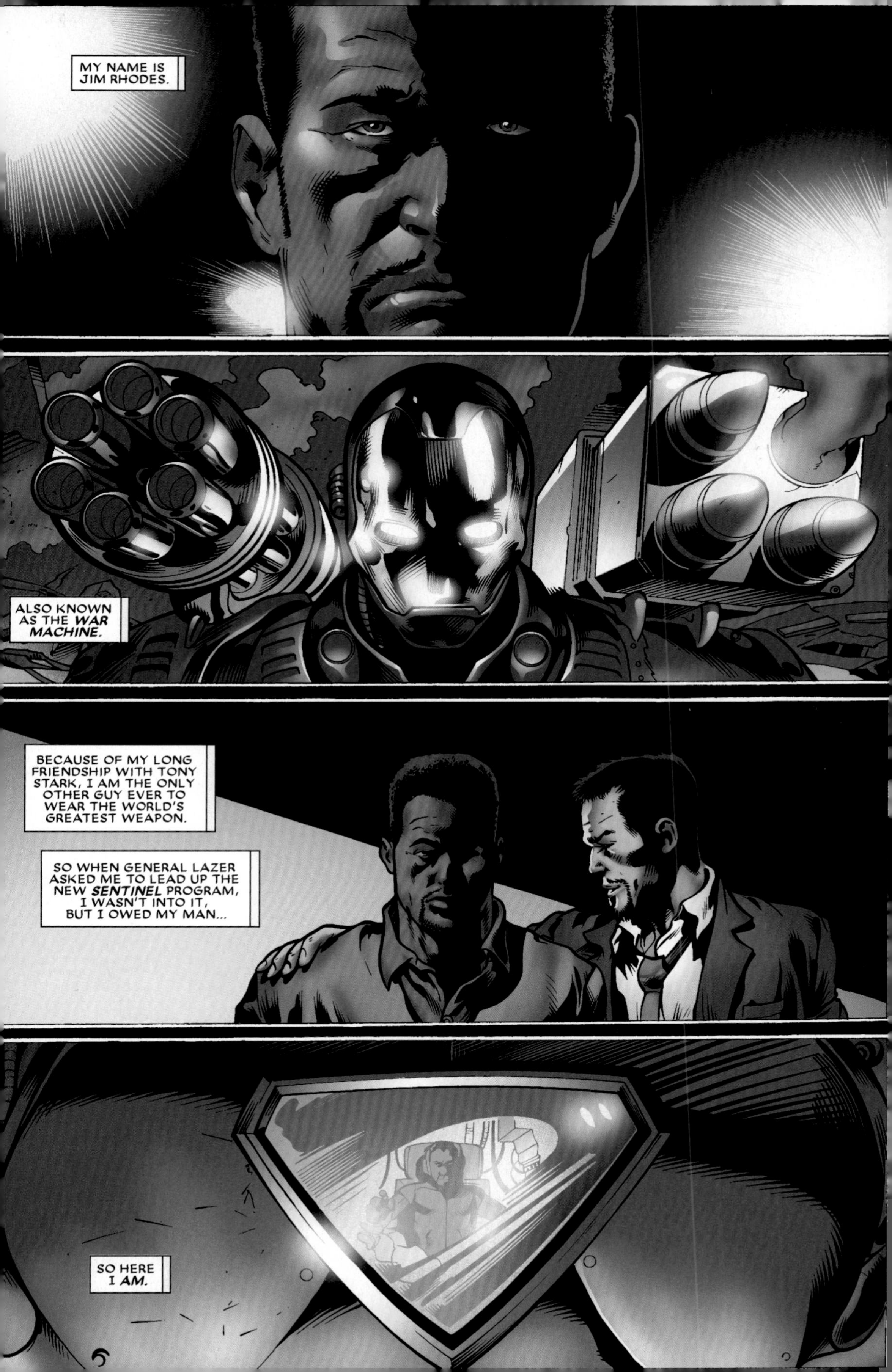
MY NAME IS JIM RHODES.
ALSO KNOWN AS THE *WAR MACHINE.*
BECAUSE OF MY LONG FRIENDSHIP WITH TONY STARK, I AM THE ONLY OTHER GUY EVER TO WEAR THE WORLD'S GREATEST WEAPON.
SO WHEN GENERAL LAZER ASKED ME TO LEAD UP THE NEW ***SENTINEL*** PROGRAM, I WASN'T INTO IT, BUT I OWED MY MAN...
SO HERE I *AM.*

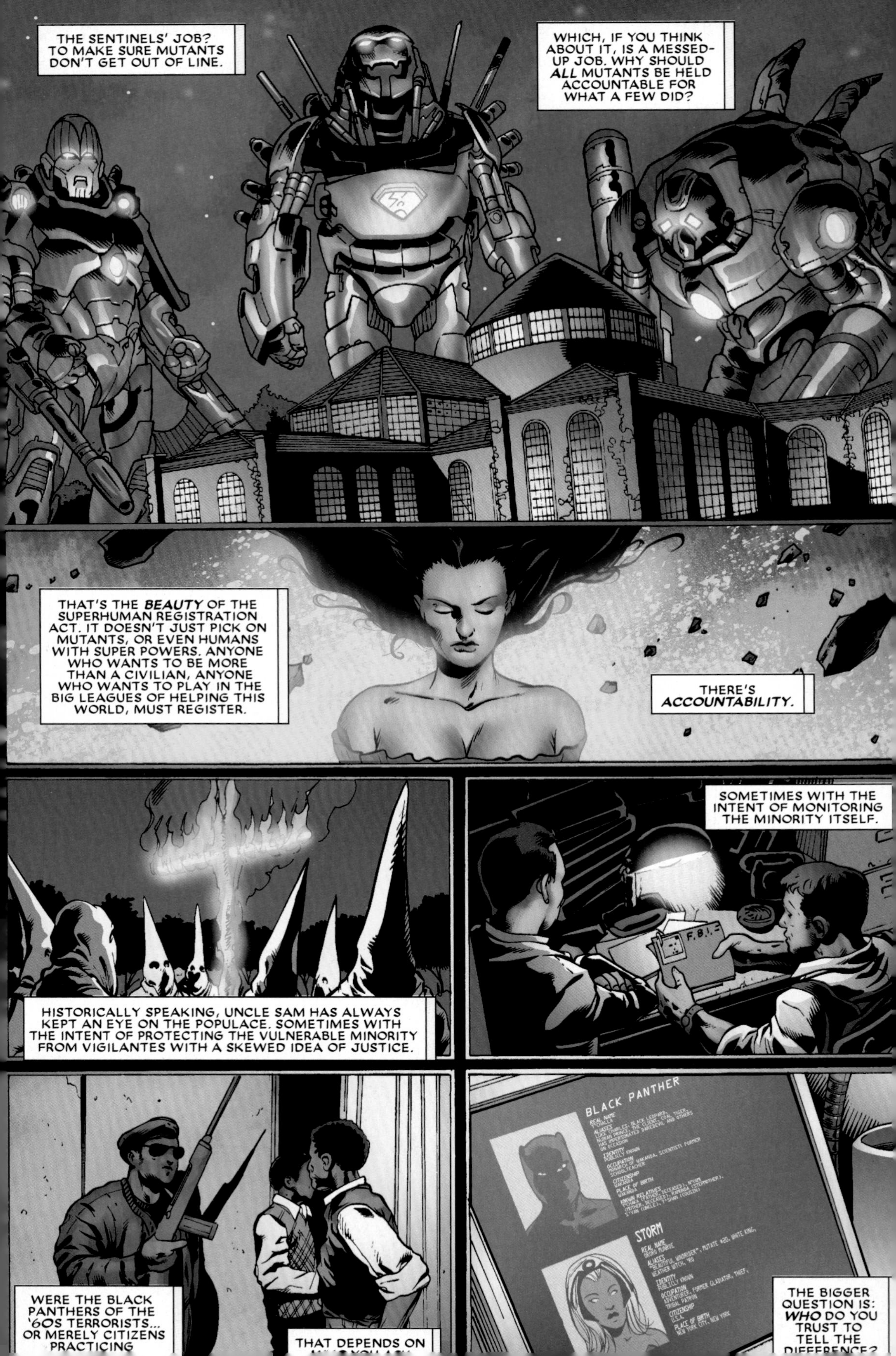

THE SENTINELS' JOB? TO MAKE SURE MUTANTS DON'T GET OUT OF LINE.
WHICH, IF YOU THINK ABOUT IT, IS A MESSED-UP JOB. WHY SHOULD *ALL* MUTANTS BE HELD ACCOUNTABLE FOR WHAT A FEW DID?
THAT'S THE *BEAUTY* OF THE SUPERHUMAN REGISTRATION ACT. IT DOESN'T JUST PICK ON MUTANTS, OR EVEN HUMANS WITH SUPER POWERS. ANYONE WHO WANTS TO BE MORE THAN A CIVILIAN, ANYONE WHO WANTS TO PLAY IN THE BIG LEAGUES OF HELPING THIS WORLD, MUST REGISTER.
THERE'S *ACCOUNTABILITY.*
HISTORICALLY SPEAKING, UNCLE SAM HAS ALWAYS KEPT AN EYE ON THE POPULACE. SOMETIMES WITH THE INTENT OF PROTECTING THE VULNERABLE MINORITY FROM VIGILANTES WITH A SKEWED IDEA OF JUSTICE.
SOMETIMES WITH THE INTENT OF MONITORING THE MINORITY ITSELF.
F.B.I.
WERE THE BLACK PANTHERS OF THE '60S TERRORISTS... OR MERELY CITIZENS PRACTICING
THAT DEPENDS ON
BLACK PANTHER
STORM
THE BIGGER QUESTION IS: *WHO* DO YOU TRUST TO TELL THE

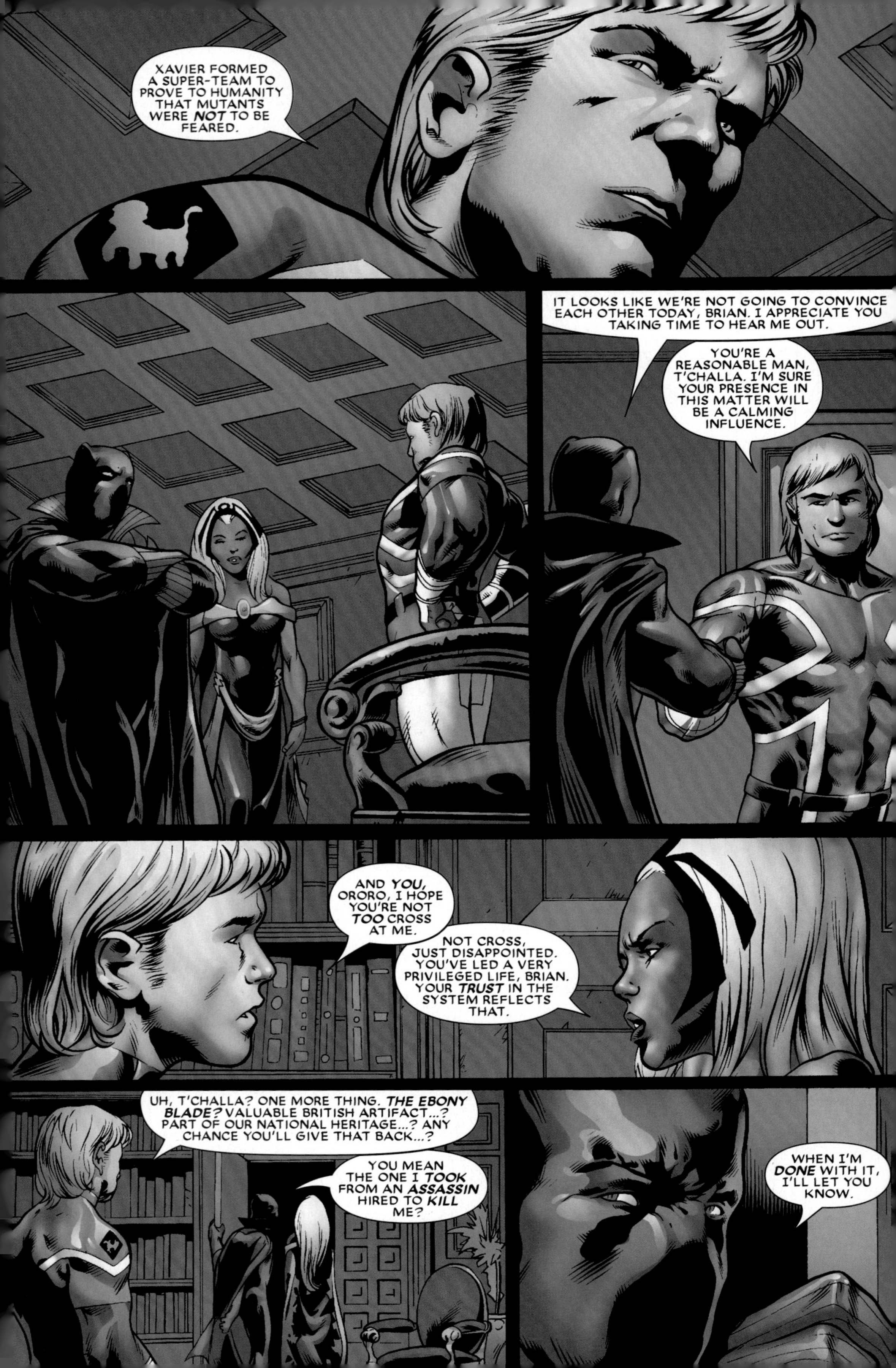
XAVIER FORMED A SUPER-TEAM TO PROVE TO HUMANITY THAT MUTANTS WERE *NOT* TO BE FEARED.
IT LOOKS LIKE WE'RE NOT GOING TO CONVINCE EACH OTHER TODAY, BRIAN. I APPRECIATE YOU TAKING TIME TO HEAR ME OUT.
YOU'RE A REASONABLE MAN, T'CHALLA. I'M SURE YOUR PRESENCE IN THIS MATTER WILL BE A CALMING INFLUENCE.
AND *YOU*, ORORO, I HOPE YOU'RE NOT *TOO* CROSS AT ME.
NOT CROSS, JUST DISAPPOINTED. YOU'VE LED A VERY PRIVILEGED LIFE, BRIAN. YOUR *TRUST* IN THE SYSTEM REFLECTS THAT.
UH, T'CHALLA? ONE MORE THING. *THE EBONY BLADE?* VALUABLE BRITISH ARTIFACT...? PART OF OUR NATIONAL HERITAGE...? ANY CHANCE YOU'LL GIVE THAT BACK...?
YOU MEAN THE ONE I *TOOK* FROM AN *ASSASSIN* HIRED TO *KILL* ME?
WHEN I'M *DONE* WITH IT, I'LL LET YOU KNOW.

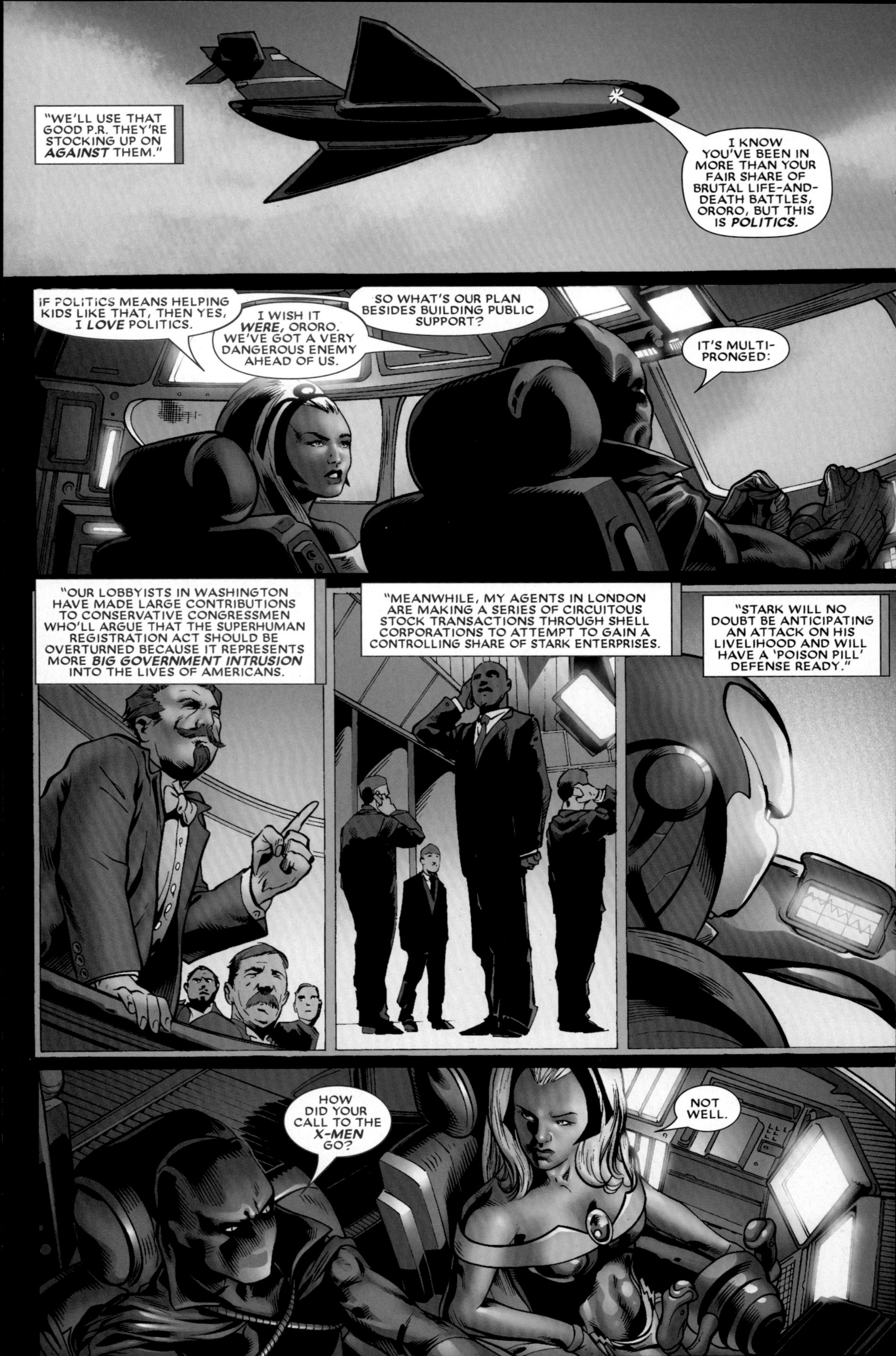
"WE'LL USE THAT GOOD P.R. THEY'RE STOCKING UP ON *AGAINST* THEM."
I KNOW YOU'VE BEEN IN MORE THAN YOUR FAIR SHARE OF BRUTAL LIFE-AND-DEATH BATTLES, ORORO, BUT THIS IS *POLITICS.*
IF POLITICS MEANS HELPING KIDS LIKE THAT, THEN YES, I *LOVE* POLITICS.
I WISH IT *WERE,* ORORO. WE'VE GOT A VERY DANGEROUS ENEMY AHEAD OF US.
SO WHAT'S OUR PLAN BESIDES BUILDING PUBLIC SUPPORT?
IT'S MULTI-PRONGED:
"OUR LOBBYISTS IN WASHINGTON HAVE MADE LARGE CONTRIBUTIONS TO CONSERVATIVE CONGRESSMEN WHO'LL ARGUE THAT THE SUPERHUMAN REGISTRATION ACT SHOULD BE OVERTURNED BECAUSE IT REPRESENTS MORE *BIG GOVERNMENT INTRUSION* INTO THE LIVES OF AMERICANS.
"MEANWHILE, MY AGENTS IN LONDON ARE MAKING A SERIES OF CIRCUITOUS STOCK TRANSACTIONS THROUGH SHELL CORPORATIONS TO ATTEMPT TO GAIN A CONTROLLING SHARE OF STARK ENTERPRISES.
"STARK WILL NO DOUBT BE ANTICIPATING AN ATTACK ON HIS LIVELIHOOD AND WILL HAVE A 'POISON PILL' DEFENSE READY."
HOW DID YOUR CALL TO THE *X-MEN* GO?
NOT WELL.

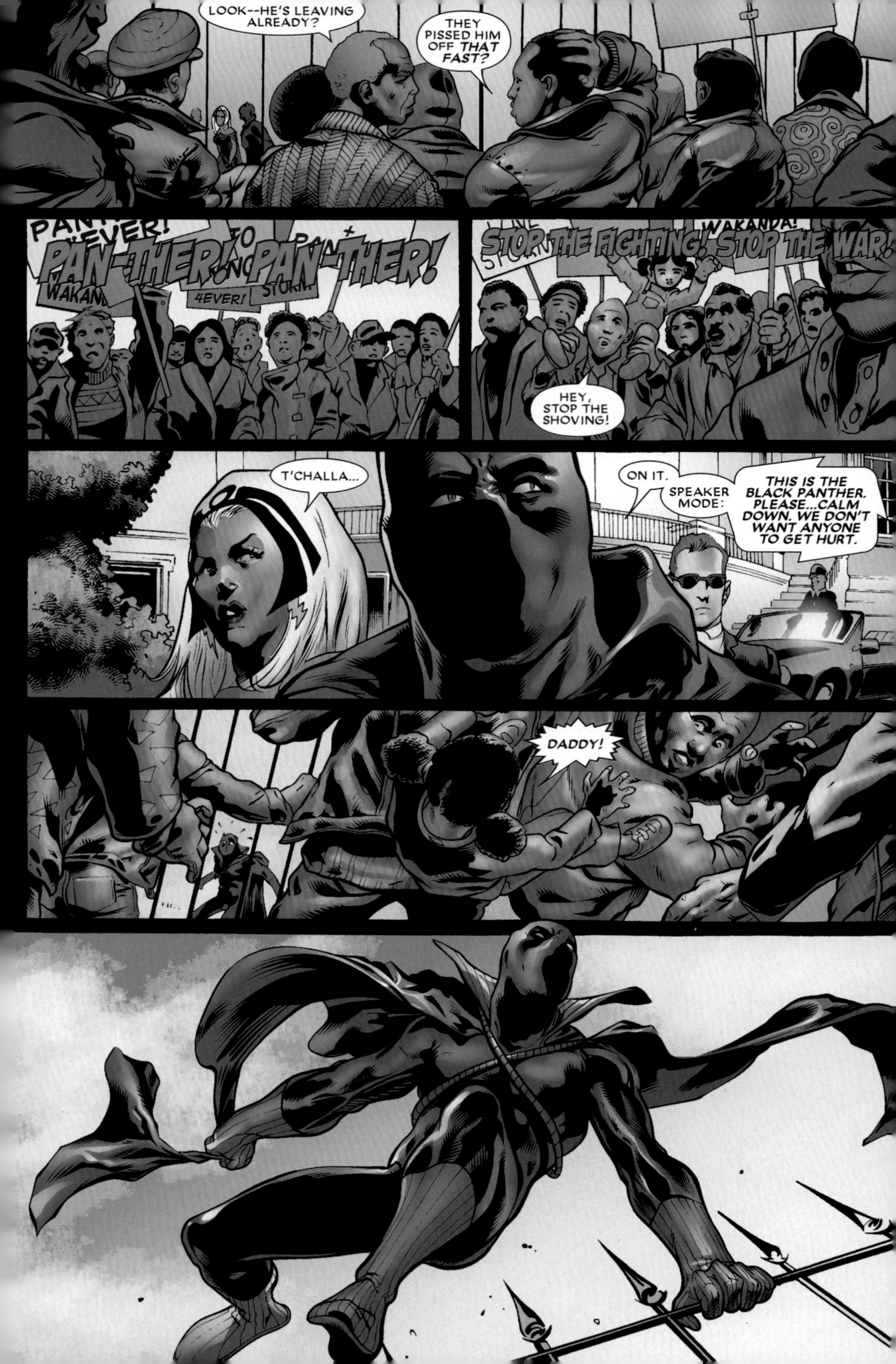

LOOK--HE'S LEAVING ALREADY?
THEY PISSED HIM OFF *THAT FAST?*
PAN-THER! PAN-THER!
4EVER!
WAKANDA!
STOP THE FIGHTING! STOP THE WAR!
HEY, STOP THE SHOVING!
T'CHALLA...
ON IT.
SPEAKER MODE:
THIS IS THE BLACK PANTHER. PLEASE...CALM DOWN. WE DON'T WANT ANYONE TO GET HURT.
DADDY!

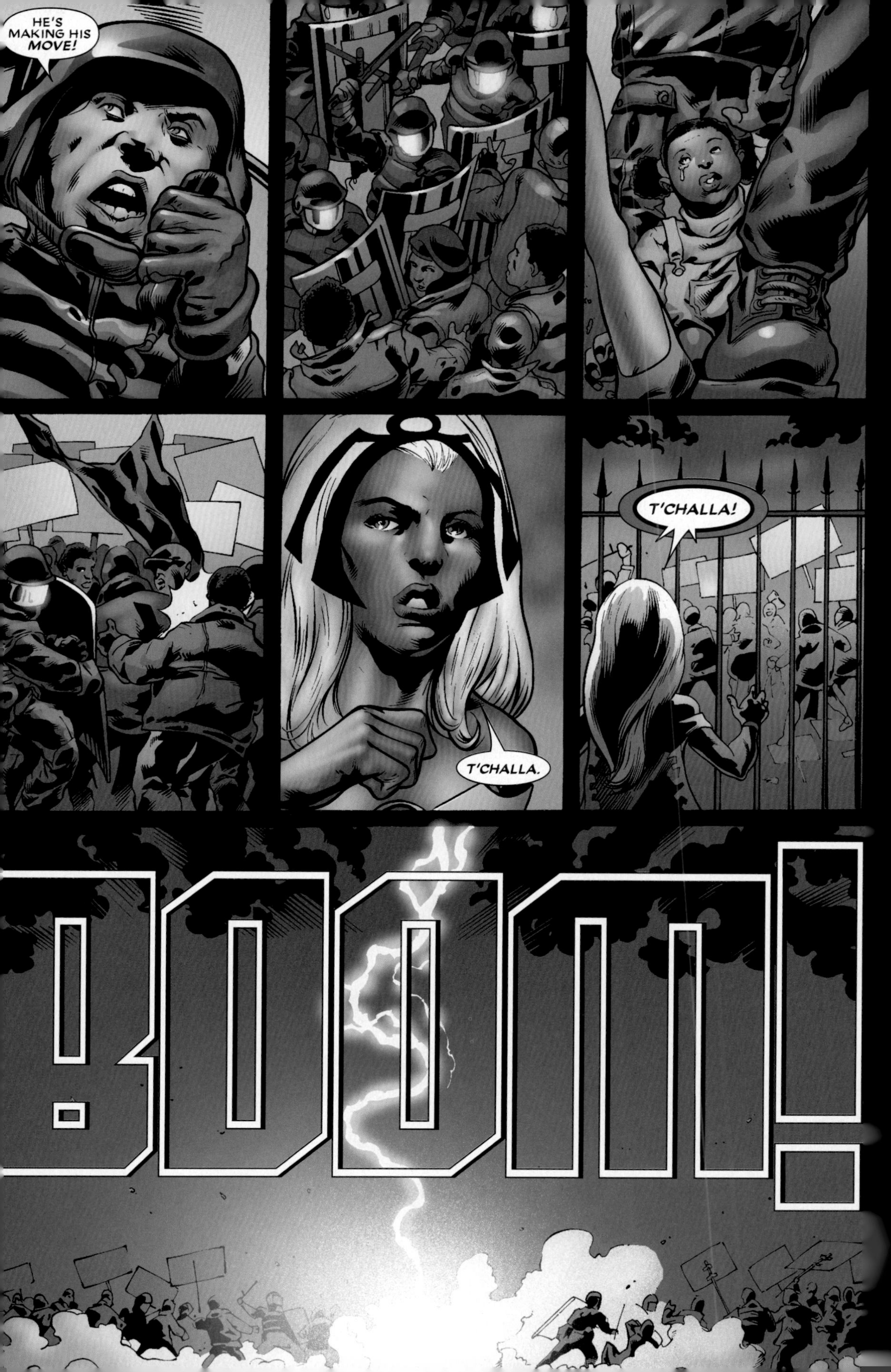
HE'S MAKING HIS MOVE!
T'CHALLA.
T'CHALLA!
BOOM!

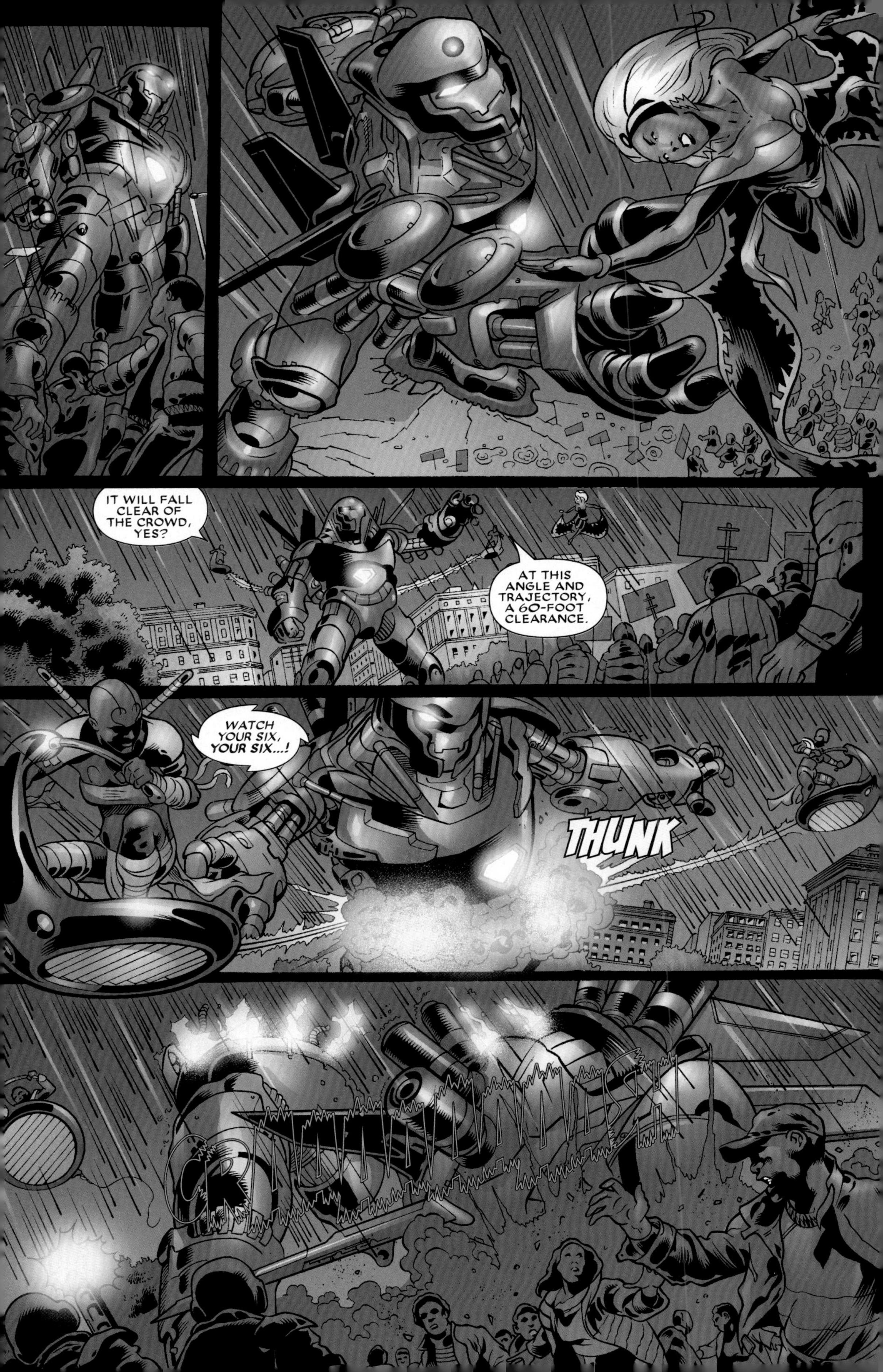
IT WILL FALL CLEAR OF THE CROWD, YES?
AT THIS ANGLE AND TRAJECTORY, A 60-FOOT CLEARANCE.
WATCH YOUR SIX, YOUR SIX...!
THUNK

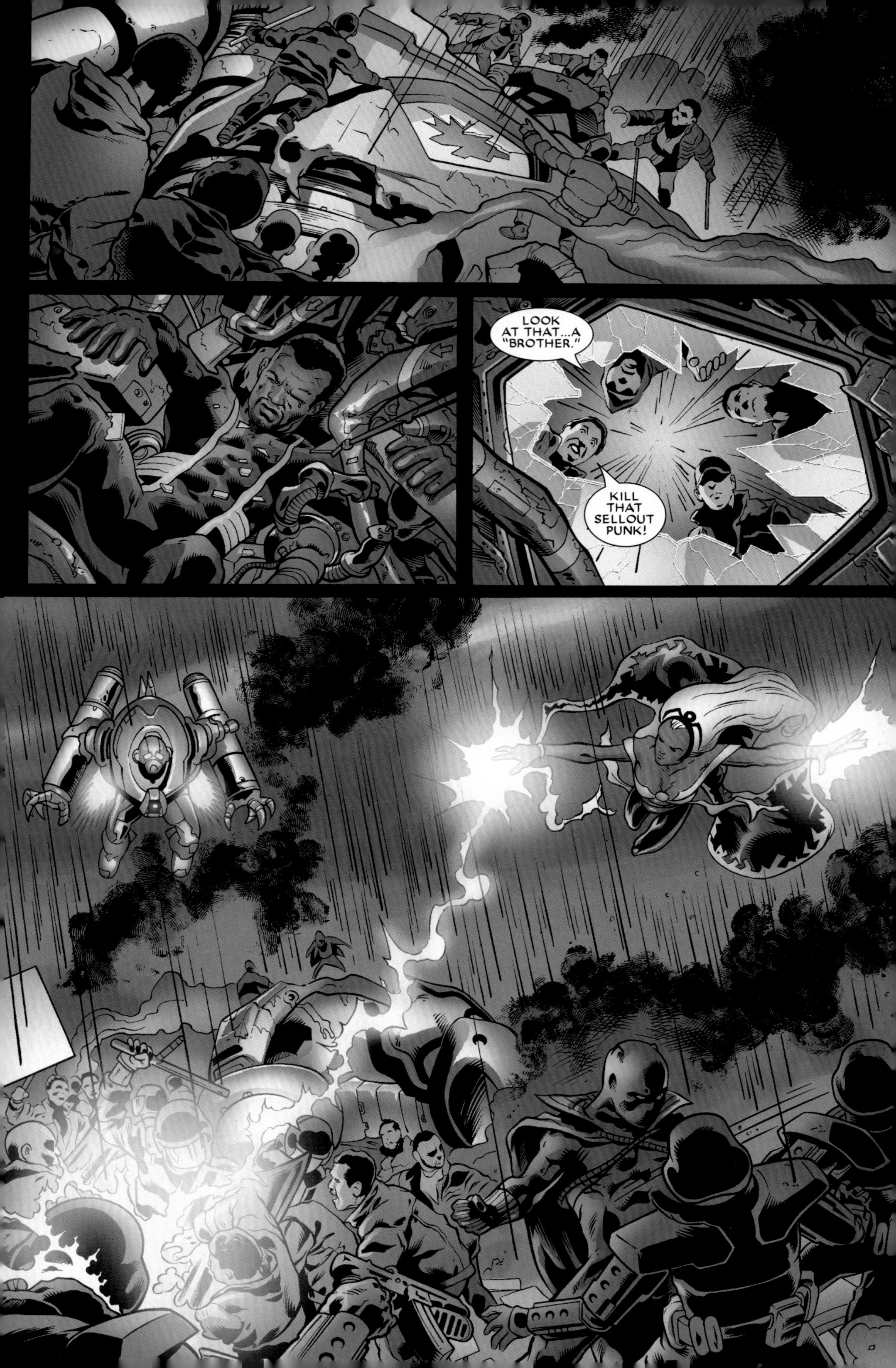
LOOK AT THAT...A "BROTHER."
KILL THAT SELLOUT PUNK!

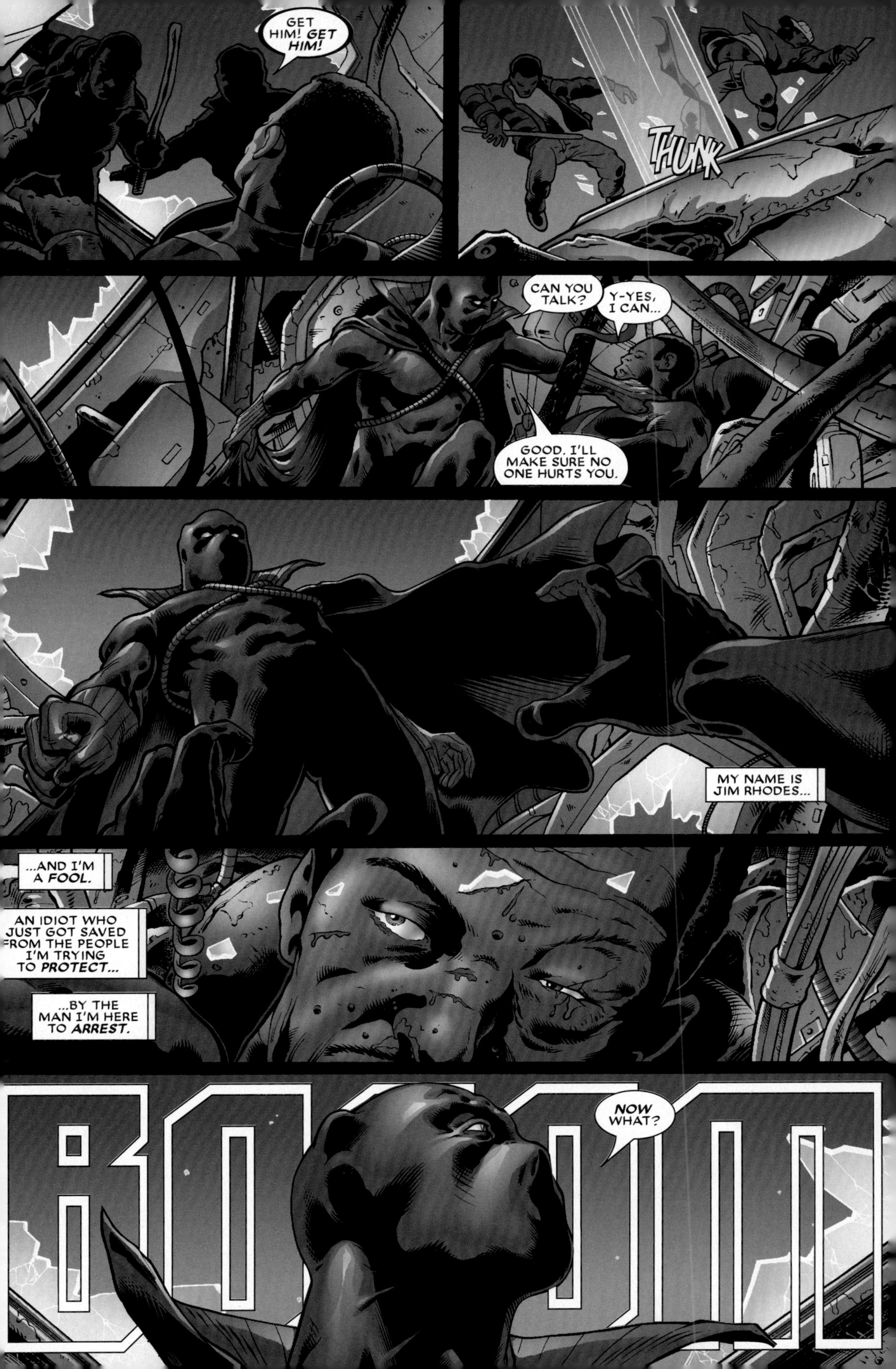
GET HIM! GET HIM!
THUNK
CAN YOU TALK?
Y-YES, I CAN...
GOOD. I'LL MAKE SURE NO ONE HURTS YOU.
MY NAME IS JIM RHODES...
...AND I'M A FOOL.
AN IDIOT WHO JUST GOT SAVED FROM THE PEOPLE I'M TRYING TO PROTECT...
...BY THE MAN I'M HERE TO ARREST.
NOW WHAT?

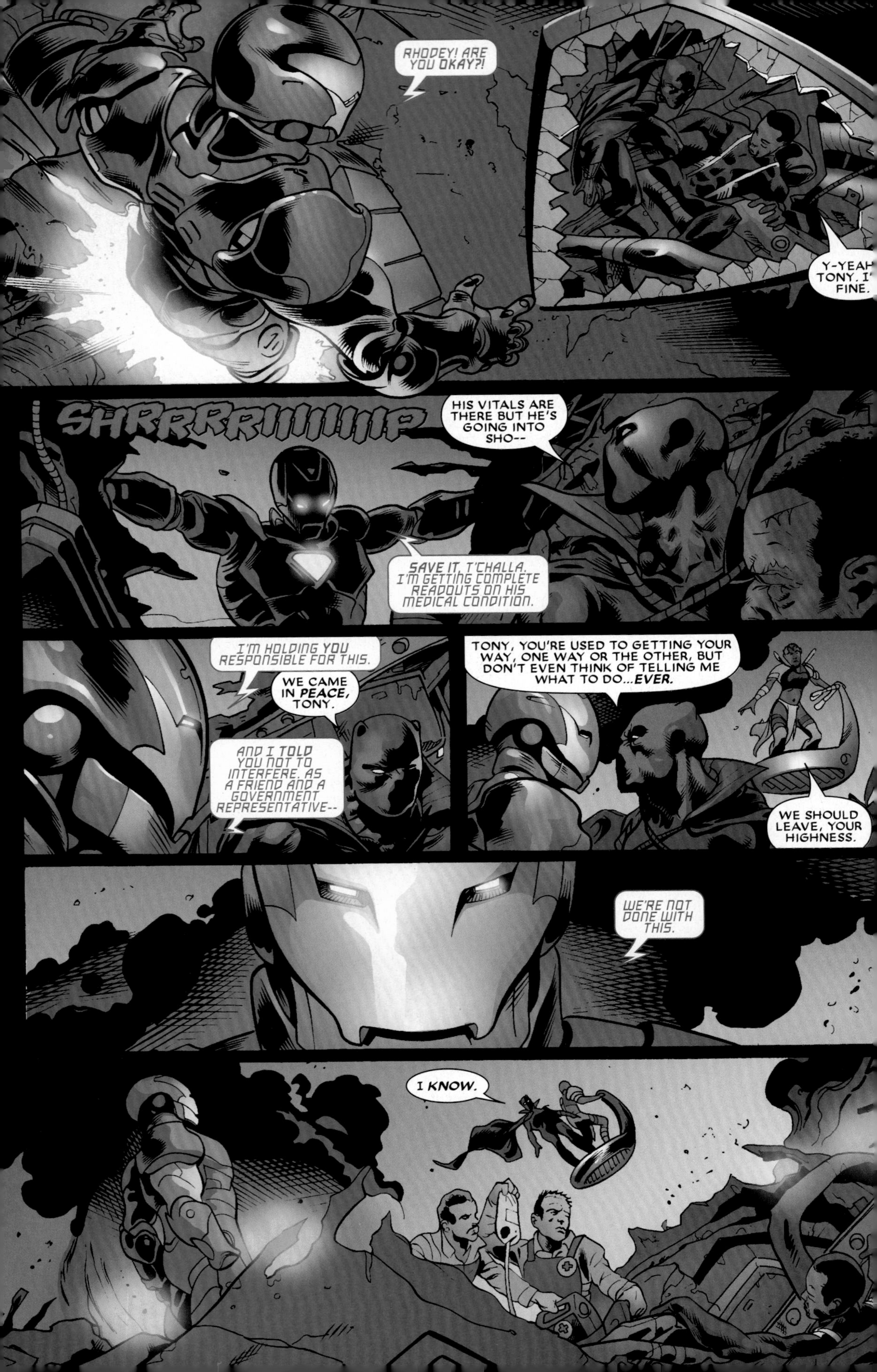
RHODEY! ARE YOU OKAY?!
Y-YEAH TONY. I' FINE.
SHRRRRIIIIIIIP
HIS VITALS ARE THERE BUT HE'S GOING INTO SHO--
SAVE IT, T'CHALLA. I'M GETTING COMPLETE READOUTS ON HIS MEDICAL CONDITION.
I'M HOLDING YOU RESPONSIBLE FOR THIS.
WE CAME IN PEACE, TONY.
AND I TOLD YOU NOT TO INTERFERE. AS A FRIEND AND A GOVERNMENT REPRESENTATIVE--
TONY, YOU'RE USED TO GETTING YOUR WAY, ONE WAY OR THE OTHER, BUT DON'T EVEN THINK OF TELLING ME WHAT TO DO...EVER.
WE SHOULD LEAVE, YOUR HIGHNESS.
WE'RE NOT DONE WITH THIS.
I KNOW.

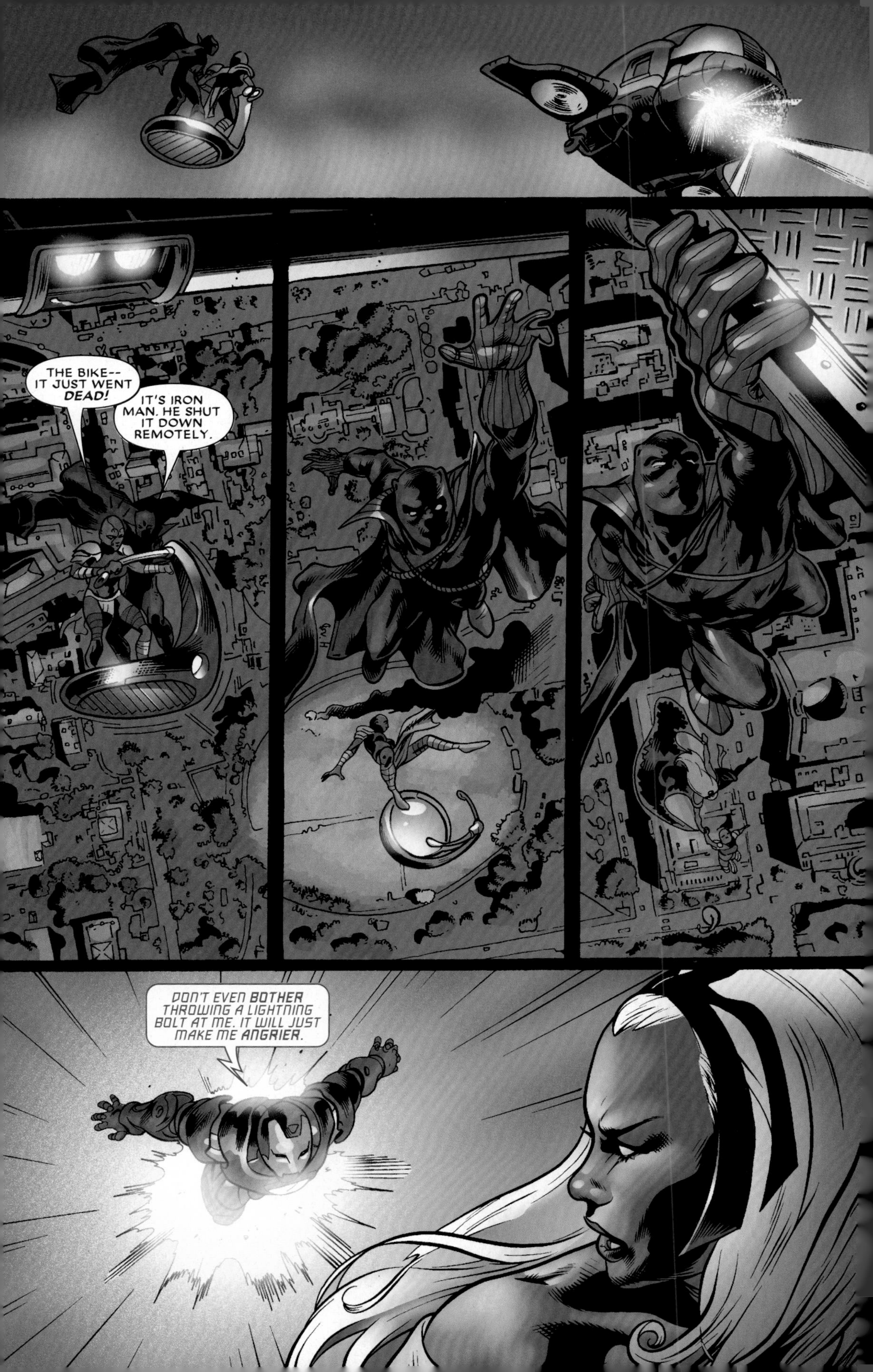
THE BIKE--
IT JUST WENT
DEAD!
IT'S IRON
MAN. HE SHUT
IT DOWN
REMOTELY.
DON'T EVEN BOTHER THROWING A LIGHTNING BOLT AT ME. IT WILL JUST MAKE ME ANGRIER.

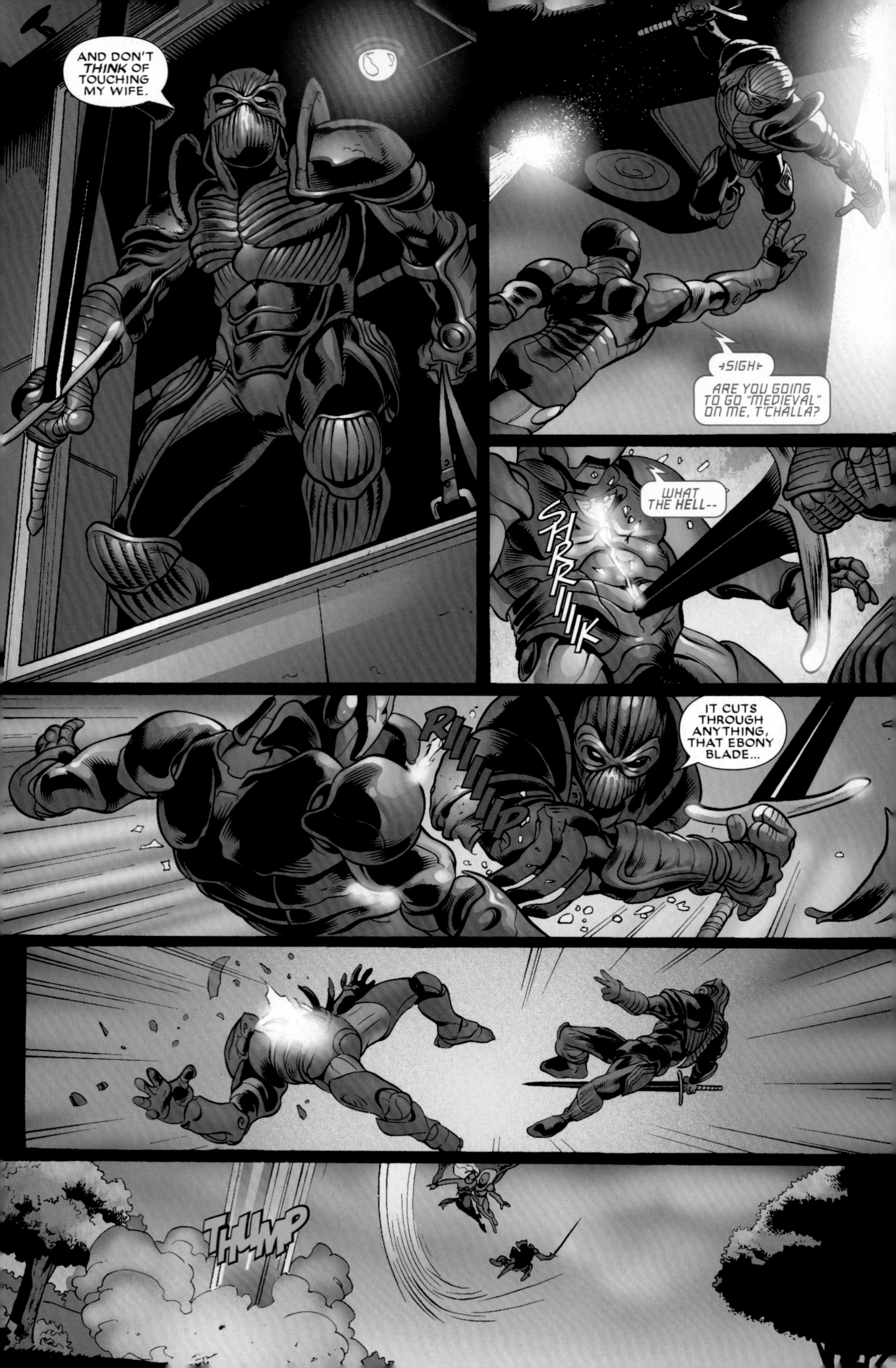
AND DON'T THINK OF TOUCHING MY WIFE.
-SIGH-
ARE YOU GOING TO GO "MEDIEVAL" ON ME, T'CHALLA?
WHAT THE HELL--
SHRRIIIIK
IT CUTS THROUGH ANYTHING, THAT EBONY BLADE...
RIIIIIIP
THUMP

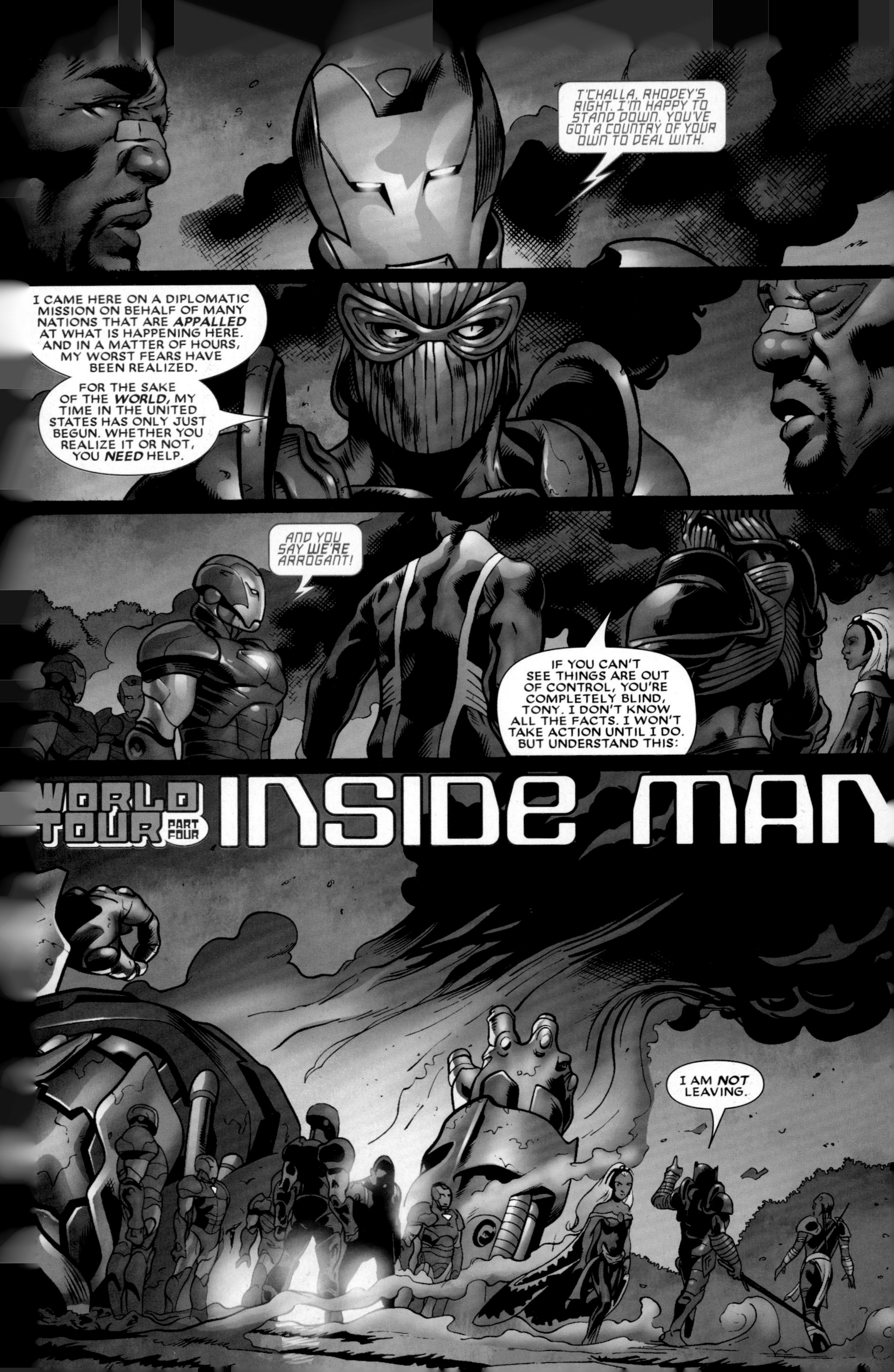
T'CHALLA. RHODEY'S RIGHT. I'M HAPPY TO STAND DOWN. YOU'VE GOT A COUNTRY OF YOUR OWN TO DEAL WITH.
I CAME HERE ON A DIPLOMATIC MISSION ON BEHALF OF MANY NATIONS THAT ARE *APPALLED* AT WHAT IS HAPPENING HERE. AND IN A MATTER OF HOURS, MY WORST FEARS HAVE BEEN REALIZED.
FOR THE SAKE OF THE *WORLD*, MY TIME IN THE UNITED STATES HAS ONLY JUST BEGUN. WHETHER YOU REALIZE IT OR NOT, YOU *NEED* HELP.
AND YOU SAY *WE'RE* ARROGANT!
IF YOU CAN'T SEE THINGS ARE OUT OF CONTROL, YOU'RE COMPLETELY BLIND, TONY. I DON'T KNOW ALL THE FACTS. I WON'T TAKE ACTION UNTIL I DO. BUT UNDERSTAND THIS:
WORLD TOUR PART FOUR
INSIDE MAN
I AM *NOT* LEAVING.

23

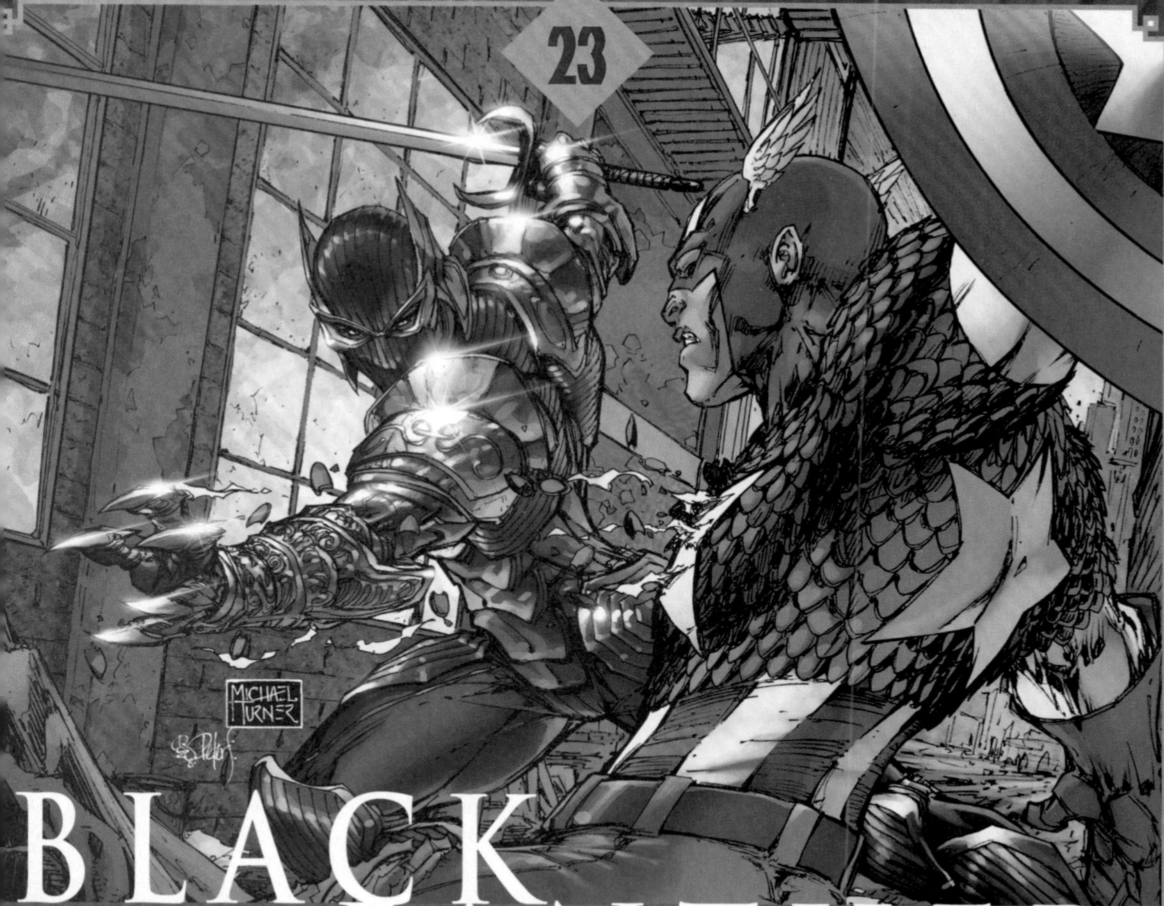
MICHAEL TURNER

BLACK PANTHER

A MARVEL COMICS EVENT

CIVIL WAR

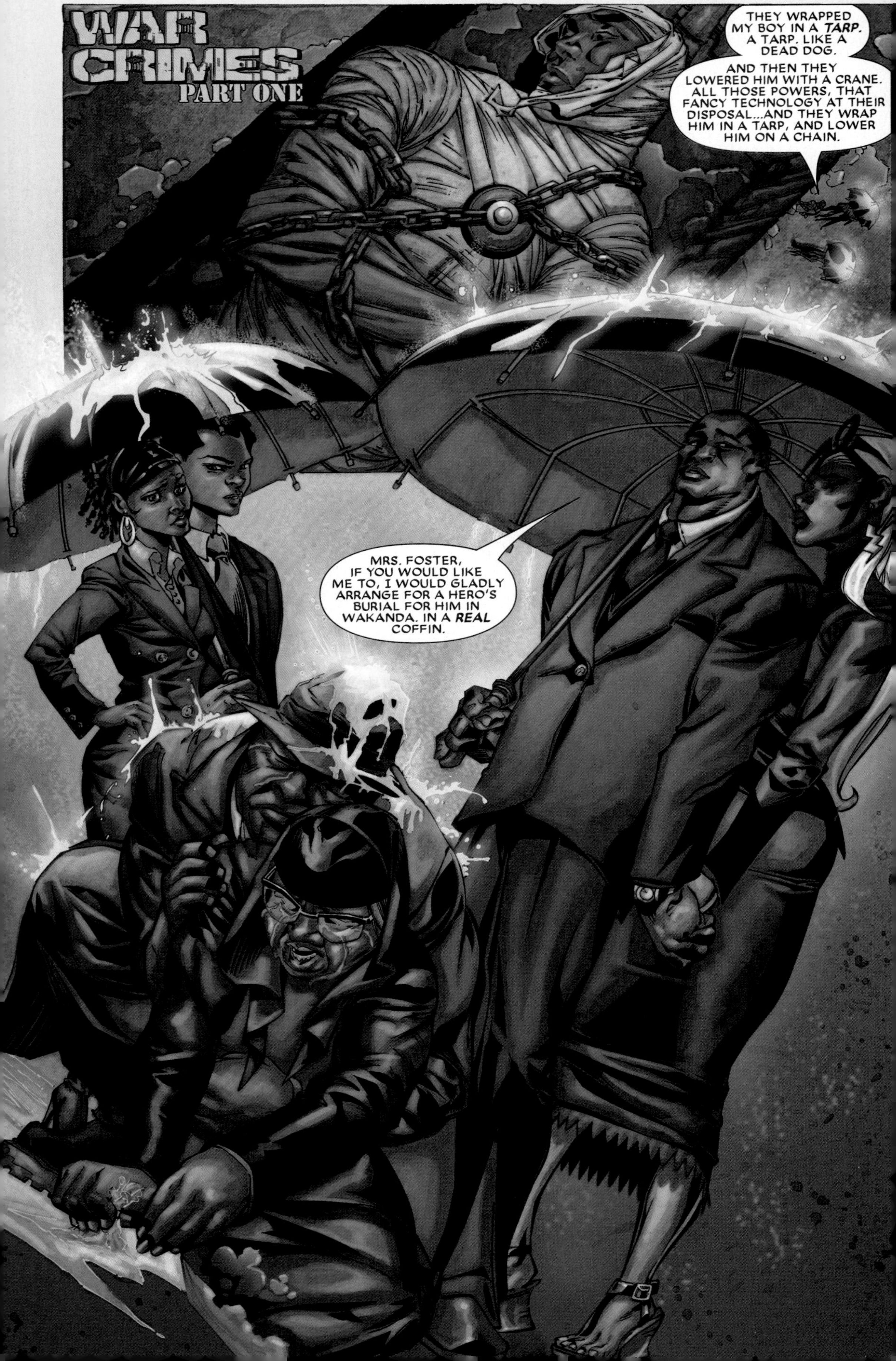
WAR CRIMES
PART ONE
THEY WRAPPED MY BOY IN A *TARP.* A TARP. LIKE A DEAD DOG.
AND THEN THEY LOWERED HIM WITH A CRANE. ALL THOSE POWERS, THAT FANCY TECHNOLOGY AT THEIR DISPOSAL...AND THEY WRAP HIM IN A TARP, AND LOWER HIM ON A CHAIN.
MRS. FOSTER, IF YOU WOULD LIKE ME TO, I WOULD GLADLY ARRANGE FOR A HERO'S BURIAL FOR HIM IN WAKANDA. IN A *REAL* COFFIN.

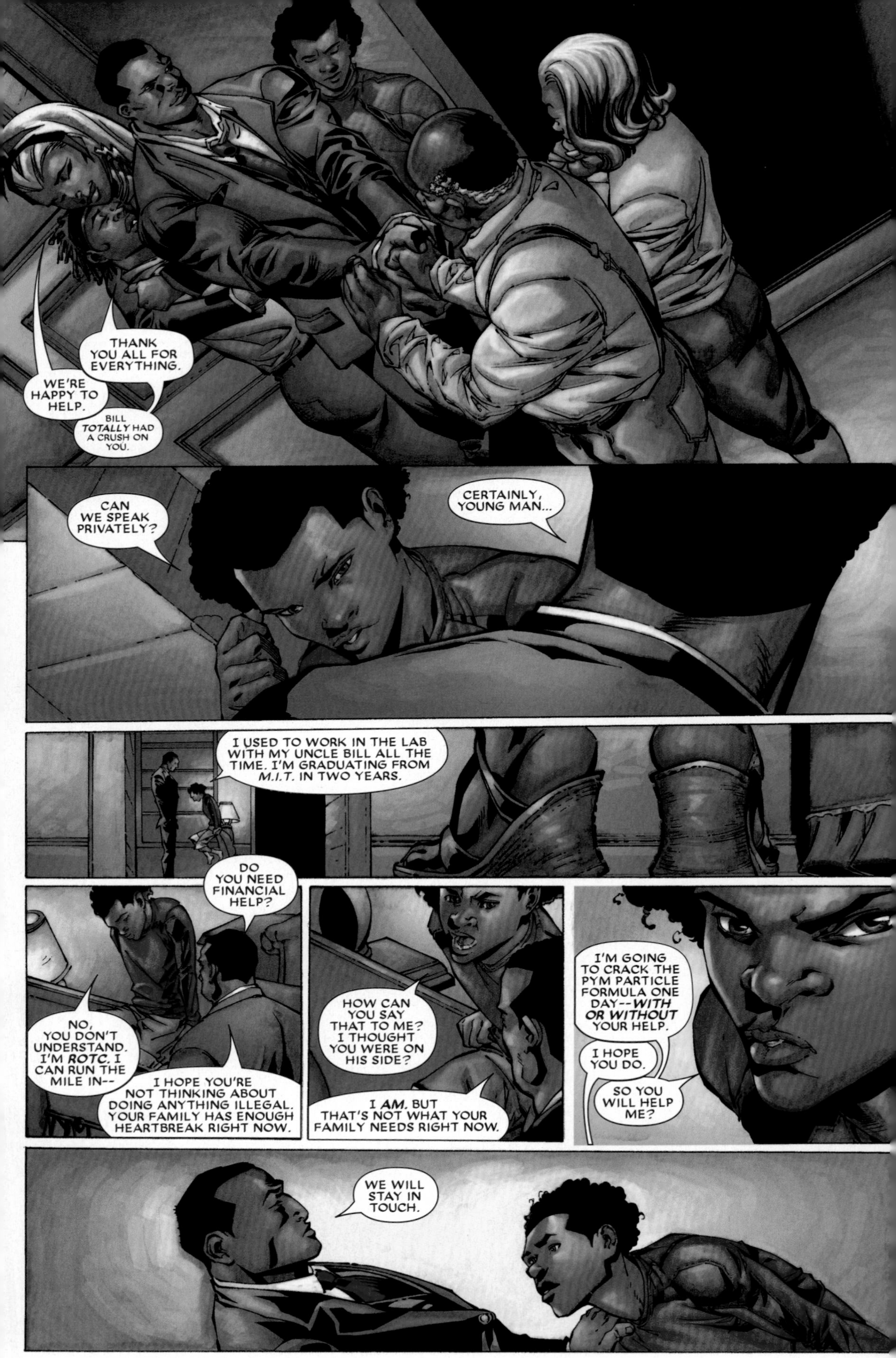
THANK YOU ALL FOR EVERYTHING.
WE'RE HAPPY TO HELP.
BILL *TOTALLY* HAD A CRUSH ON YOU.
CAN WE SPEAK PRIVATELY?
CERTAINLY, YOUNG MAN...
I USED TO WORK IN THE LAB WITH MY UNCLE BILL ALL THE TIME. I'M GRADUATING FROM *M.I.T.* IN TWO YEARS.
DO YOU NEED FINANCIAL HELP?
NO, YOU DON'T UNDERSTAND. I'M *ROTC*. I CAN RUN THE MILE IN--
I HOPE YOU'RE NOT THINKING ABOUT DOING ANYTHING ILLEGAL. YOUR FAMILY HAS ENOUGH HEARTBREAK RIGHT NOW.
HOW CAN YOU SAY THAT TO ME? I THOUGHT YOU WERE ON HIS SIDE?
I *AM*. BUT THAT'S NOT WHAT YOUR FAMILY NEEDS RIGHT NOW.
I'M GOING TO CRACK THE PYM PARTICLE FORMULA ONE DAY--*WITH OR WITHOUT* YOUR HELP.
I HOPE YOU DO.
SO YOU WILL HELP ME?
WE WILL STAY IN TOUCH.

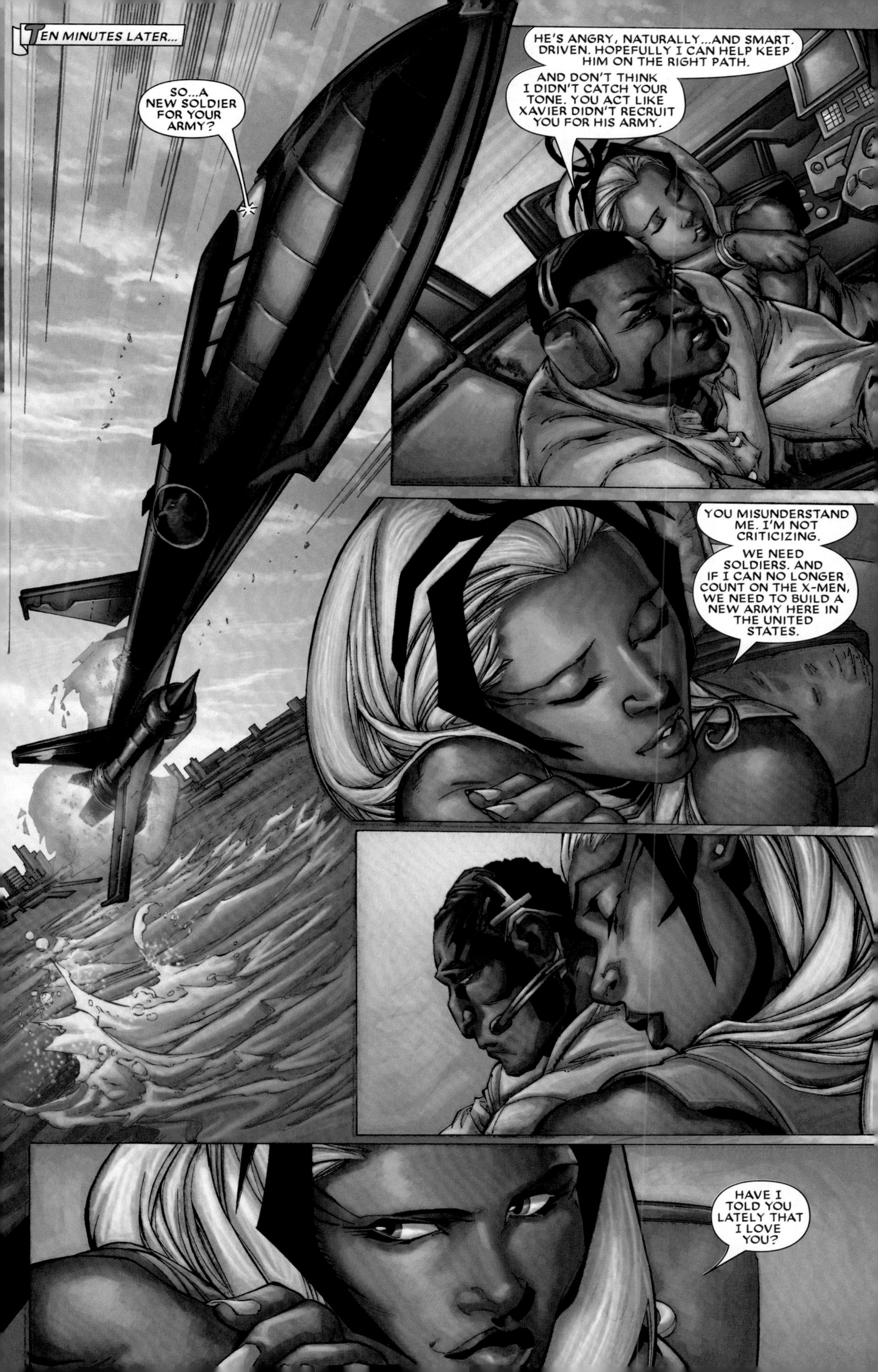
TEN MINUTES LATER...
SO...A NEW SOLDIER FOR YOUR ARMY?
HE'S ANGRY, NATURALLY...AND SMART. DRIVEN. HOPEFULLY I CAN HELP KEEP HIM ON THE RIGHT PATH.
AND DON'T THINK I DIDN'T CATCH YOUR TONE. YOU ACT LIKE XAVIER DIDN'T RECRUIT YOU FOR HIS ARMY.
YOU MISUNDERSTAND ME. I'M NOT CRITICIZING.
WE NEED SOLDIERS. AND IF I CAN NO LONGER COUNT ON THE X-MEN, WE NEED TO BUILD A NEW ARMY HERE IN THE UNITED STATES.
HAVE I TOLD YOU LATELY THAT I LOVE YOU?

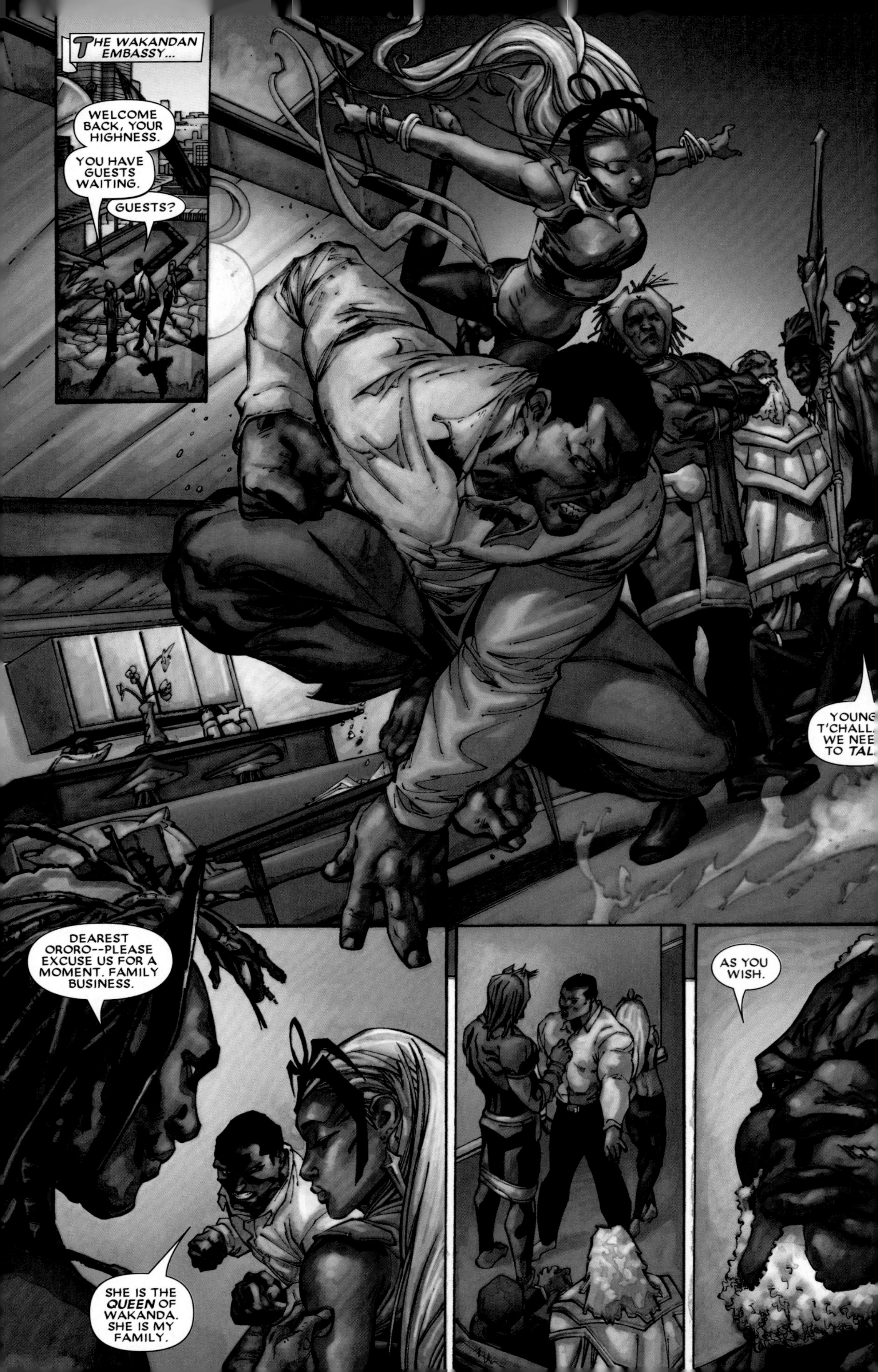

THE WAKANDAN EMBASSY...
WELCOME BACK, YOUR HIGHNESS.
YOU HAVE GUESTS WAITING.
GUESTS?
YOUNG T'CHALL WE NEE TO TAL
DEAREST ORORO--PLEASE EXCUSE US FOR A MOMENT. FAMILY BUSINESS.
SHE IS THE QUEEN OF WAKANDA. SHE IS MY FAMILY.
AS YOU WISH.

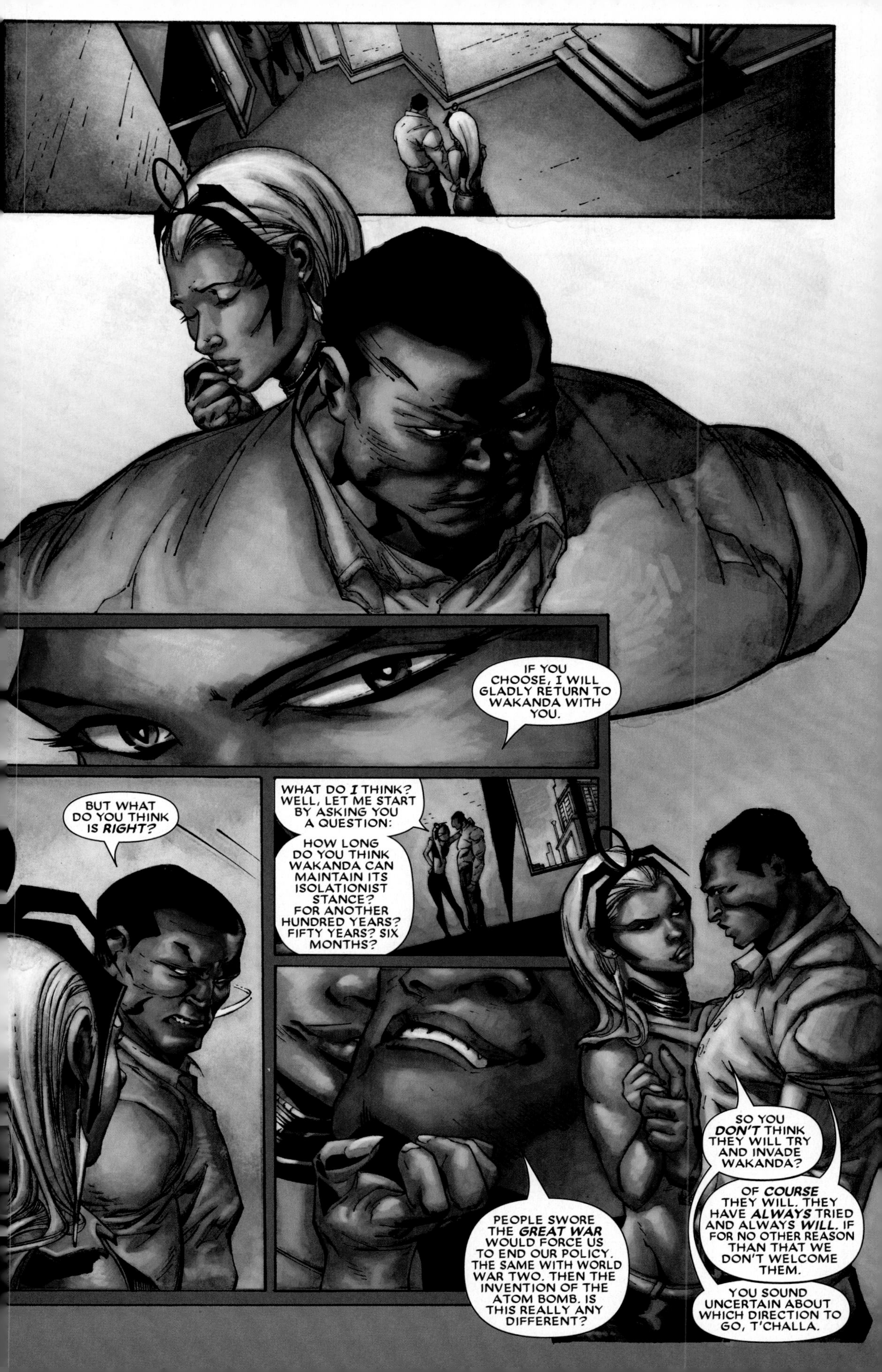
IF YOU CHOOSE, I WILL GLADLY RETURN TO WAKANDA WITH YOU.
BUT WHAT DO YOU THINK IS *RIGHT?*
WHAT DO *I* THINK? WELL, LET ME START BY ASKING YOU A QUESTION:
HOW LONG DO YOU THINK WAKANDA CAN MAINTAIN ITS ISOLATIONIST STANCE? FOR ANOTHER HUNDRED YEARS? FIFTY YEARS? SIX MONTHS?
PEOPLE SWORE THE *GREAT WAR* WOULD FORCE US TO END OUR POLICY. THE SAME WITH WORLD WAR TWO. THEN THE INVENTION OF THE ATOM BOMB. IS THIS REALLY ANY DIFFERENT?
SO YOU *DON'T* THINK THEY WILL TRY AND INVADE WAKANDA?
OF *COURSE* THEY WILL. THEY HAVE *ALWAYS* TRIED AND ALWAYS *WILL*. IF FOR NO OTHER REASON THAN THAT WE DON'T WELCOME THEM.
YOU SOUND UNCERTAIN ABOUT WHICH DIRECTION TO GO, T'CHALLA.

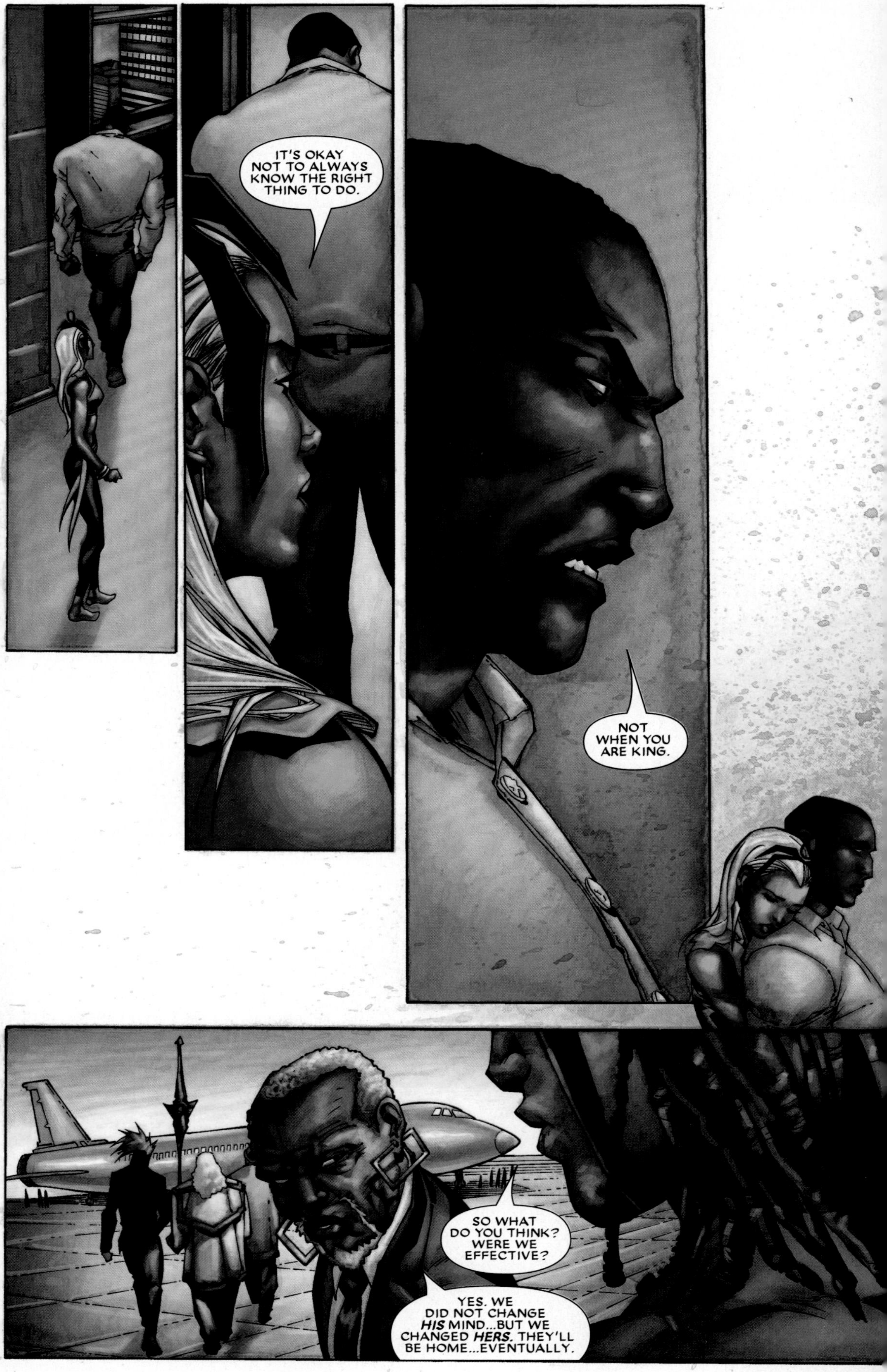
IT'S OKAY NOT TO ALWAYS KNOW THE RIGHT THING TO DO.
NOT WHEN YOU ARE KING.
SO WHAT DO YOU THINK? WERE WE EFFECTIVE?
YES. WE DID NOT CHANGE *HIS* MIND...BUT WE CHANGED *HERS.* THEY'LL BE HOME...EVENTUALLY.

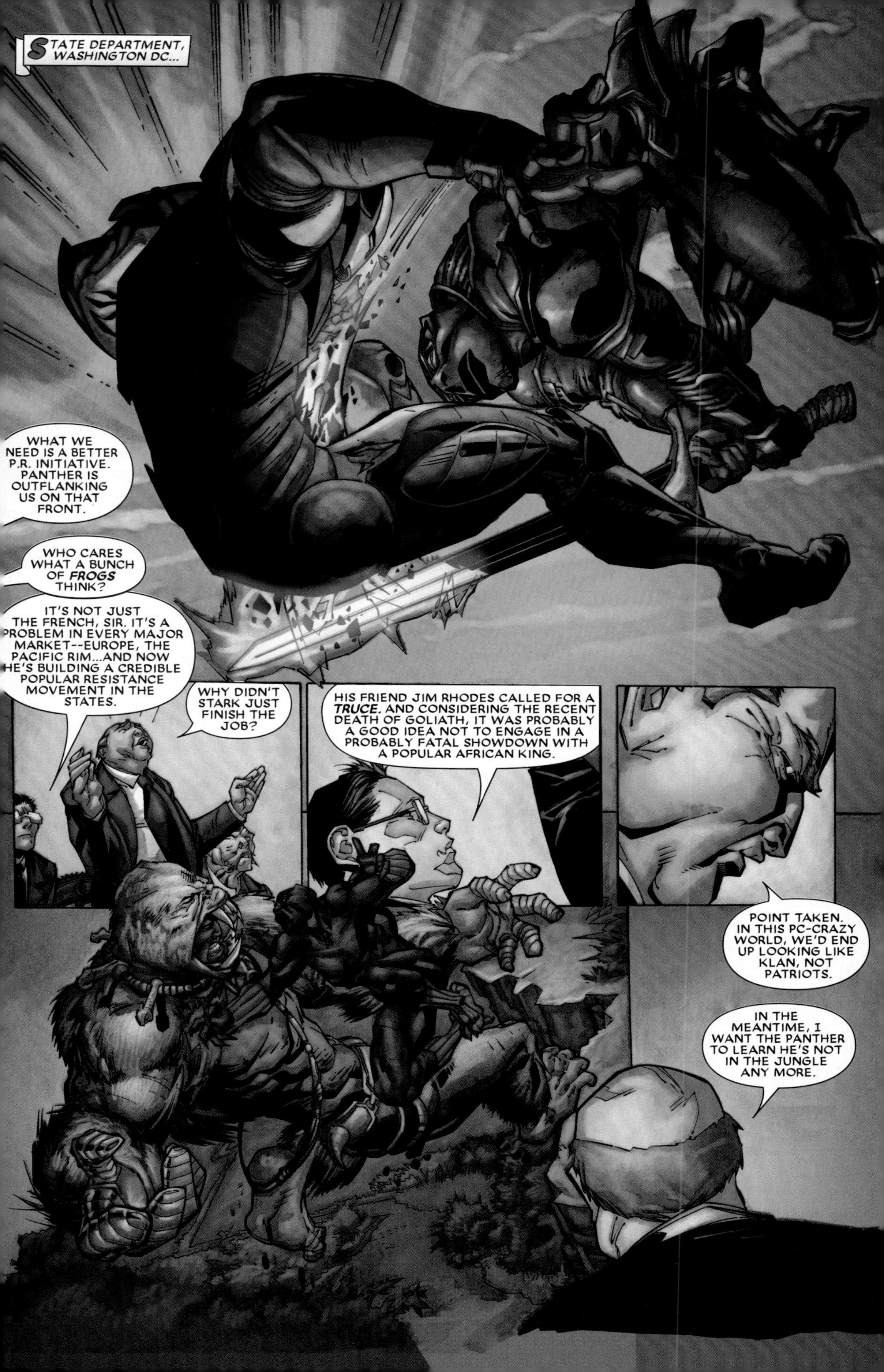
STATE DEPARTMENT, WASHINGTON DC...
WHAT WE NEED IS A BETTER P.R. INITIATIVE. PANTHER IS OUTFLANKING US ON THAT FRONT.
WHO CARES WHAT A BUNCH OF FROGS THINK?
IT'S NOT JUST THE FRENCH, SIR. IT'S A PROBLEM IN EVERY MAJOR MARKET--EUROPE, THE PACIFIC RIM...AND NOW HE'S BUILDING A CREDIBLE POPULAR RESISTANCE MOVEMENT IN THE STATES.
WHY DIDN'T STARK JUST FINISH THE JOB?
HIS FRIEND JIM RHODES CALLED FOR A TRUCE. AND CONSIDERING THE RECENT DEATH OF GOLIATH, IT WAS PROBABLY A GOOD IDEA NOT TO ENGAGE IN A PROBABLY FATAL SHOWDOWN WITH A POPULAR AFRICAN KING.
POINT TAKEN. IN THIS PC-CRAZY WORLD, WE'D END UP LOOKING LIKE KLAN, NOT PATRIOTS.
IN THE MEANTIME, I WANT THE PANTHER TO LEARN HE'S NOT IN THE JUNGLE ANY MORE.

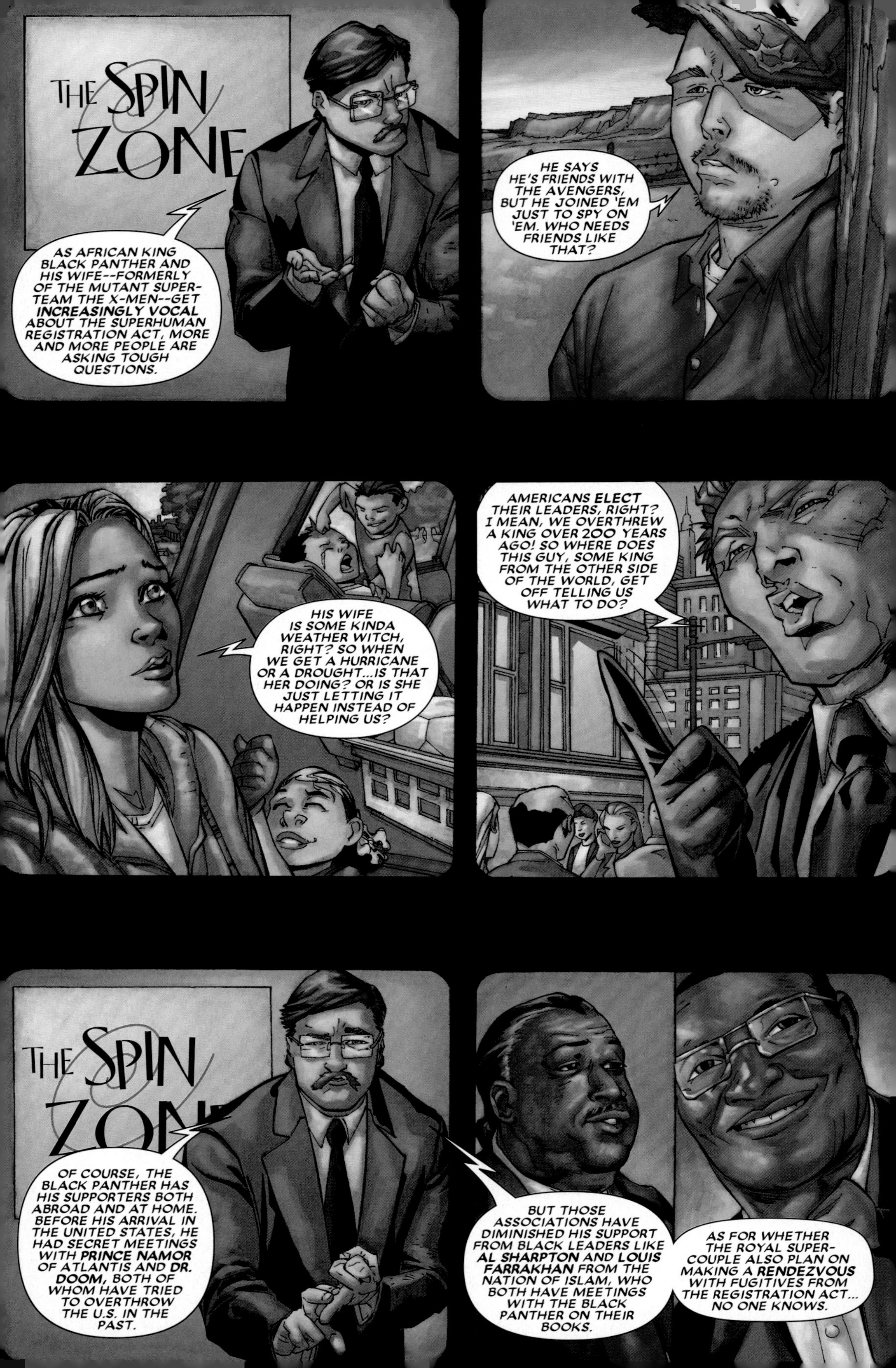
THE SPIN ZONE
AS AFRICAN KING BLACK PANTHER AND HIS WIFE--FORMERLY OF THE MUTANT SUPER-TEAM THE X-MEN--GET INCREASINGLY VOCAL ABOUT THE SUPERHUMAN REGISTRATION ACT, MORE AND MORE PEOPLE ARE ASKING TOUGH QUESTIONS.
HE SAYS HE'S FRIENDS WITH THE AVENGERS, BUT HE JOINED 'EM JUST TO SPY ON 'EM. WHO NEEDS FRIENDS LIKE THAT?
HIS WIFE IS SOME KINDA WEATHER WITCH, RIGHT? SO WHEN WE GET A HURRICANE OR A DROUGHT...IS THAT HER DOING? OR IS SHE JUST LETTING IT HAPPEN INSTEAD OF HELPING US?
AMERICANS ELECT THEIR LEADERS, RIGHT? I MEAN, WE OVERTHREW A KING OVER 200 YEARS AGO! SO WHERE DOES THIS GUY, SOME KING FROM THE OTHER SIDE OF THE WORLD, GET OFF TELLING US WHAT TO DO?
THE SPIN ZONE
OF COURSE, THE BLACK PANTHER HAS HIS SUPPORTERS BOTH ABROAD AND AT HOME. BEFORE HIS ARRIVAL IN THE UNITED STATES, HE HAD SECRET MEETINGS WITH PRINCE NAMOR OF ATLANTIS AND DR. DOOM, BOTH OF WHOM HAVE TRIED TO OVERTHROW THE U.S. IN THE PAST.
BUT THOSE ASSOCIATIONS HAVE DIMINISHED HIS SUPPORT FROM BLACK LEADERS LIKE AL SHARPTON AND LOUIS FARRAKHAN FROM THE NATION OF ISLAM, WHO BOTH HAVE MEETINGS WITH THE BLACK PANTHER ON THEIR BOOKS.
AS FOR WHETHER THE ROYAL SUPER-COUPLE ALSO PLAN ON MAKING A RENDEZVOUS WITH FUGITIVES FROM THE REGISTRATION ACT... NO ONE KNOWS.

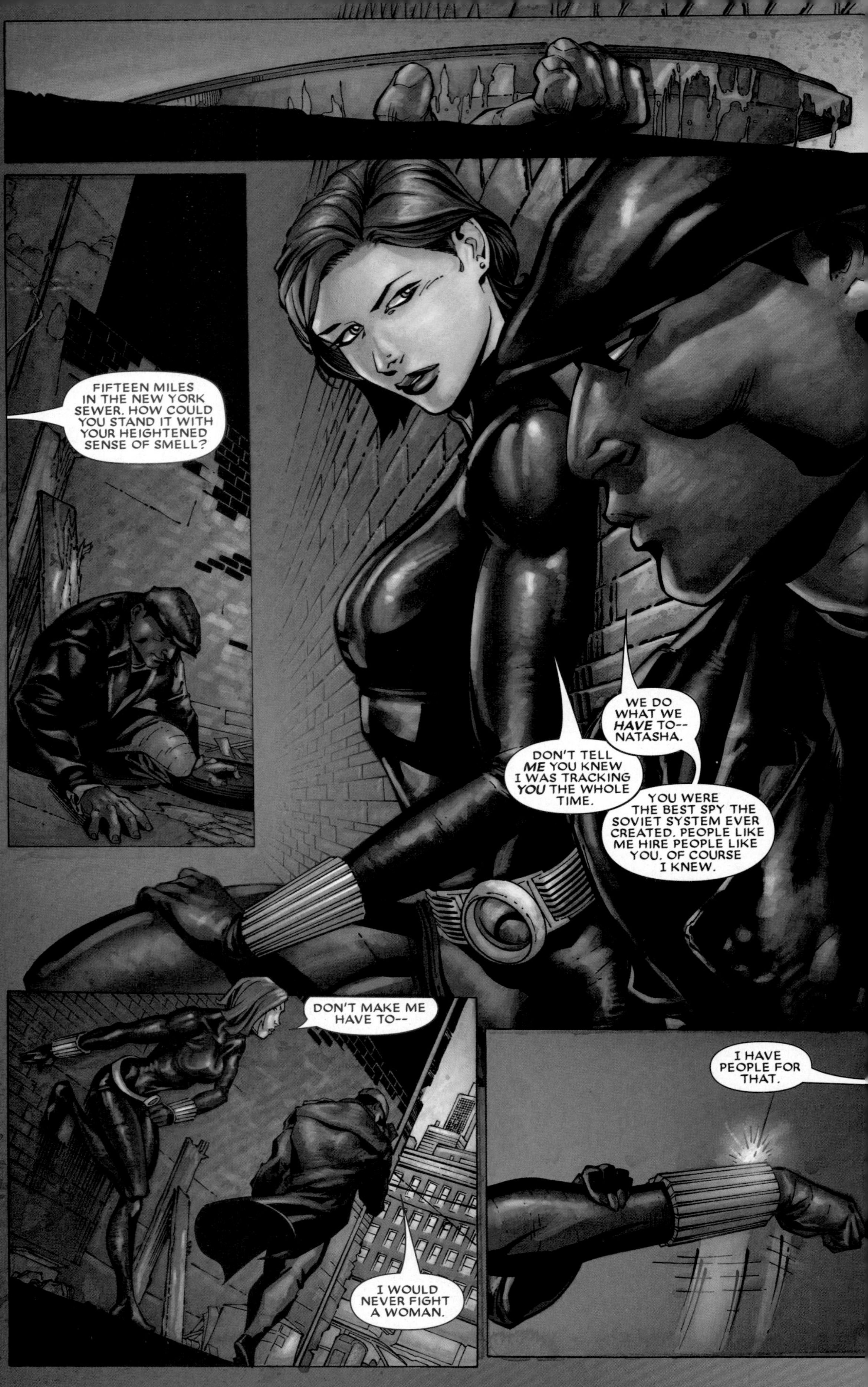
FIFTEEN MILES IN THE NEW YORK SEWER. HOW COULD YOU STAND IT WITH YOUR HEIGHTENED SENSE OF SMELL?
DON'T TELL *ME* YOU KNEW I WAS TRACKING *YOU* THE WHOLE TIME.
WE DO WHAT WE *HAVE* TO-- NATASHA.
YOU WERE THE BEST SPY THE SOVIET SYSTEM EVER CREATED. PEOPLE LIKE ME HIRE PEOPLE LIKE YOU. OF COURSE I KNEW.
DON'T MAKE ME HAVE TO--
I WOULD NEVER FIGHT A WOMAN.
I HAVE PEOPLE FOR THAT.

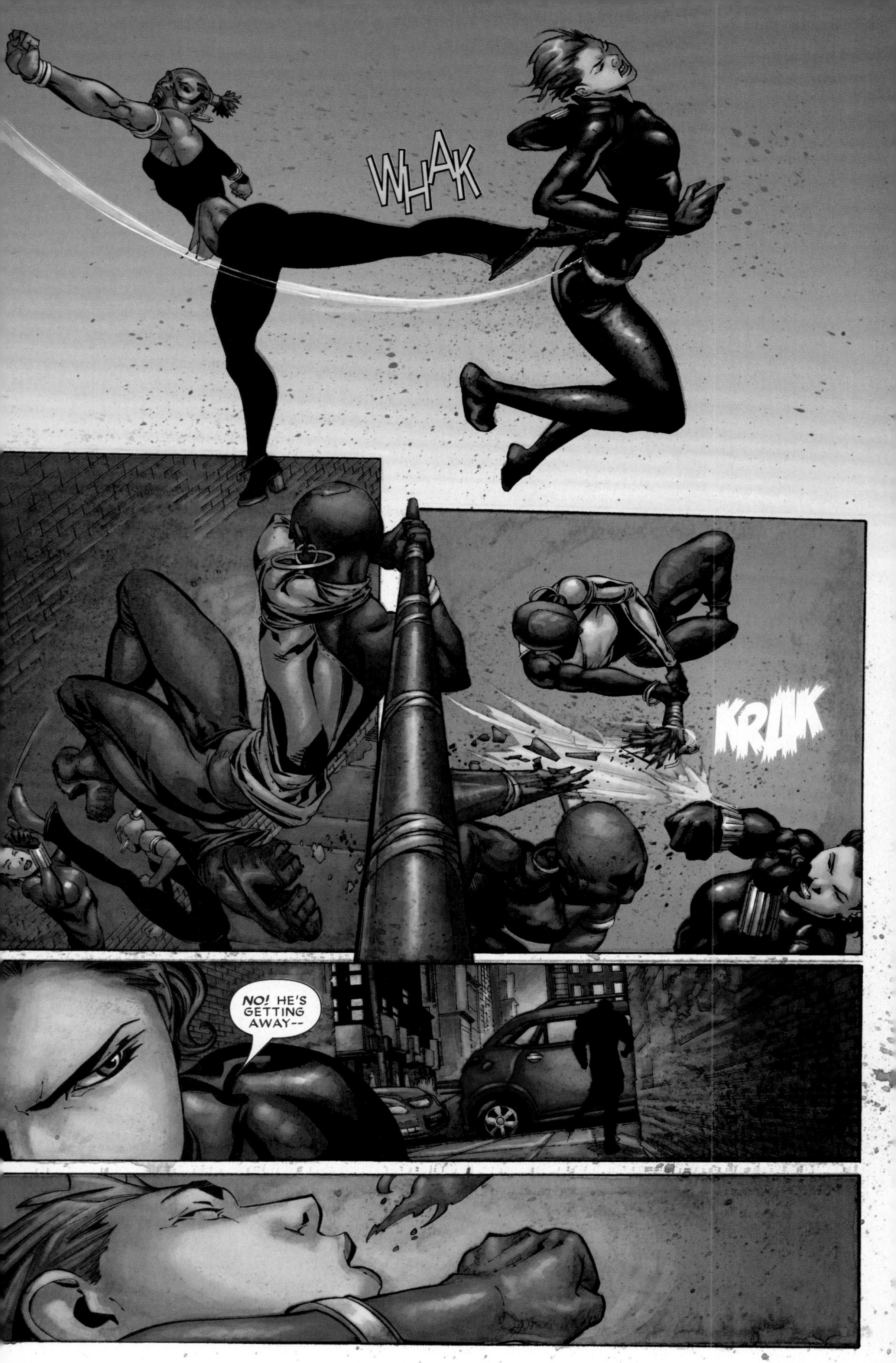
WHAK
KRAK
NO! HE'S GETTING AWAY--

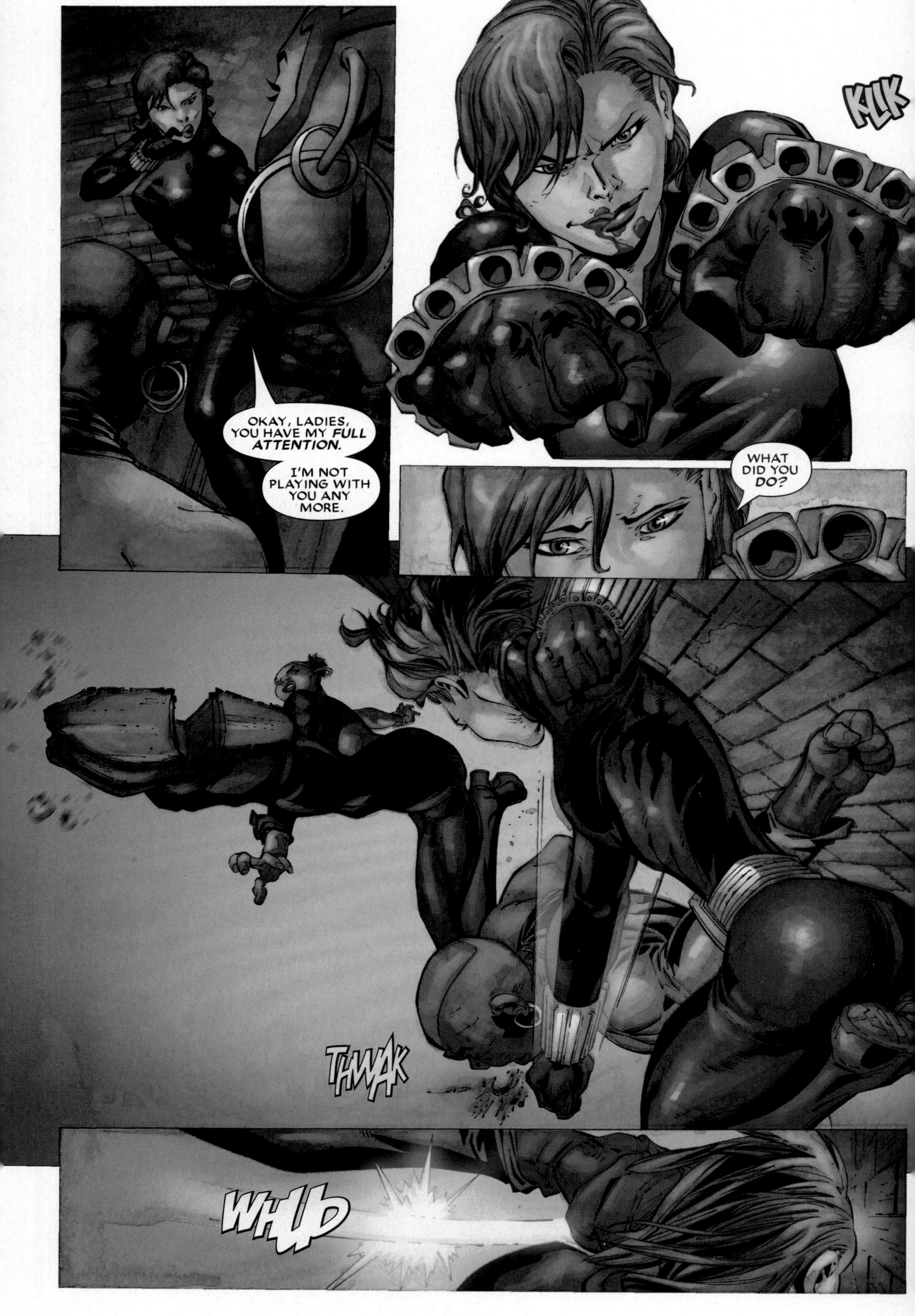

OKAY, LADIES, YOU HAVE MY *FULL ATTENTION.*
I'M NOT PLAYING WITH YOU ANY MORE.
KLIK
WHAT DID YOU *DO?*
THWAK
WHUD

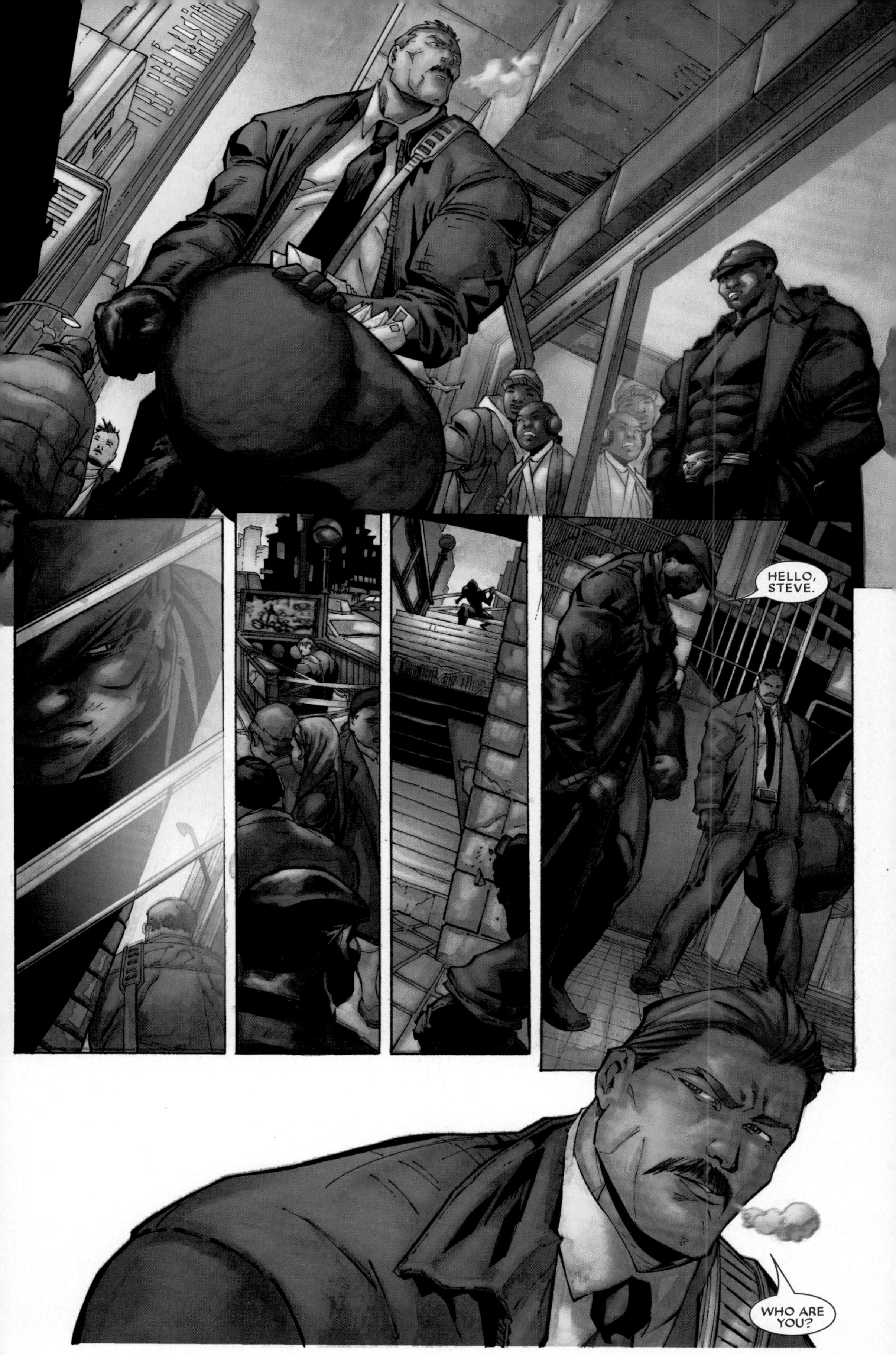
HELLO, STEVE.
WHO ARE YOU?

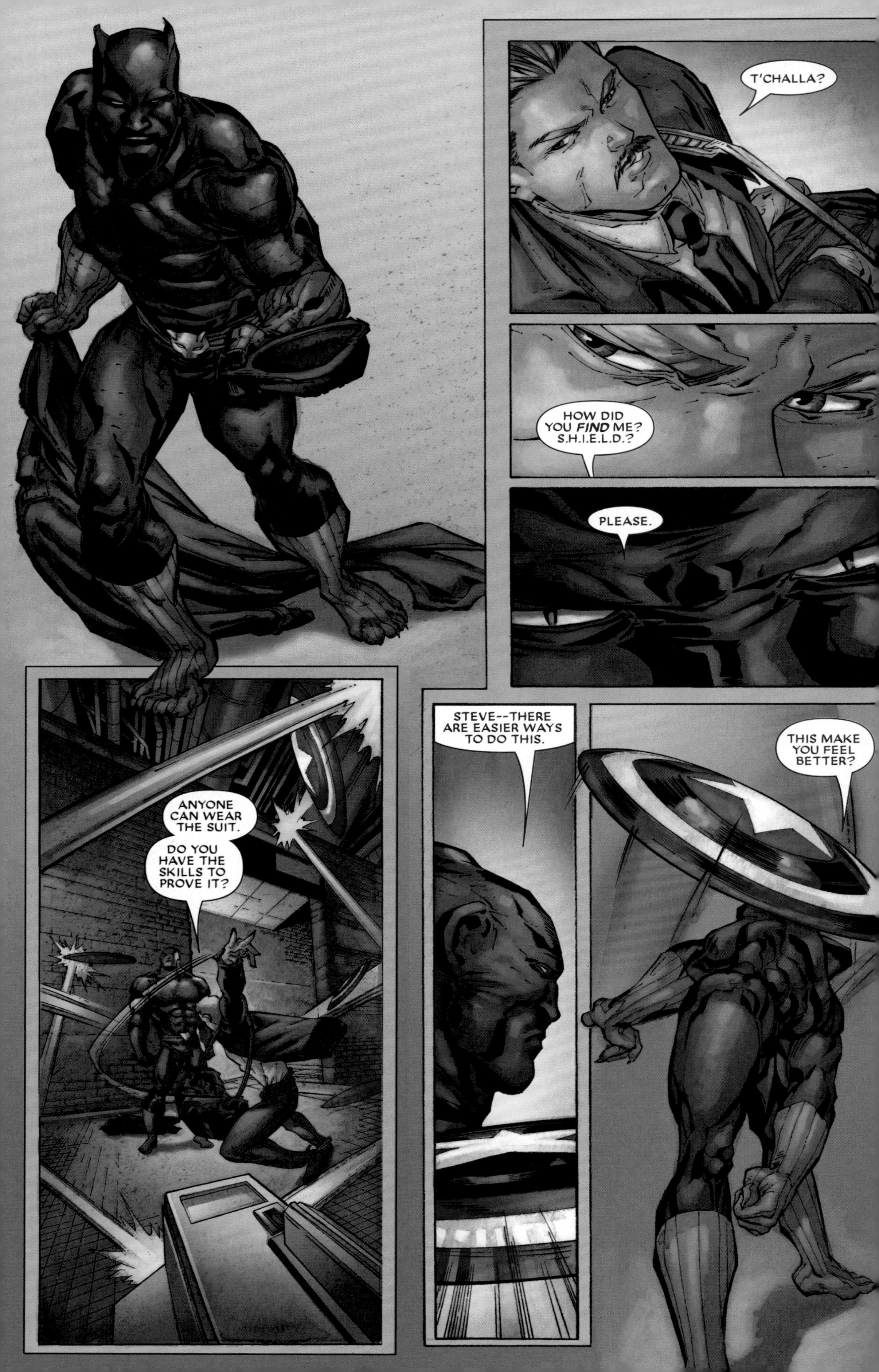
T'CHALLA?
HOW DID YOU *FIND* ME? S.H.I.E.L.D.?
PLEASE.
ANYONE CAN WEAR THE SUIT.
DO YOU HAVE THE SKILLS TO PROVE IT?
STEVE--THERE ARE EASIER WAYS TO DO THIS.
THIS MAKE YOU FEEL BETTER?

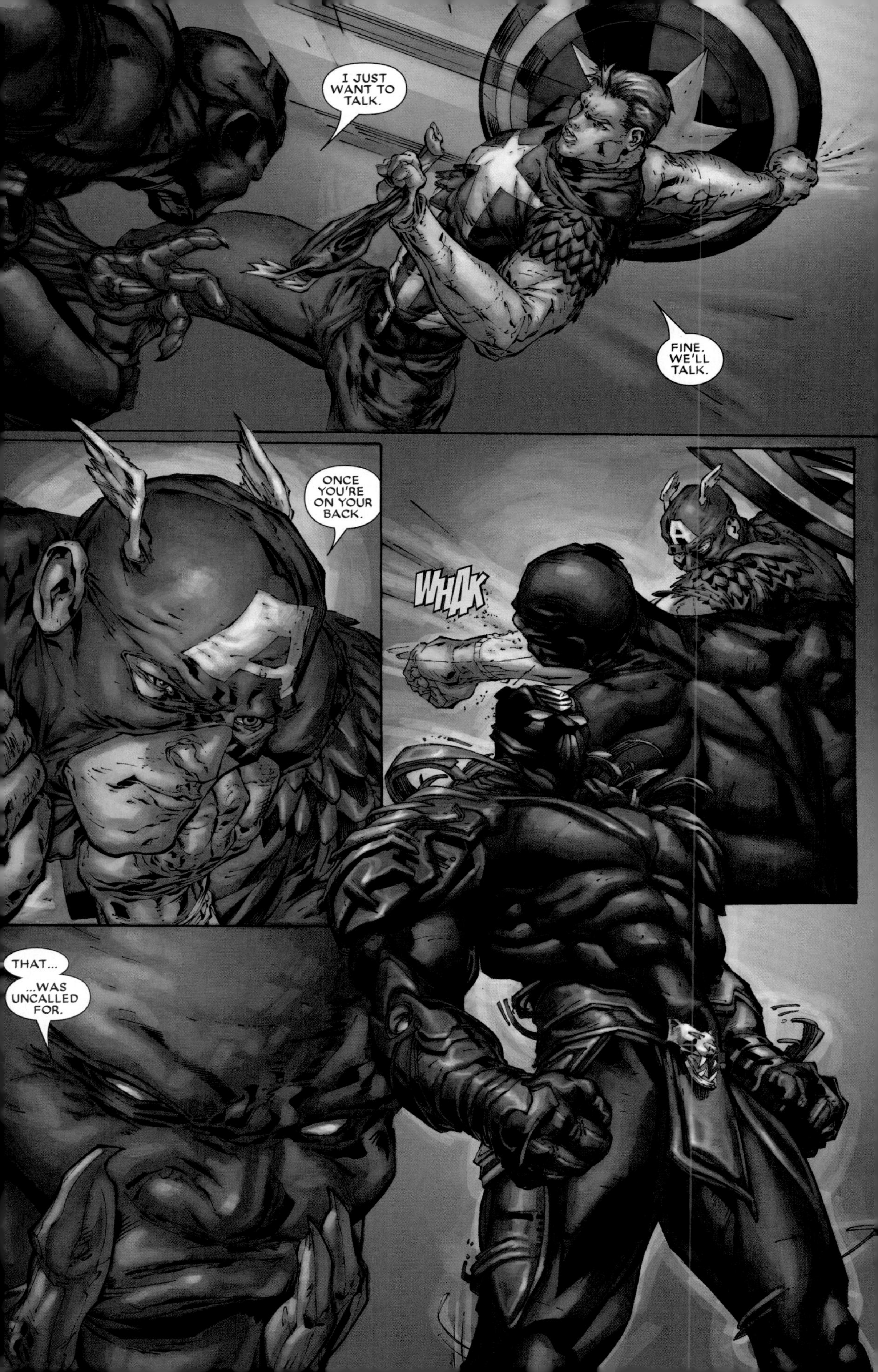
I JUST WANT TO TALK.
FINE. WE'LL TALK.
ONCE YOU'RE ON YOUR BACK.
WHAK
THAT...
...WAS UNCALLED FOR.

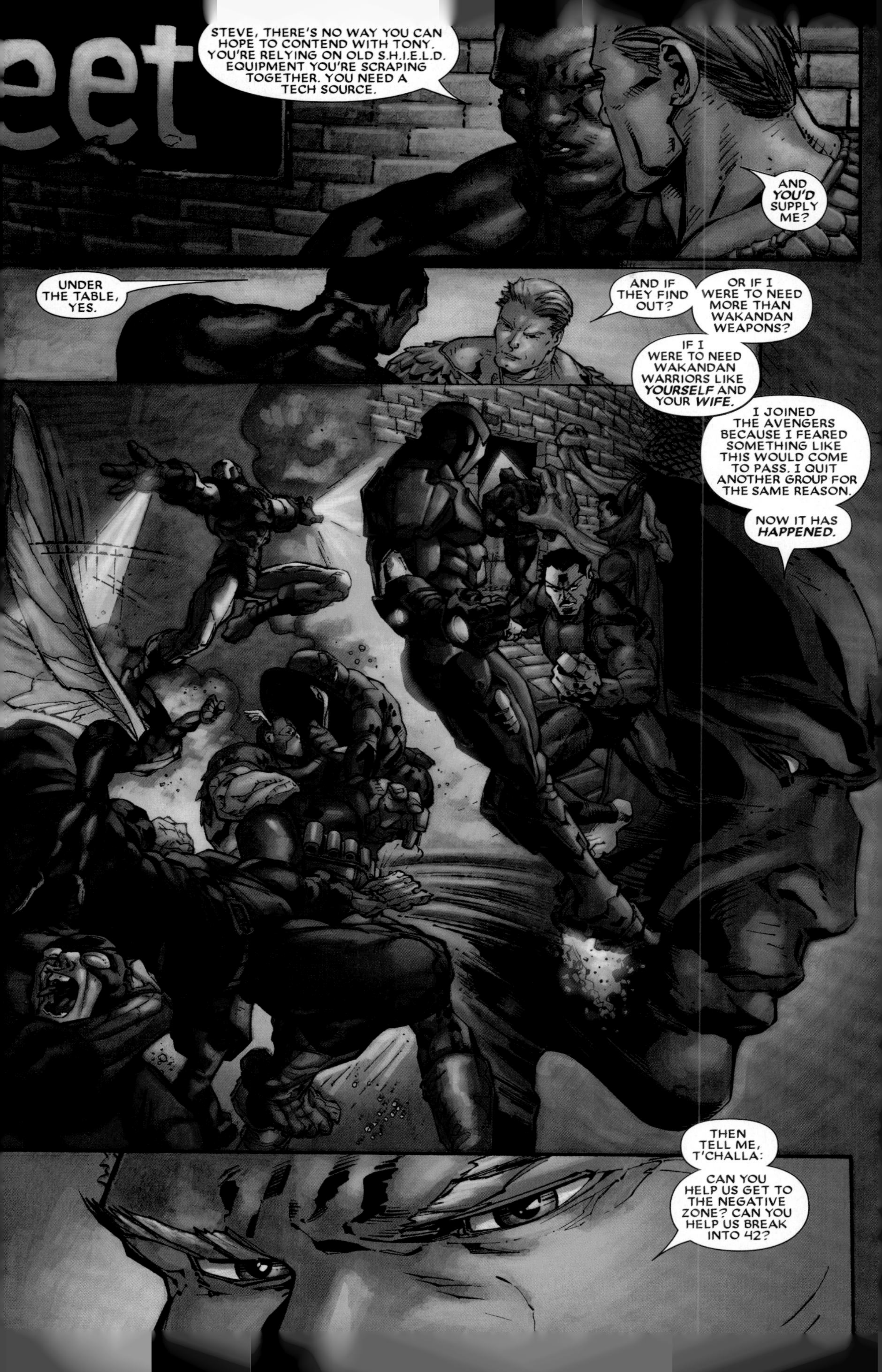
STEVE, THERE'S NO WAY YOU CAN HOPE TO CONTEND WITH TONY. YOU'RE RELYING ON OLD S.H.I.E.L.D. EQUIPMENT YOU'RE SCRAPING TOGETHER. YOU NEED A TECH SOURCE.
AND YOU'D SUPPLY ME?
UNDER THE TABLE, YES.
AND IF THEY FIND OUT?
OR IF I WERE TO NEED MORE THAN WAKANDAN WEAPONS?
IF I WERE TO NEED WAKANDAN WARRIORS LIKE YOURSELF AND YOUR WIFE.
I JOINED THE AVENGERS BECAUSE I FEARED SOMETHING LIKE THIS WOULD COME TO PASS. I QUIT ANOTHER GROUP FOR THE SAME REASON.
NOW IT HAS HAPPENED.
THEN TELL ME, T'CHALLA:
CAN YOU HELP US GET TO THE NEGATIVE ZONE? CAN YOU HELP US BREAK INTO 42?

...IT WAS *TWO* OF THEM, SO LAY OFF.

I CAN'T TALK. A GUY WITH NO POWERS CUT MY CHEST PLATE OFF IN MID-AIR.

OF COURSE, IF RHODEY HADN'T JUMPED IN, I WOULD HAVE SOLVED THE WHOLE PROBLEM RIGHT *THEN*...

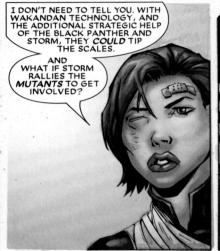

I DON'T NEED TO TELL YOU. WITH WAKANDAN TECHNOLOGY, AND THE ADDITIONAL STRATEGIC HELP OF THE BLACK PANTHER AND STORM, THEY *COULD* TIP THE SCALES.

AND WHAT IF STORM RALLIES THE *MUTANTS* TO GET INVOLVED?

TIME FOR THE *BIG GUNS.*

BLACK PANTHER

A MARVEL COMICS EVENT

CIVIL WAR

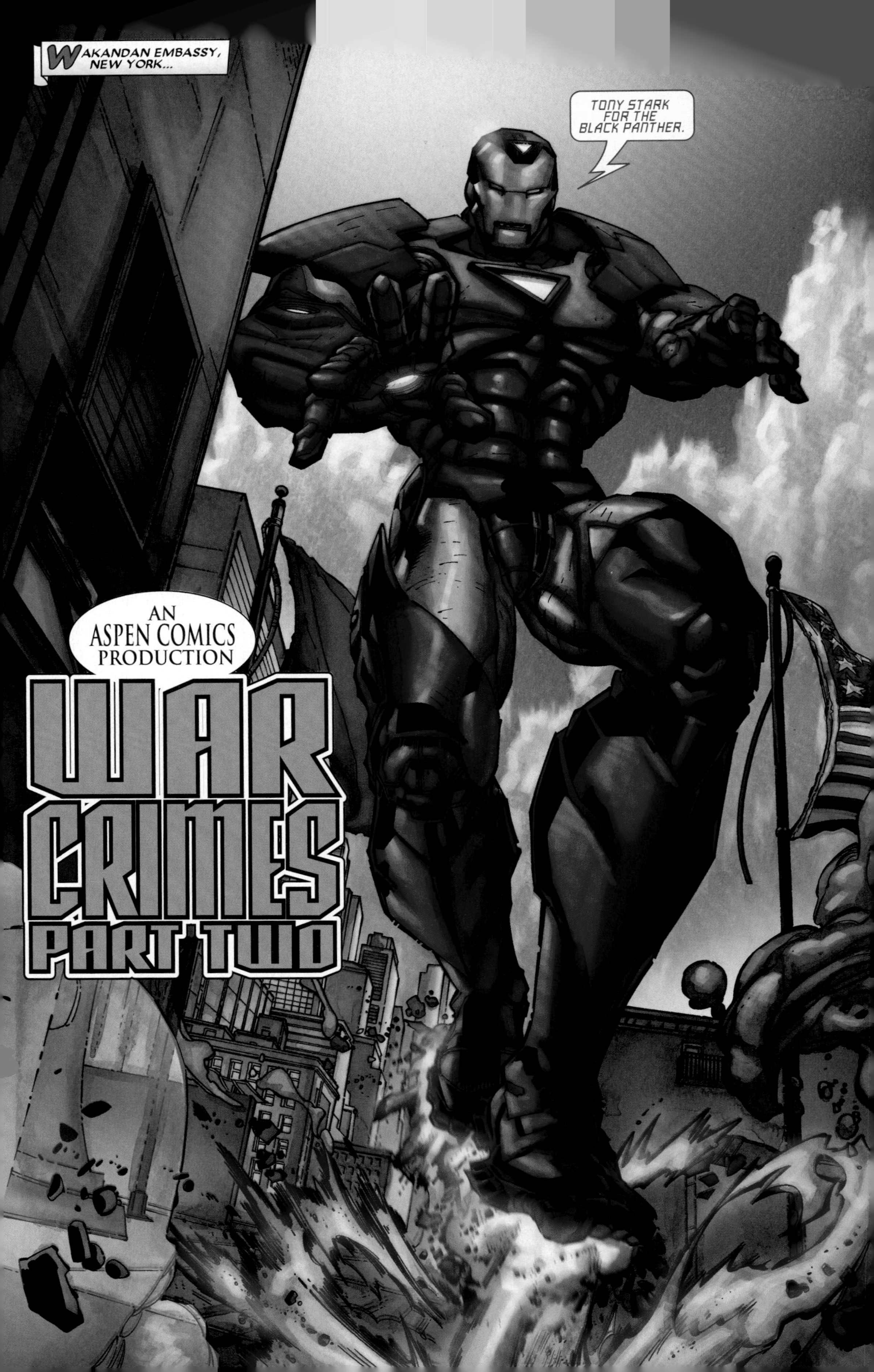
WAKANDAN EMBASSY, NEW YORK...
TONY STARK FOR THE BLACK PANTHER.
AN ASPEN COMICS PRODUCTION
WAR CRIMES
PART TWO

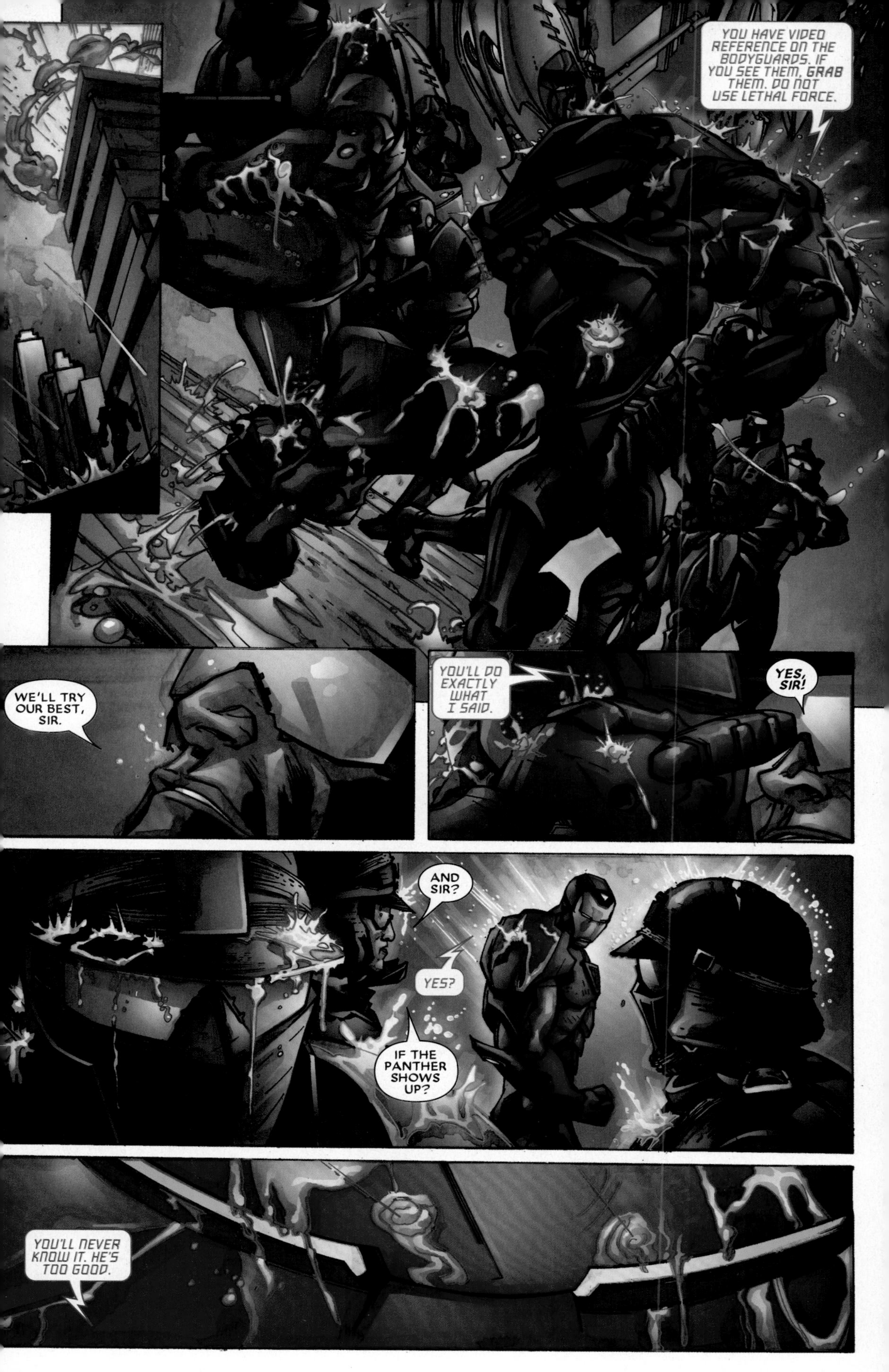
YOU HAVE VIDEO REFERENCE ON THE BODYGUARDS. IF YOU SEE THEM, GRAB THEM. DO NOT USE LETHAL FORCE.
WE'LL TRY OUR BEST, SIR.
YOU'LL DO EXACTLY WHAT I SAID.
YES, SIR!
AND SIR?
YES?
IF THE PANTHER SHOWS UP?
YOU'LL NEVER KNOW IT. HE'S TOO GOOD.

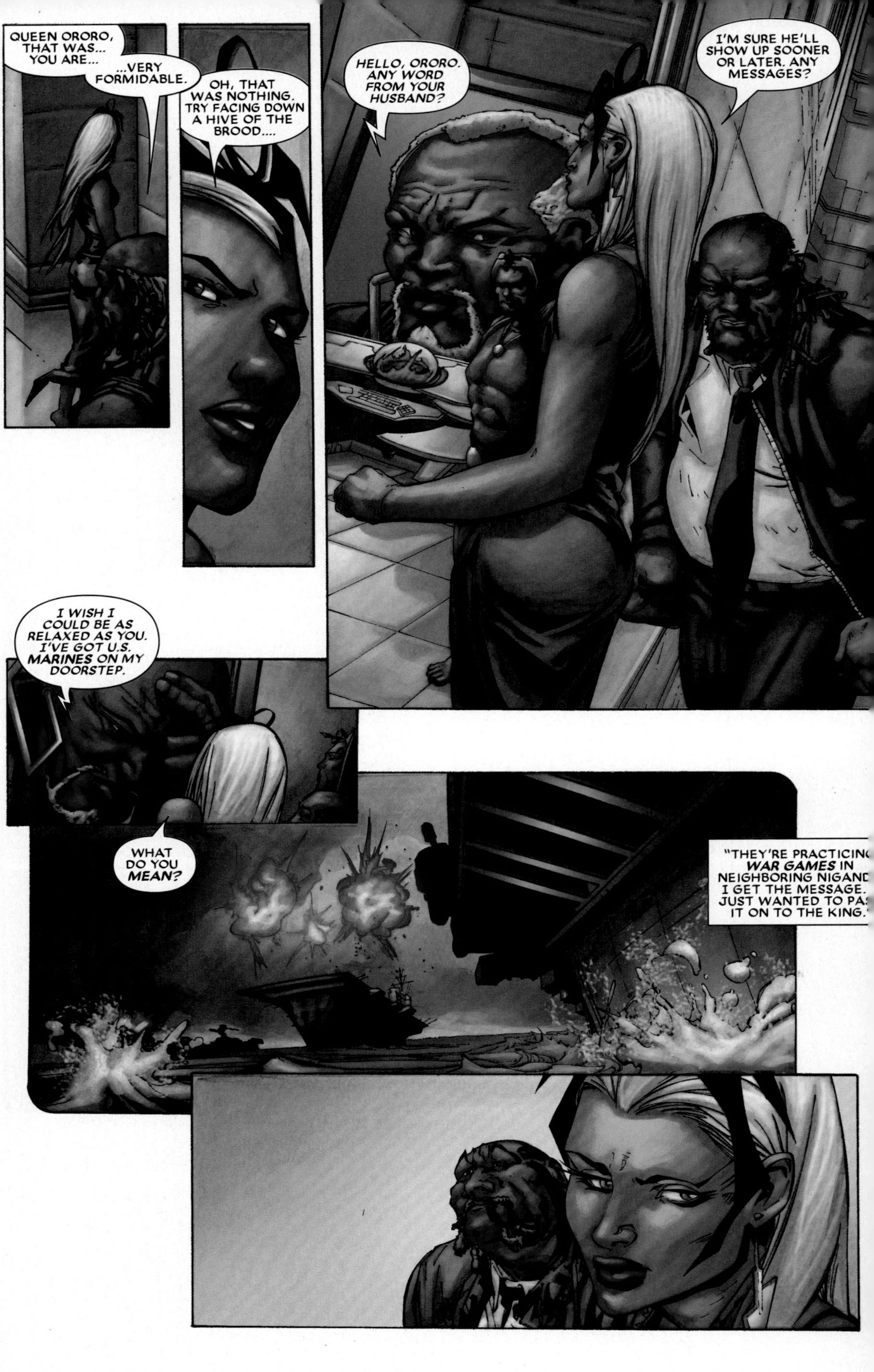
QUEEN ORORO, THAT WAS... YOU ARE...
...VERY FORMIDABLE.
OH, THAT WAS NOTHING. TRY FACING DOWN A HIVE OF THE BROOD....
HELLO, ORORO. ANY WORD FROM YOUR HUSBAND?
I'M SURE HE'LL SHOW UP SOONER OR LATER. ANY MESSAGES?
I WISH I COULD BE AS RELAXED AS YOU. I'VE GOT U.S. MARINES ON MY DOORSTEP.
WHAT DO YOU MEAN?
"THEY'RE PRACTICIN WAR GAMES IN NEIGHBORING NIGAND I GET THE MESSAGE. JUST WANTED TO PAS IT ON TO THE KING."

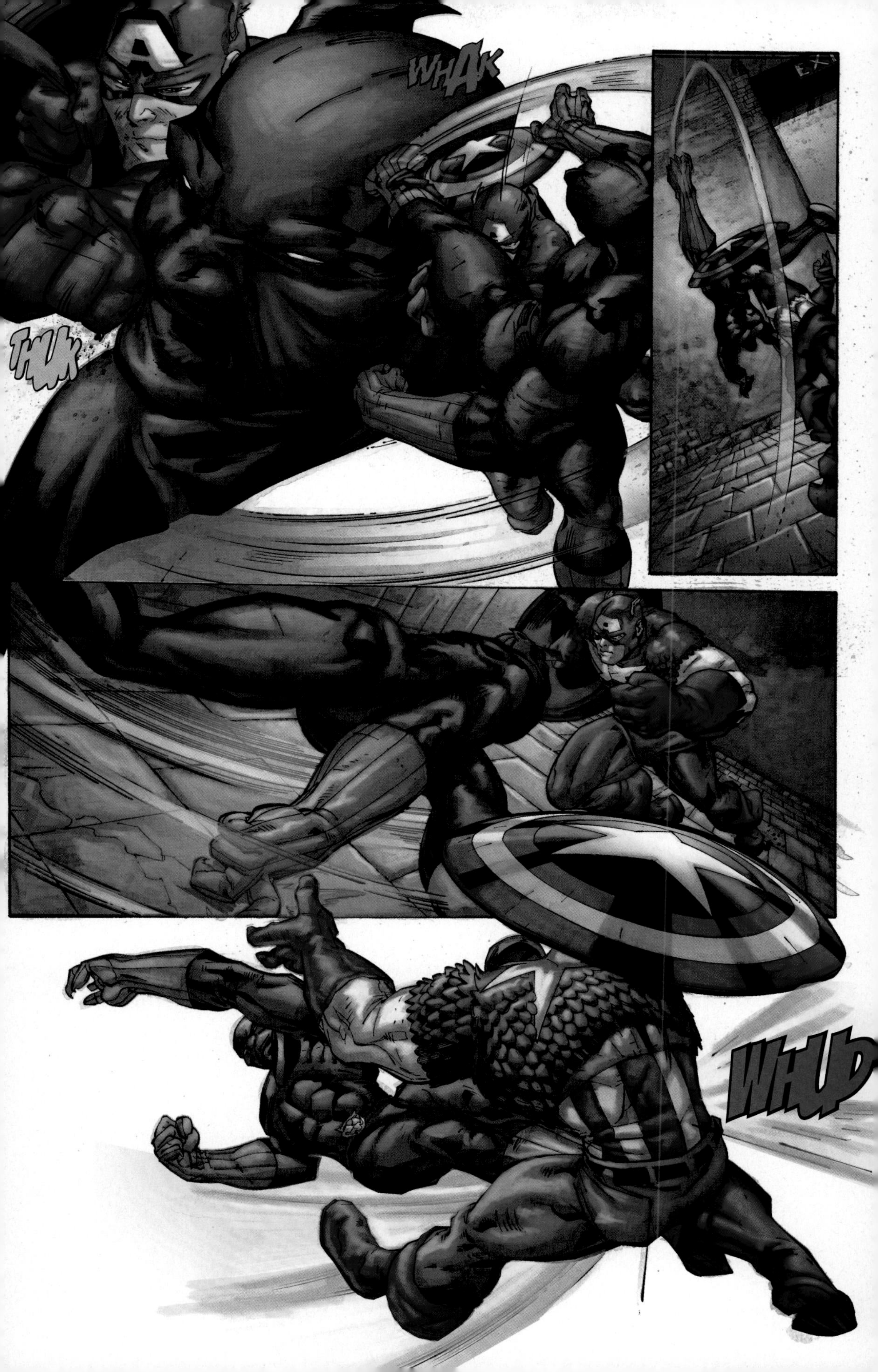
WHAK
THUK
WHUP

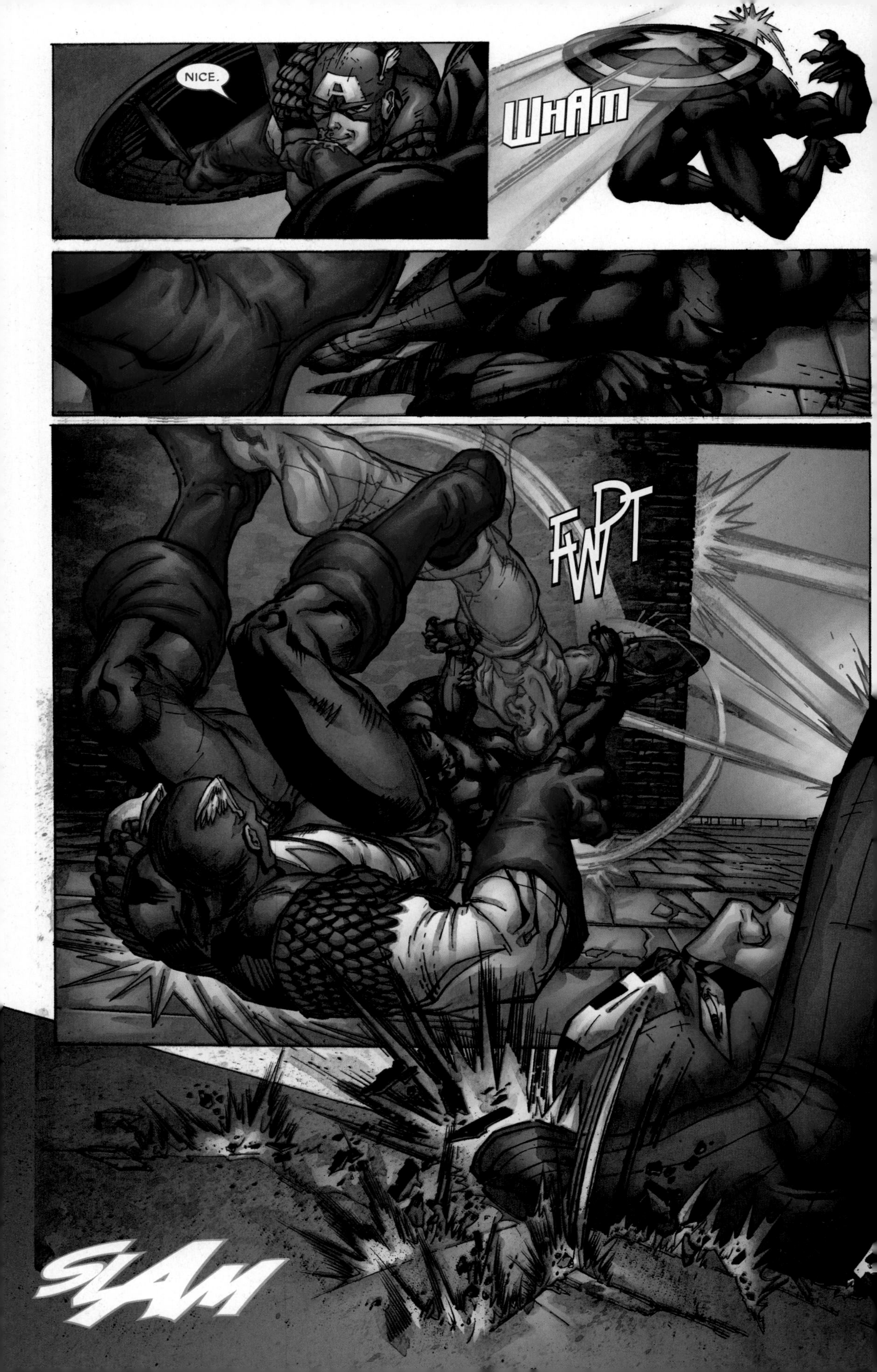
NICE.
WHAM
FWPT
SLAM

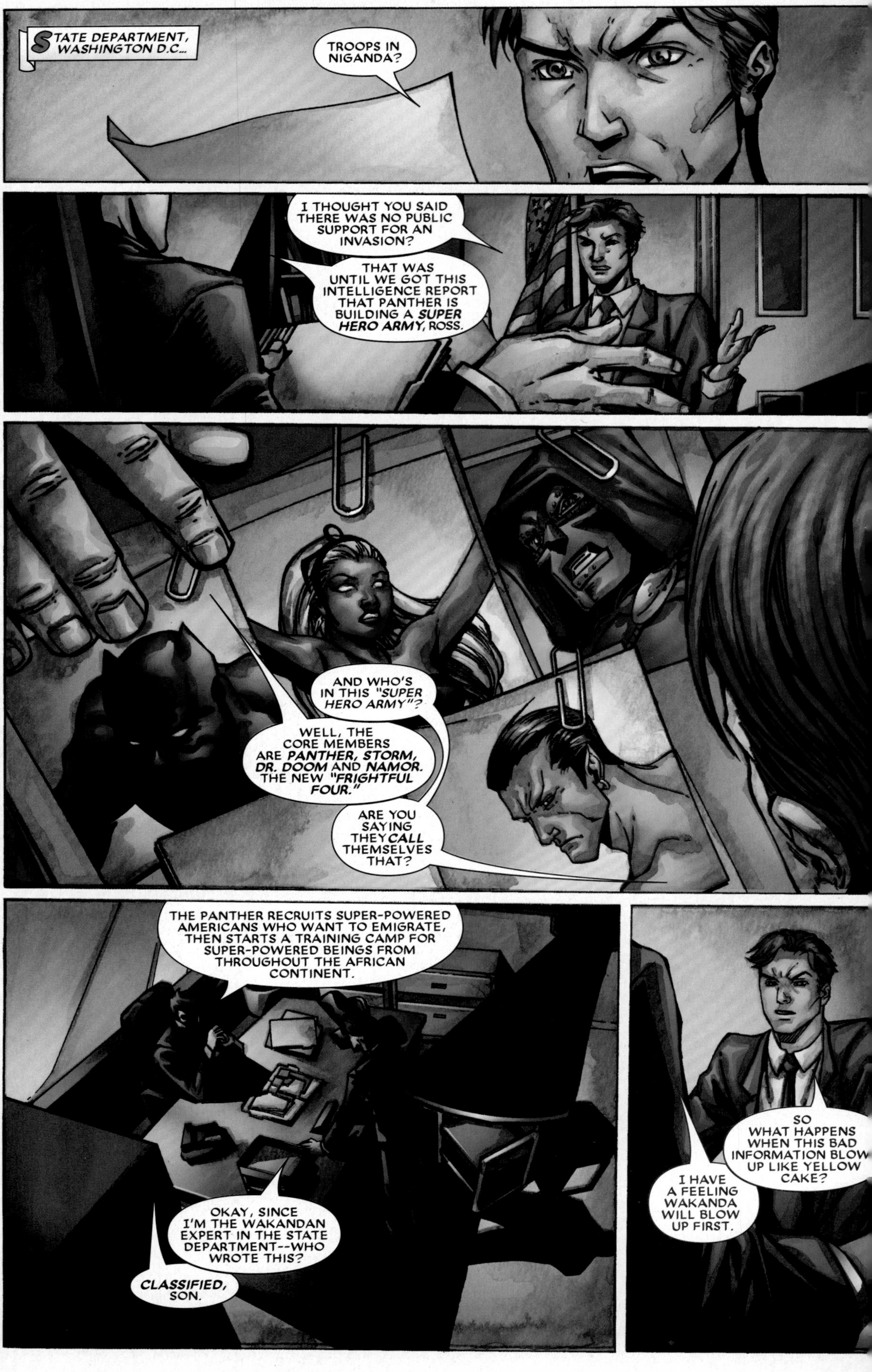
STATE DEPARTMENT, WASHINGTON D.C...
TROOPS IN NIGANDA?
I THOUGHT YOU SAID THERE WAS NO PUBLIC SUPPORT FOR AN INVASION?
THAT WAS UNTIL WE GOT THIS INTELLIGENCE REPORT THAT PANTHER IS BUILDING A SUPER HERO ARMY, ROSS.
AND WHO'S IN THIS "SUPER HERO ARMY"?
WELL, THE CORE MEMBERS ARE PANTHER, STORM, DR. DOOM AND NAMOR. THE NEW "FRIGHTFUL FOUR."
ARE YOU SAYING THEY CALL THEMSELVES THAT?
THE PANTHER RECRUITS SUPER-POWERED AMERICANS WHO WANT TO EMIGRATE, THEN STARTS A TRAINING CAMP FOR SUPER-POWERED BEINGS FROM THROUGHOUT THE AFRICAN CONTINENT.
OKAY, SINCE I'M THE WAKANDAN EXPERT IN THE STATE DEPARTMENT--WHO WROTE THIS?
CLASSIFIED, SON.
SO WHAT HAPPENS WHEN THIS BAD INFORMATION BLOW UP LIKE YELLOW CAKE?
I HAVE A FEELING WAKANDA WILL BLOW UP FIRST.

BROTHER VOODOO! HOW GOES IT?

WELL, THANK YOU. WAKANDAN HOSPITALITY IS EXTRAORDINARY.

DO YOU THINK MORE OF YOUR COUNTRYMEN WILL TAKE UP T'CHALLA'S OFFER?

WELL, I HOPE A SPEEDY RESOLUTION OF THE REGISTRATION CRISIS IN THE UNITED STATES WILL MAKE IT A NONISSUE.

BUT IN THE MEANTIME, I HAVE BEEN WORKING WITH YOUR PRIESTS HERE. THERE'S BEEN A FASCINATING EXCHANGE OF IDEAS. I HAD NO IDEA HOW CLOSELY THE SPIRITUAL AND THE SCIENTIFIC WERE IN WAKANDA.

IT'S ALL A CONTINUUM TO US.

I'M STILL SEARCHING FOR THE WHEREABOUTS OF THAT SHAPE-SHIFTER OR BODY STEALER WHO WAS AT THE WEDDING.

STILL NO PERCEPTION OF HIM? OR HER?

NOT YET. THEY KNOW THEY ARE BEING HUNTED. BUT EVENTUALLY THEY WILL MAKE A PLAY FOR A POWERFUL HOST. AND THAT'S WHEN THEY WILL BE CAUGHT.

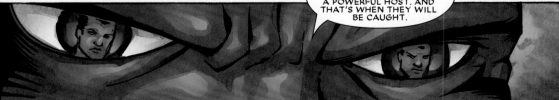

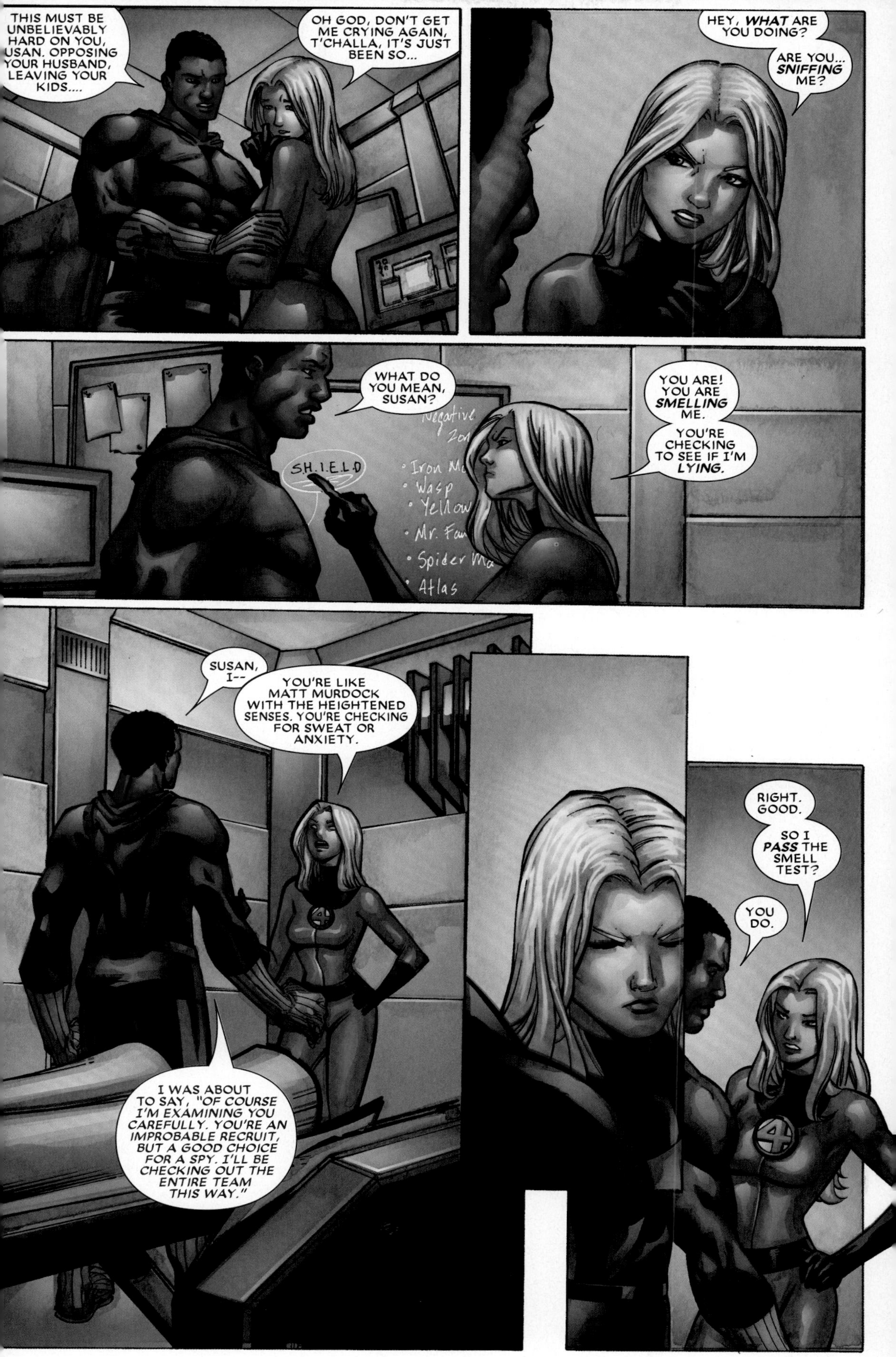
THIS MUST BE UNBELIEVABLY HARD ON YOU, SUSAN. OPPOSING YOUR HUSBAND, LEAVING YOUR KIDS....
OH GOD, DON'T GET ME CRYING AGAIN, T'CHALLA, IT'S JUST BEEN SO...
HEY, ***WHAT*** ARE YOU DOING?
ARE YOU... ***SNIFFING*** ME?
WHAT DO YOU MEAN, SUSAN?
Negative Zon
S.H.I.E.L.D
• Iron M
• Wasp
• Yellow
• Mr. Fan
• Spider Ma
• Atlas
YOU ARE! YOU ARE ***SMELLING*** ME.
YOU'RE CHECKING TO SEE IF I'M ***LYING.***
SUSAN, I--
YOU'RE LIKE MATT MURDOCK WITH THE HEIGHTENED SENSES. YOU'RE CHECKING FOR SWEAT OR ANXIETY.
I WAS ABOUT TO SAY, *"OF COURSE I'M EXAMINING YOU CAREFULLY. YOU'RE AN IMPROBABLE RECRUIT, BUT A GOOD CHOICE FOR A SPY. I'LL BE CHECKING OUT THE ENTIRE TEAM THIS WAY."*
RIGHT. GOOD.
SO I ***PASS*** THE SMELL TEST?
YOU DO.

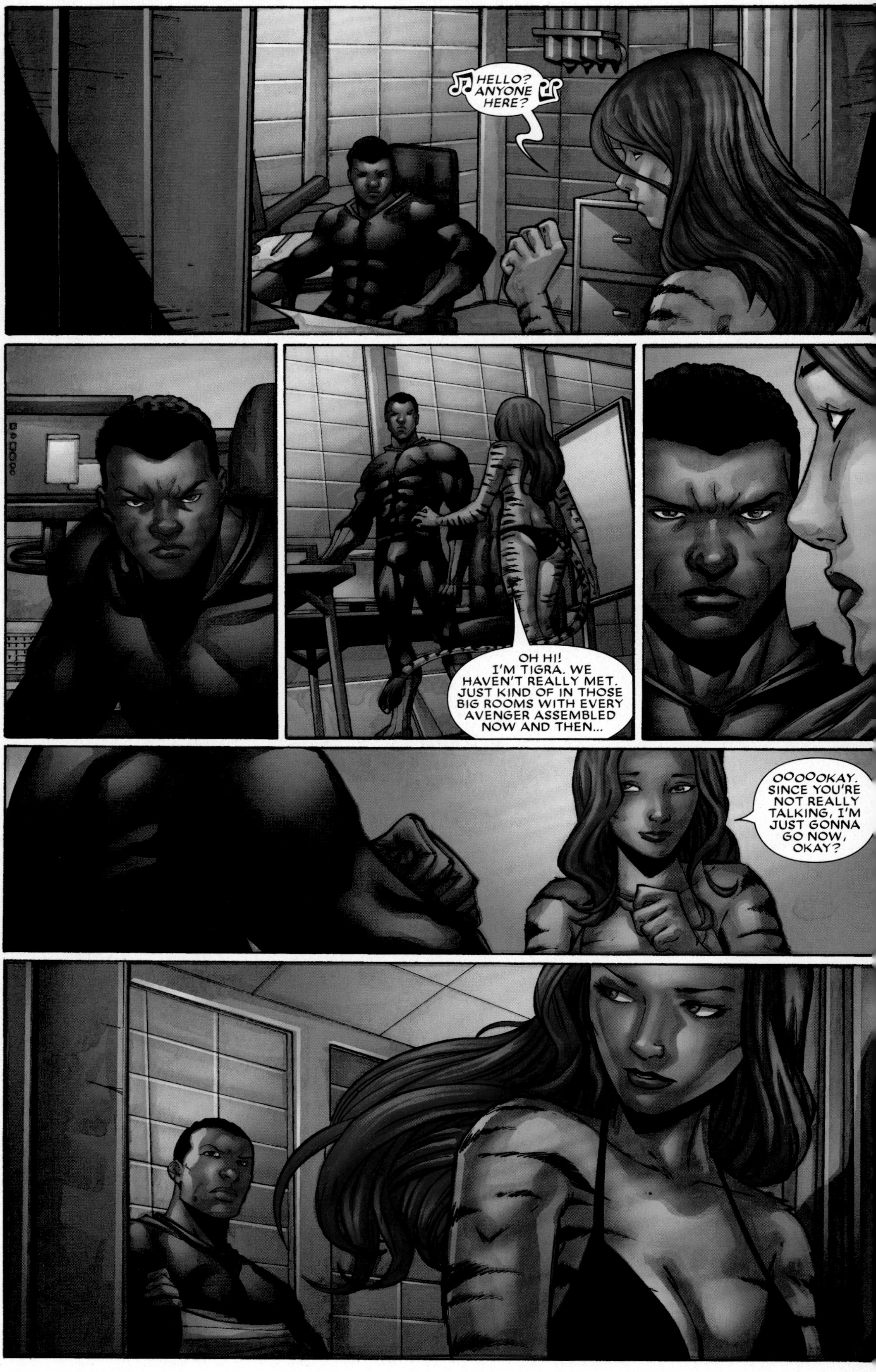
HELLO? ANYONE HERE?
OH HI! I'M TIGRA. WE HAVEN'T REALLY MET. JUST KIND OF IN THOSE BIG ROOMS WITH EVERY AVENGER ASSEMBLED NOW AND THEN...
OOOOOKAY. SINCE YOU'RE NOT REALLY TALKING, I'M JUST GONNA GO NOW, OKAY?

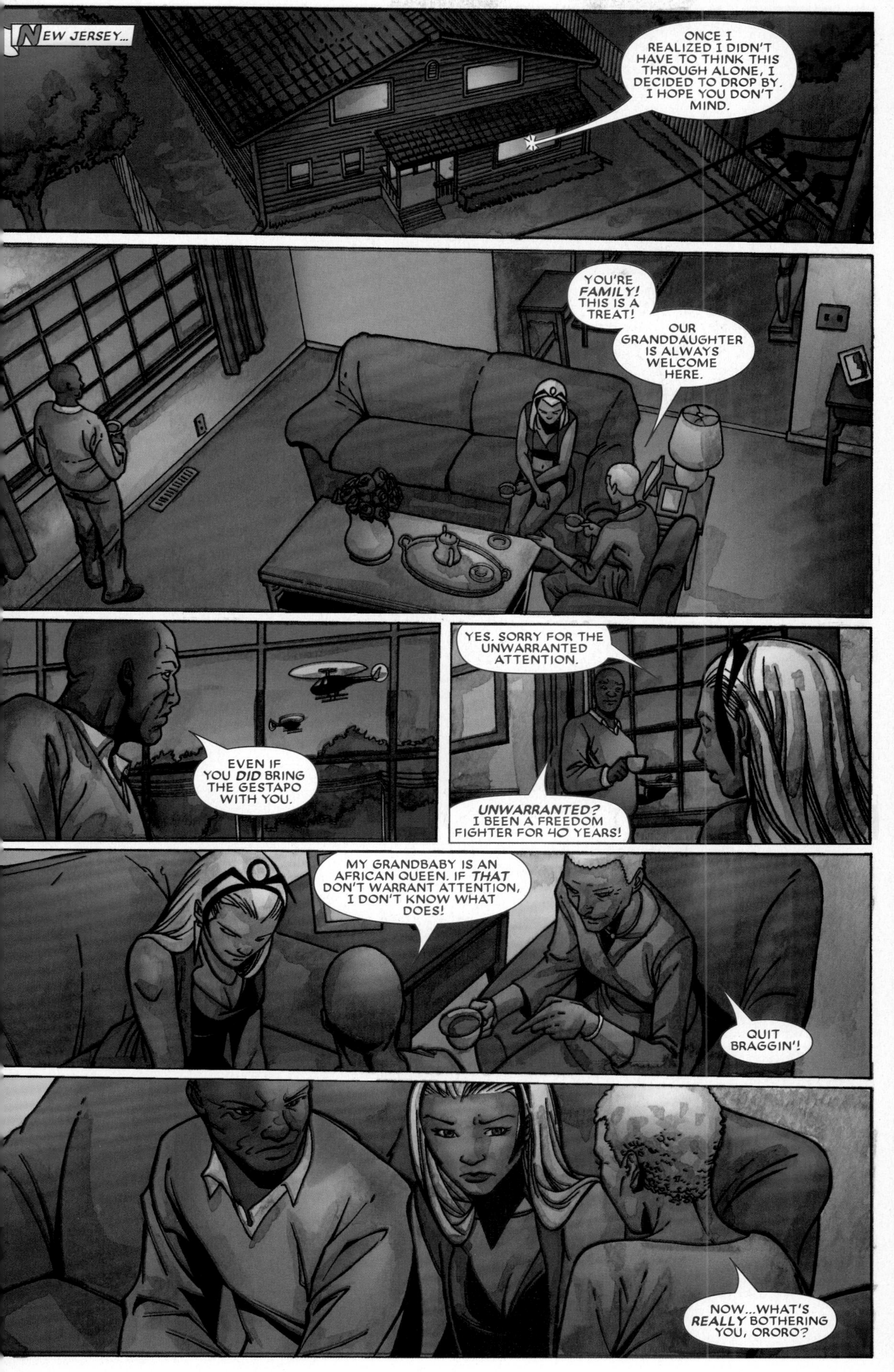
NEW JERSEY...
ONCE I REALIZED I DIDN'T HAVE TO THINK THIS THROUGH ALONE, I DECIDED TO DROP BY. I HOPE YOU DON'T MIND.
YOU'RE *FAMILY!* THIS IS A TREAT!
OUR GRANDDAUGHTER IS ALWAYS WELCOME HERE.
EVEN IF YOU *DID* BRING THE GESTAPO WITH YOU.
YES. SORRY FOR THE UNWARRANTED ATTENTION.
UNWARRANTED? I BEEN A FREEDOM FIGHTER FOR 40 YEARS!
MY GRANDBABY IS AN AFRICAN QUEEN. IF *THAT* DON'T WARRANT ATTENTION, I DON'T KNOW WHAT DOES!
QUIT BRAGGIN'!
NOW...WHAT'S *REALLY* BOTHERING YOU, ORORO?

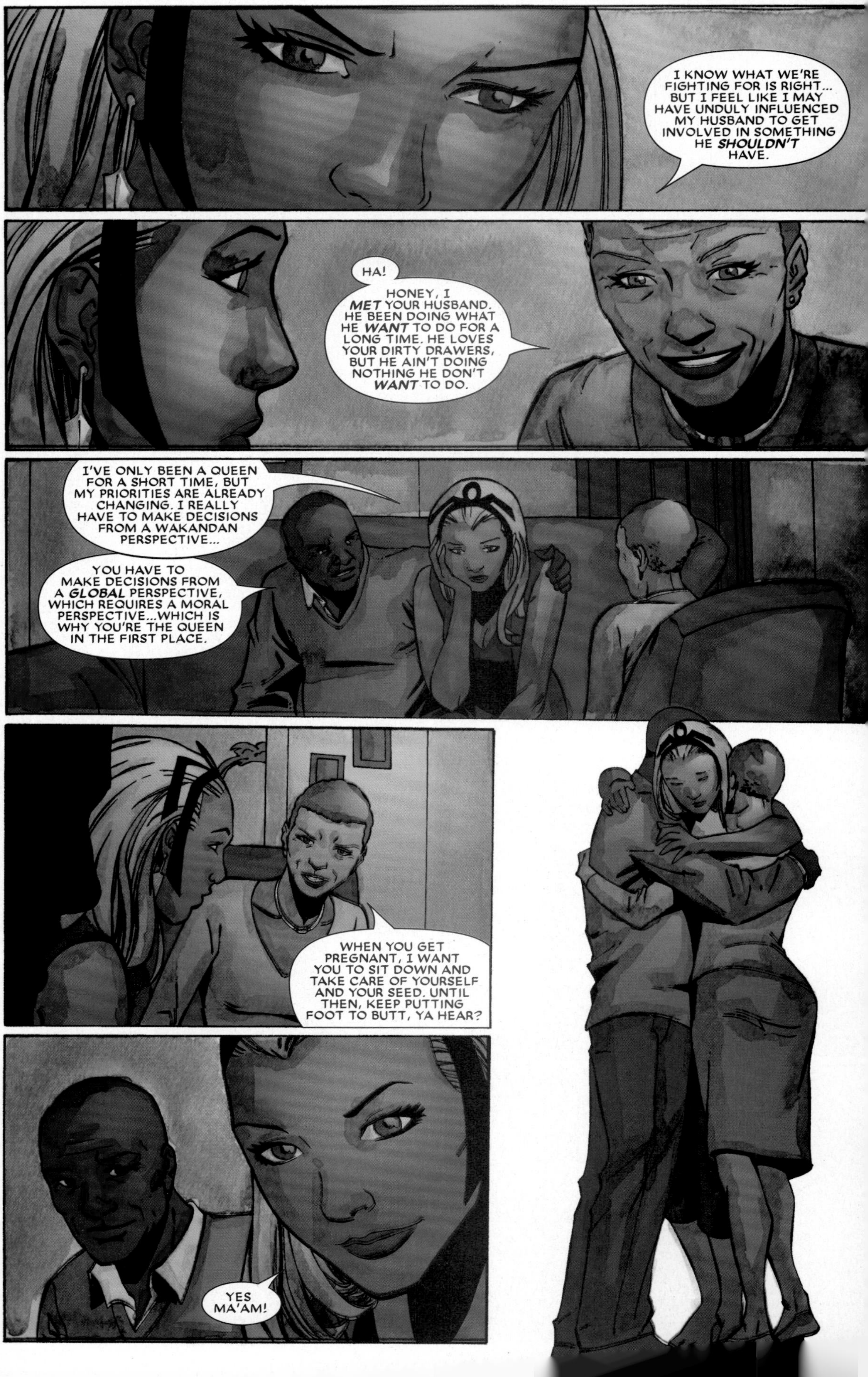
I KNOW WHAT WE'RE FIGHTING FOR IS RIGHT... BUT I FEEL LIKE I MAY HAVE UNDULY INFLUENCED MY HUSBAND TO GET INVOLVED IN SOMETHING HE SHOULDN'T HAVE.
HA!
HONEY, I MET YOUR HUSBAND. HE BEEN DOING WHAT HE WANT TO DO FOR A LONG TIME. HE LOVES YOUR DIRTY DRAWERS, BUT HE AIN'T DOING NOTHING HE DON'T WANT TO DO.
I'VE ONLY BEEN A QUEEN FOR A SHORT TIME, BUT MY PRIORITIES ARE ALREADY CHANGING. I REALLY HAVE TO MAKE DECISIONS FROM A WAKANDAN PERSPECTIVE...
YOU HAVE TO MAKE DECISIONS FROM A GLOBAL PERSPECTIVE, WHICH REQUIRES A MORAL PERSPECTIVE...WHICH IS WHY YOU'RE THE QUEEN IN THE FIRST PLACE.
WHEN YOU GET PREGNANT, I WANT YOU TO SIT DOWN AND TAKE CARE OF YOURSELF AND YOUR SEED. UNTIL THEN, KEEP PUTTING FOOT TO BUTT, YA HEAR?
YES MA'AM!

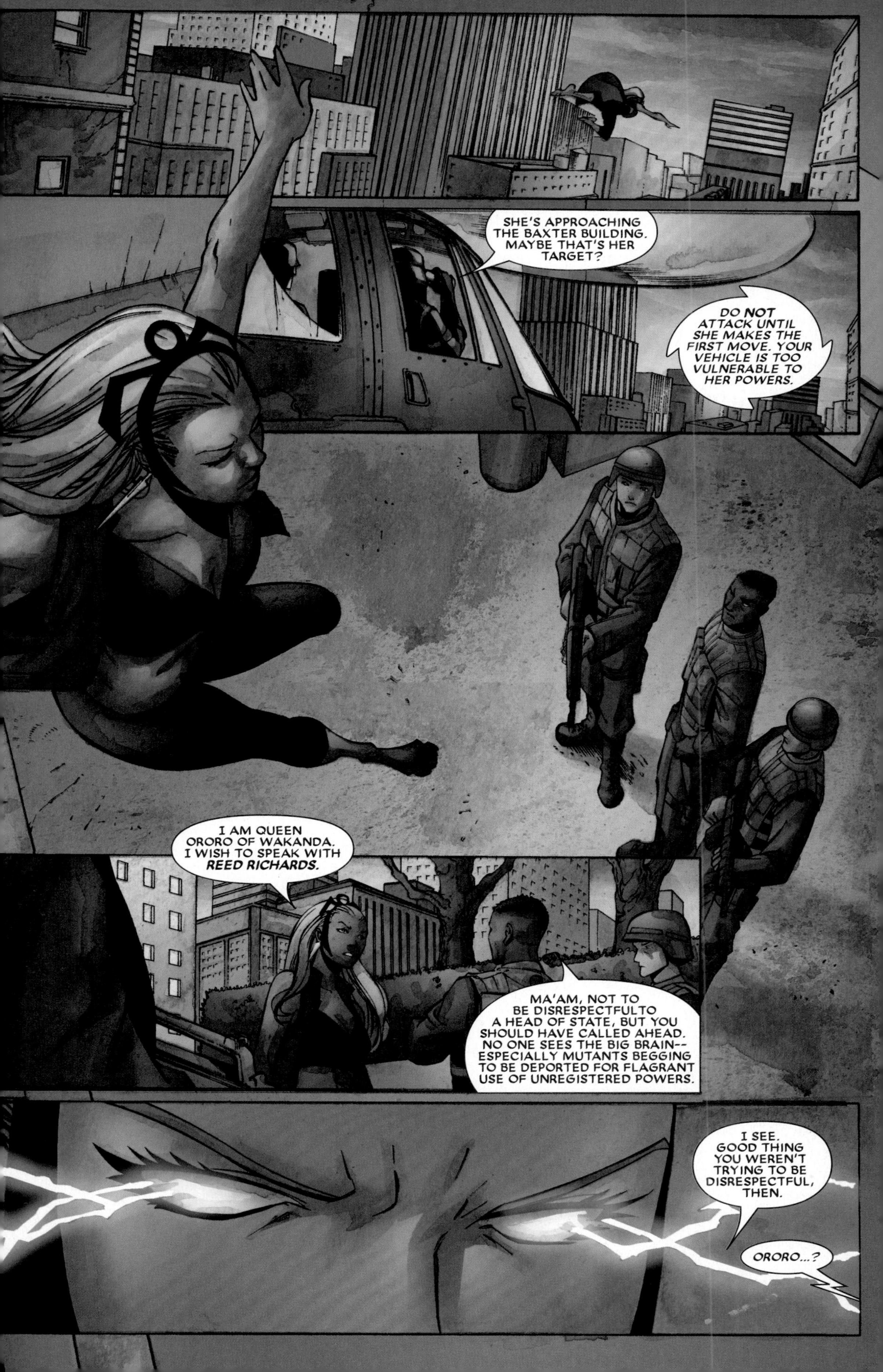
SHE'S APPROACHING THE BAXTER BUILDING. MAYBE THAT'S HER TARGET?
DO NOT ATTACK UNTIL SHE MAKES THE FIRST MOVE. YOUR VEHICLE IS TOO VULNERABLE TO HER POWERS.
I AM QUEEN ORORO OF WAKANDA. I WISH TO SPEAK WITH REED RICHARDS.
MA'AM, NOT TO BE DISRESPECTFULTO A HEAD OF STATE, BUT YOU SHOULD HAVE CALLED AHEAD. NO ONE SEES THE BIG BRAIN-- ESPECIALLY MUTANTS BEGGING TO BE DEPORTED FOR FLAGRANT USE OF UNREGISTERED POWERS.
I SEE. GOOD THING YOU WEREN'T TRYING TO BE DISRESPECTFUL, THEN.
ORORO...?

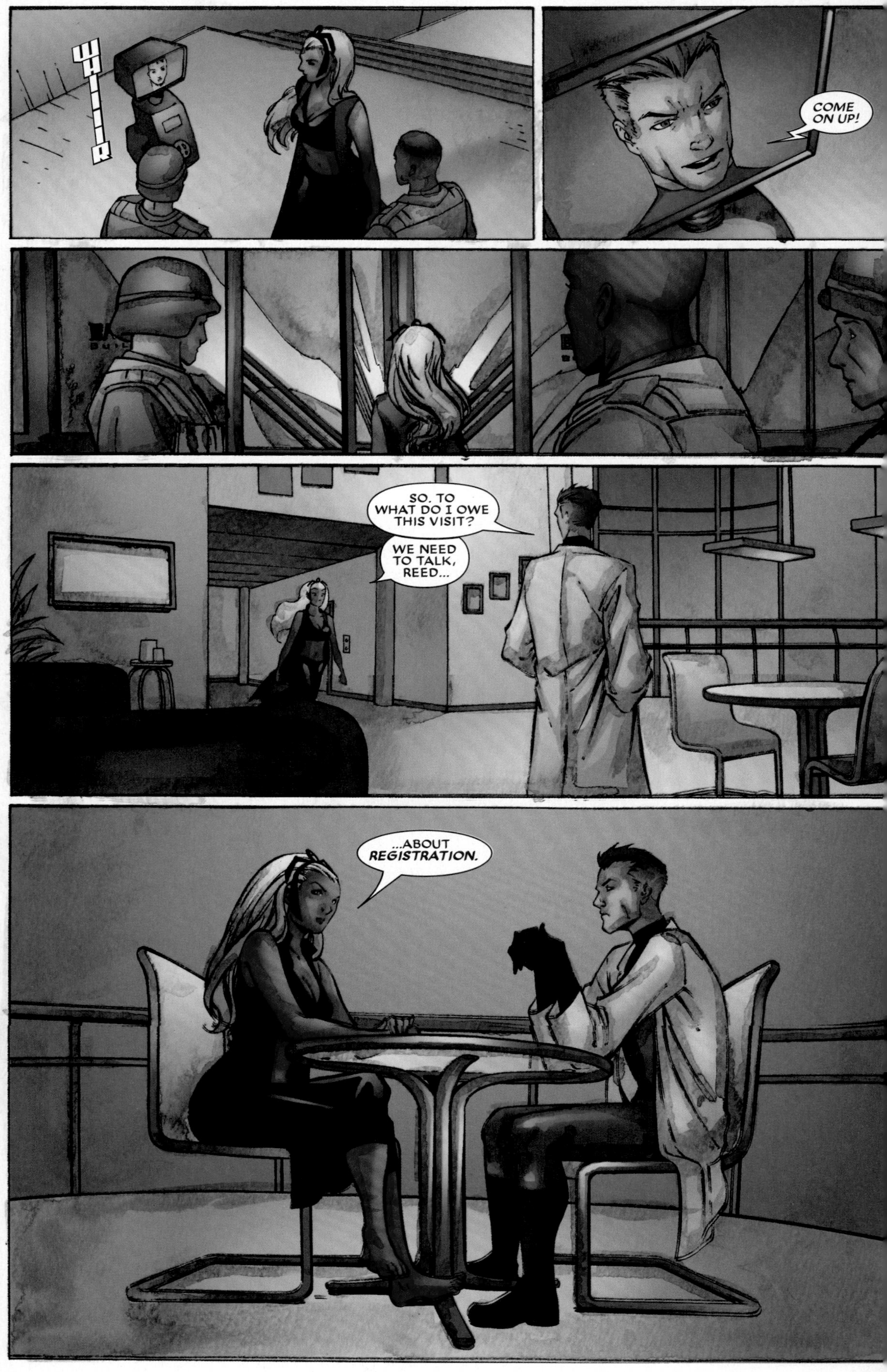
WHIIIR
COME ON UP!
SO. TO WHAT DO I OWE THIS VISIT?
WE NEED TO TALK, REED...
...ABOUT REGISTRATION.

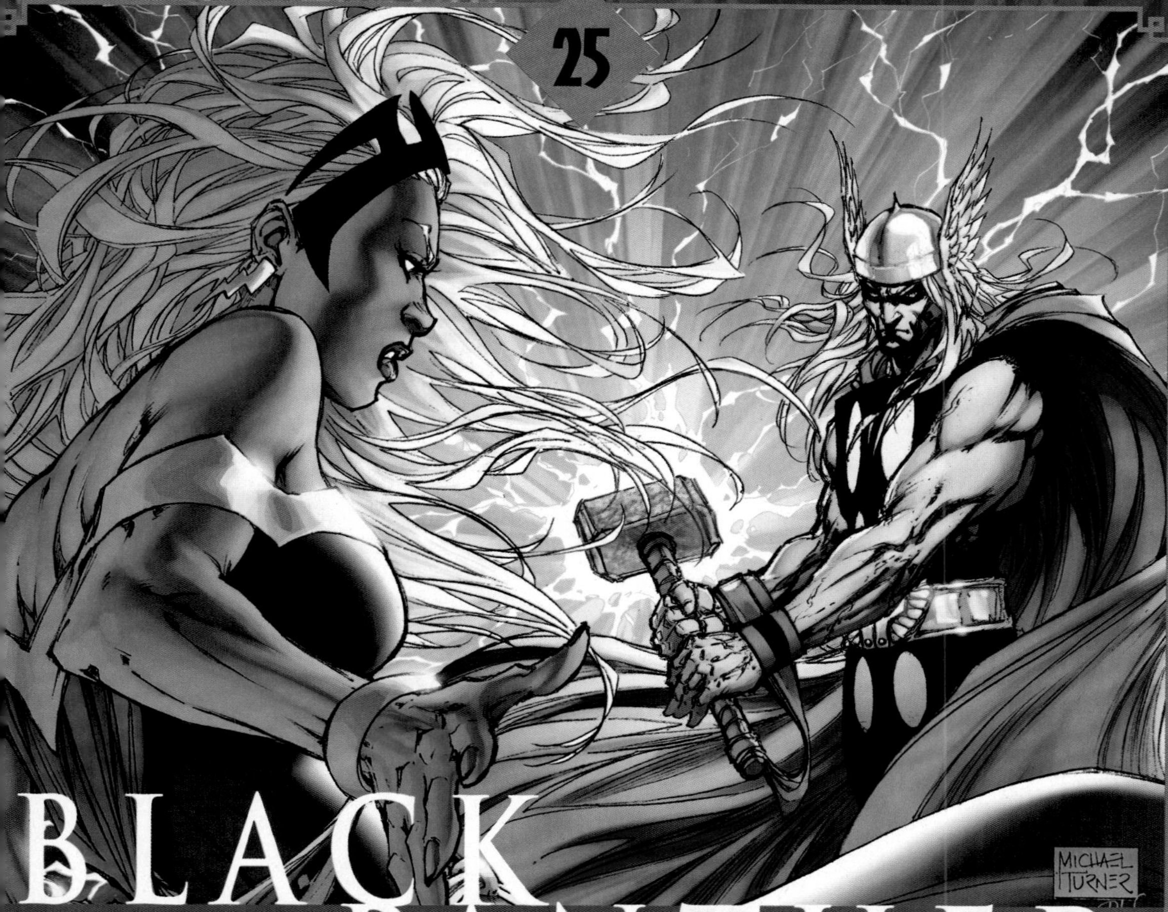
25
MICHAEL TURNER

BLACK PANTHER

A MARVEL COMICS EVENT

CIVIL WAR

25

ASPEN VARIANT BY MICHAEL TURNER

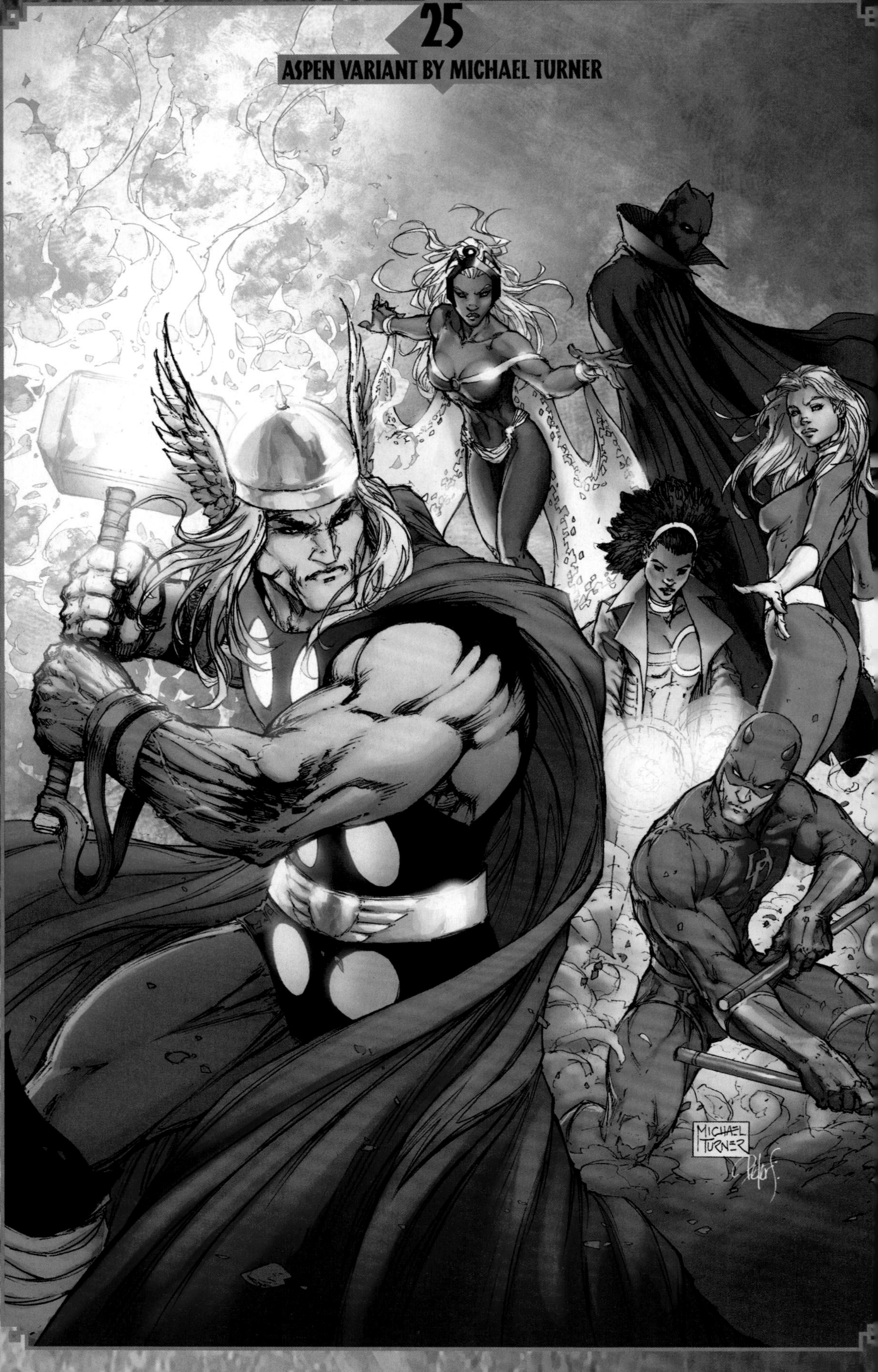
MICHAEL TURNER

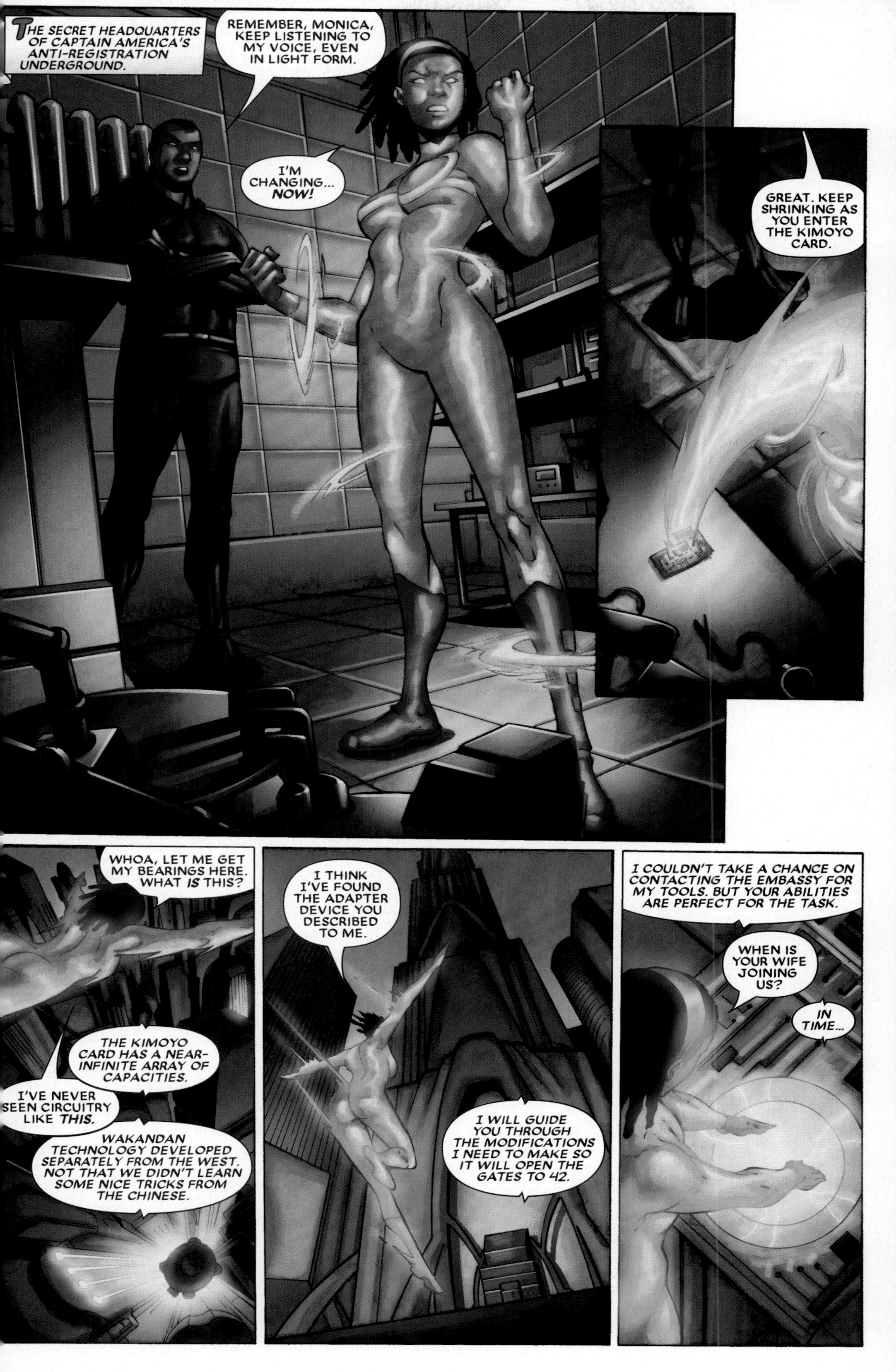
THE SECRET HEADQUARTERS OF CAPTAIN AMERICA'S ANTI-REGISTRATION UNDERGROUND.
REMEMBER, MONICA, KEEP LISTENING TO MY VOICE, EVEN IN LIGHT FORM.
I'M CHANGING... NOW!
GREAT. KEEP SHRINKING AS YOU ENTER THE KIMOYO CARD.
WHOA, LET ME GET MY BEARINGS HERE. WHAT IS THIS?
THE KIMOYO CARD HAS A NEAR-INFINITE ARRAY OF CAPACITIES.
I'VE NEVER SEEN CIRCUITRY LIKE THIS.
WAKANDAN TECHNOLOGY DEVELOPED SEPARATELY FROM THE WEST. NOT THAT WE DIDN'T LEARN SOME NICE TRICKS FROM THE CHINESE.
I THINK I'VE FOUND THE ADAPTER DEVICE YOU DESCRIBED TO ME.
I WILL GUIDE YOU THROUGH THE MODIFICATIONS I NEED TO MAKE SO IT WILL OPEN THE GATES TO 42.
I COULDN'T TAKE A CHANCE ON CONTACTING THE EMBASSY FOR MY TOOLS. BUT YOUR ABILITIES ARE PERFECT FOR THE TASK.
WHEN IS YOUR WIFE JOINING US?
IN TIME...

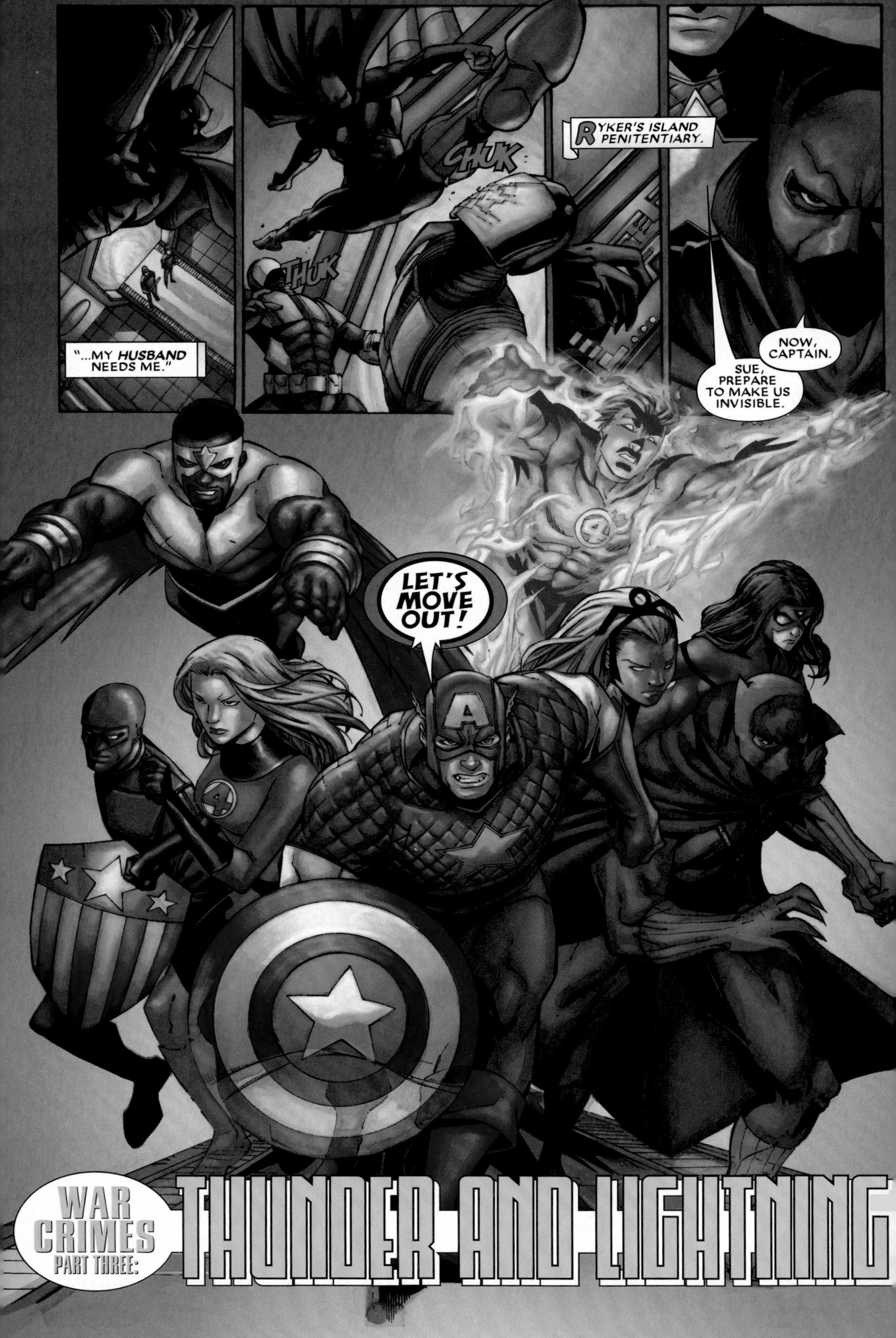
"...MY HUSBAND NEEDS ME."
THUK
CHUK
RYKER'S ISLAND PENITENTIARY.
NOW, CAPTAIN.
SUE, PREPARE TO MAKE US INVISIBLE.
LET'S MOVE OUT!
WAR CRIMES PART THREE:
THUNDER AND LIGHTNING

ATTENTION ALL EMBASSY PERSONNEL!

THIS IS THE BLACK PANTHER. IF YOU ARE RECEIVING THIS MESSAGE, IT MEANS A CRISIS THAT THREATENS YOUR SAFETY IS IMMINENT.

EVACUATE THE BUILDING IMMEDIATELY!

FILES DELETED

LOOKS LIKE EVERYBODY'S BUGGING OUT OF THE WAKANDAN EMBASSY. FIGURE THEY KNOW SOMETHING WE DON'T?

FWOOSH

WHAT THE HELL IS *THAT?*

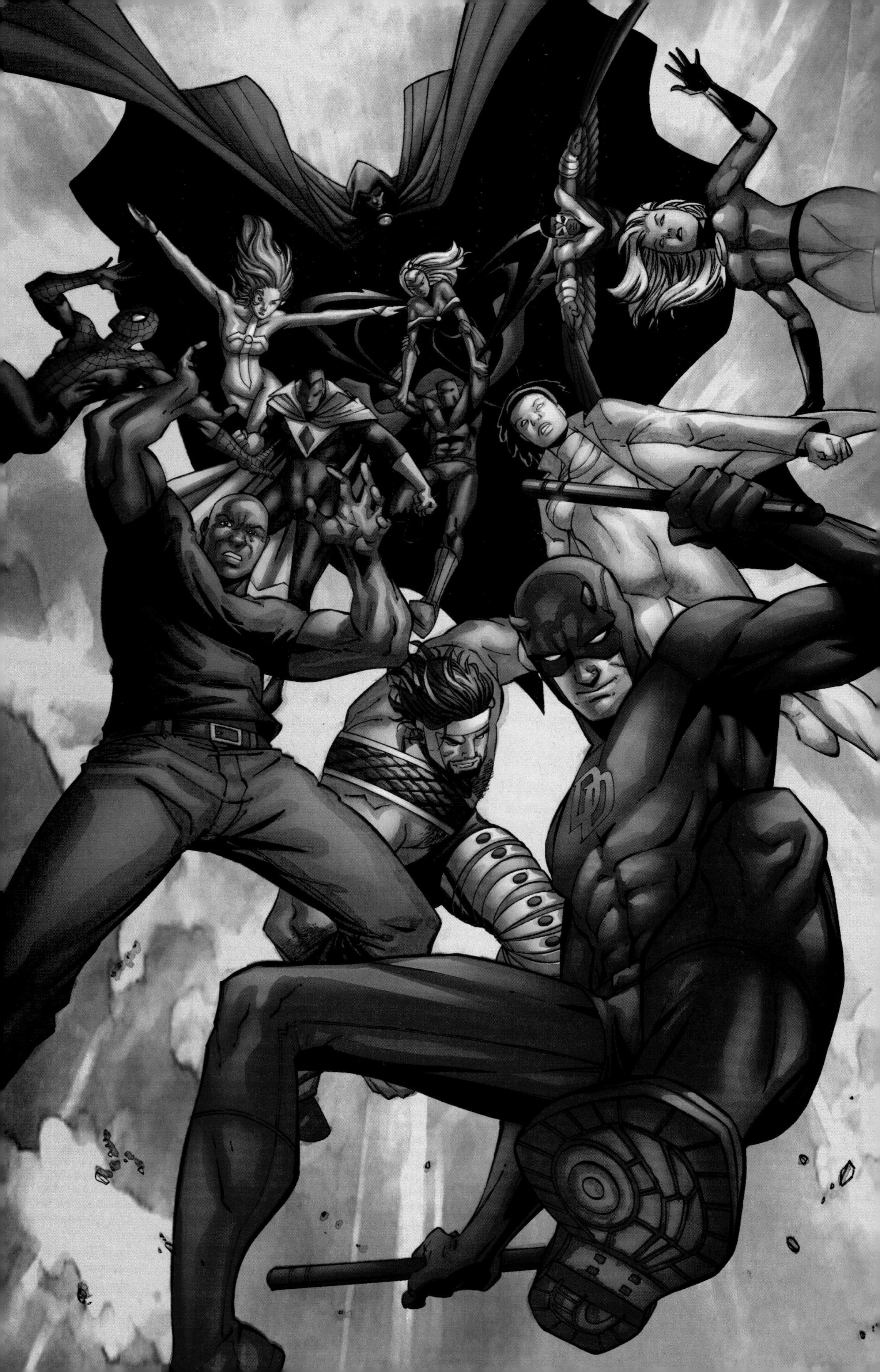

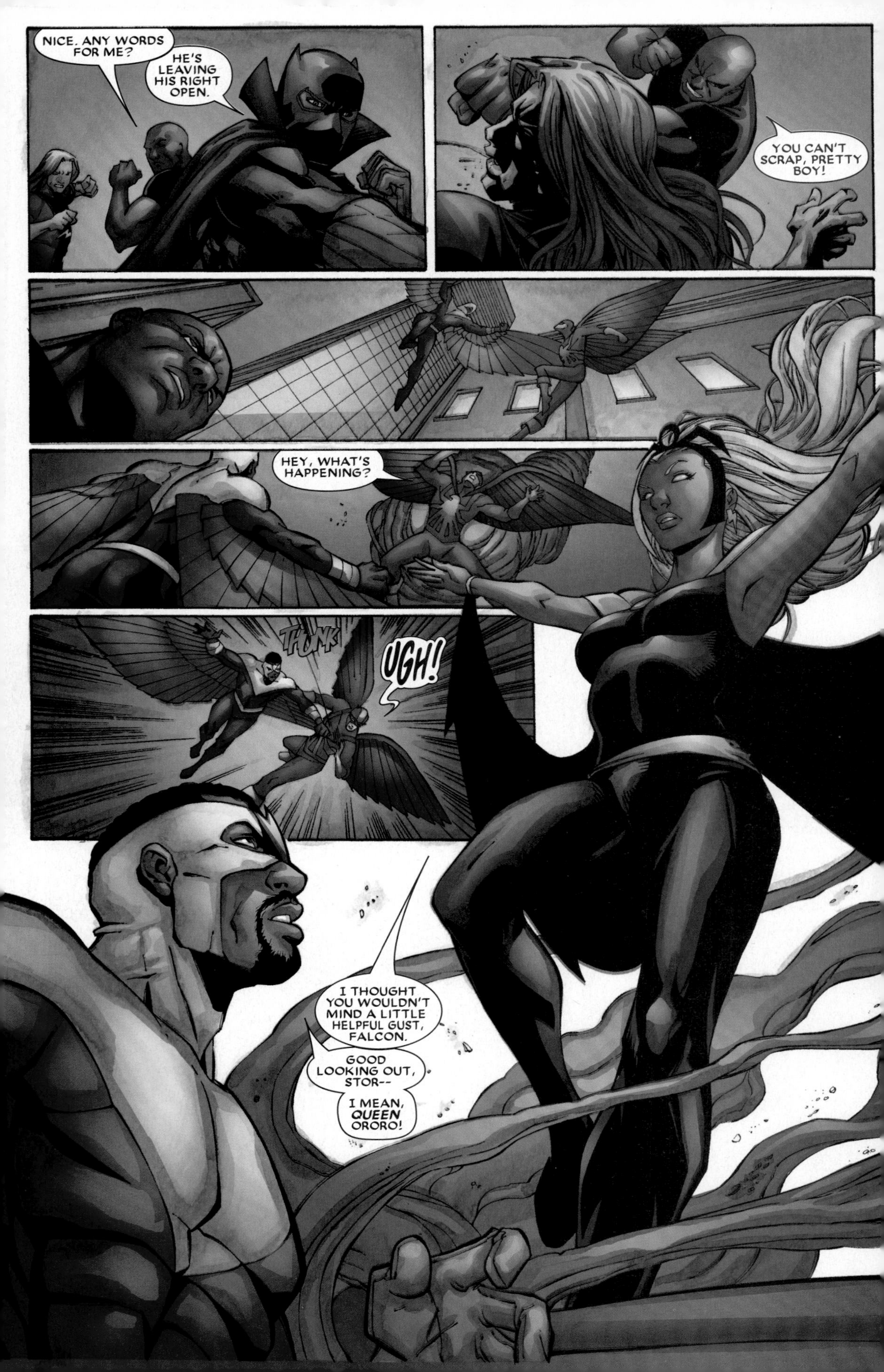
NICE. ANY WORDS FOR ME?
HE'S LEAVING HIS RIGHT OPEN.
YOU CAN'T SCRAP, PRETTY BOY!
HEY, WHAT'S HAPPENING?
THUNK
UGH!
I THOUGHT YOU WOULDN'T MIND A LITTLE HELPFUL GUST, FALCON.
GOOD LOOKING OUT, STOR--
I MEAN, QUEEN ORORO!

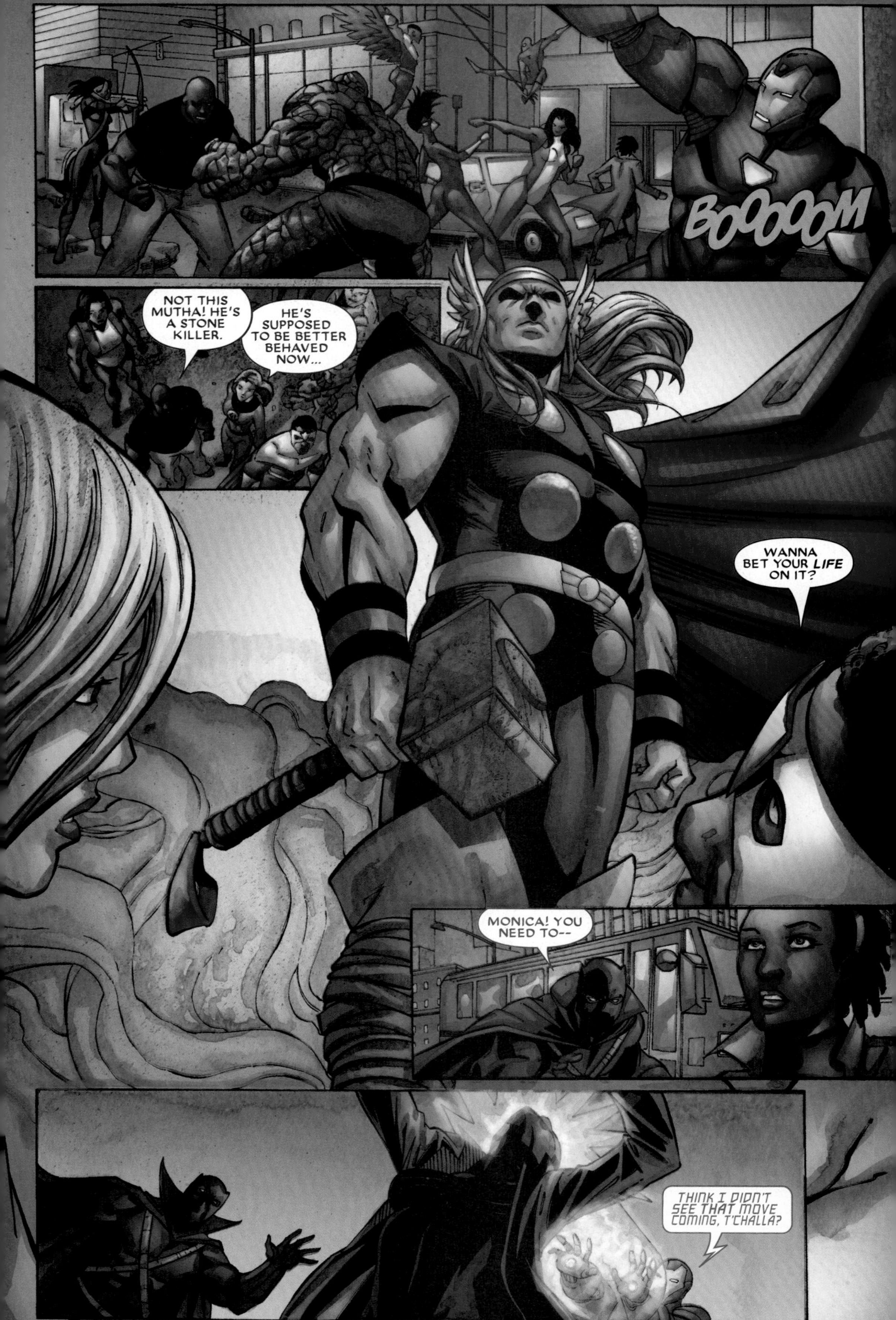
BOOOOOM
NOT THIS MUTHA! HE'S A STONE KILLER.
HE'S SUPPOSED TO BE BETTER BEHAVED NOW...
WANNA BET YOUR *LIFE* ON IT?
MONICA! YOU NEED TO--
THINK I DIDN'T SEE *THAT* MOVE COMING, T'CHALLA?

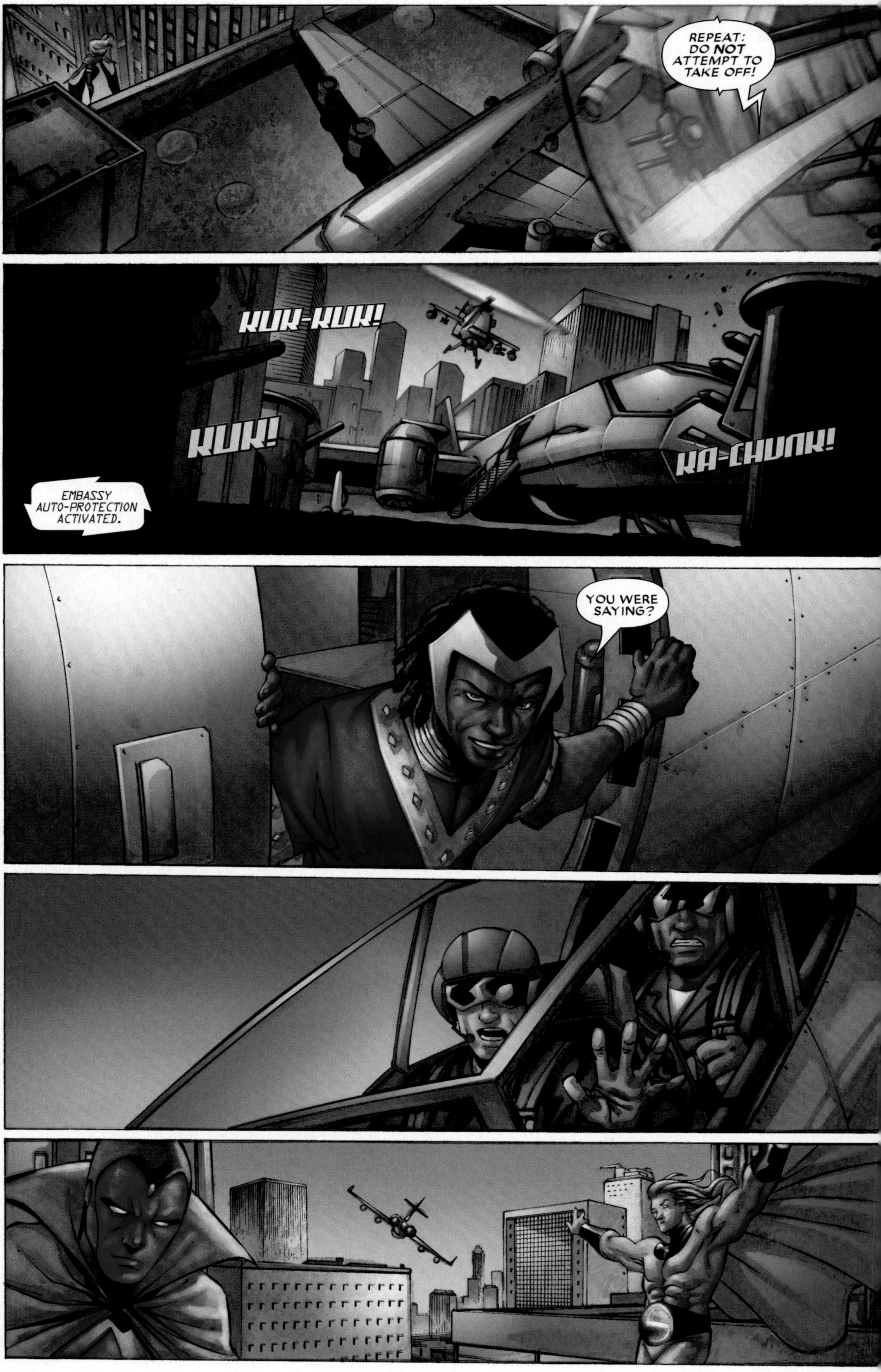
REPEAT: DO NOT ATTEMPT TO TAKE OFF!
KUK-KUK!
KUK!
KA-CHUNK!
EMBASSY AUTO-PROTECTION ACTIVATED.
YOU WERE SAYING?

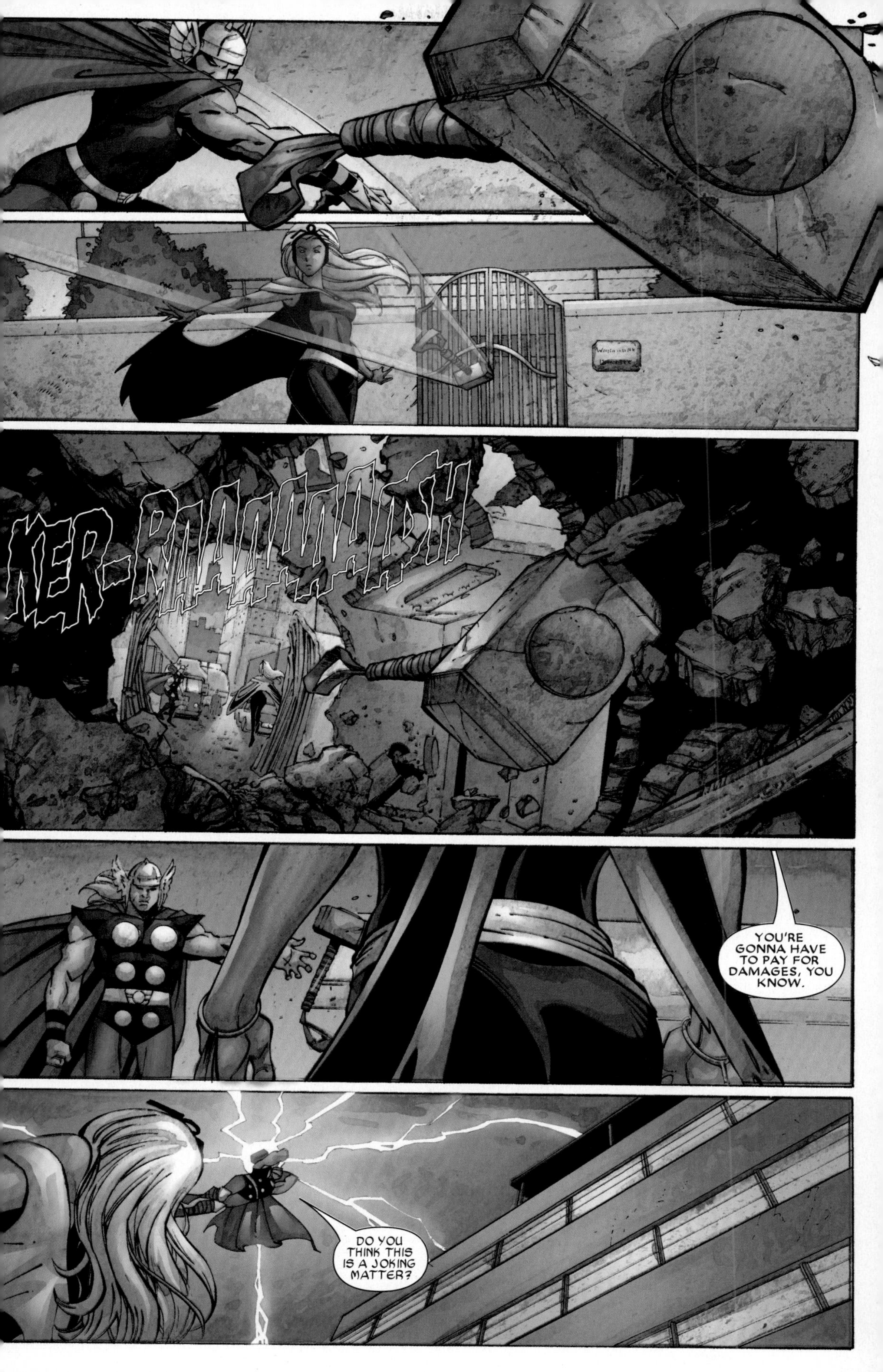
KER-RAAAAAAASH
YOU'RE GONNA HAVE TO PAY FOR DAMAGES, YOU KNOW.
DO YOU THINK THIS IS A JOKING MATTER?

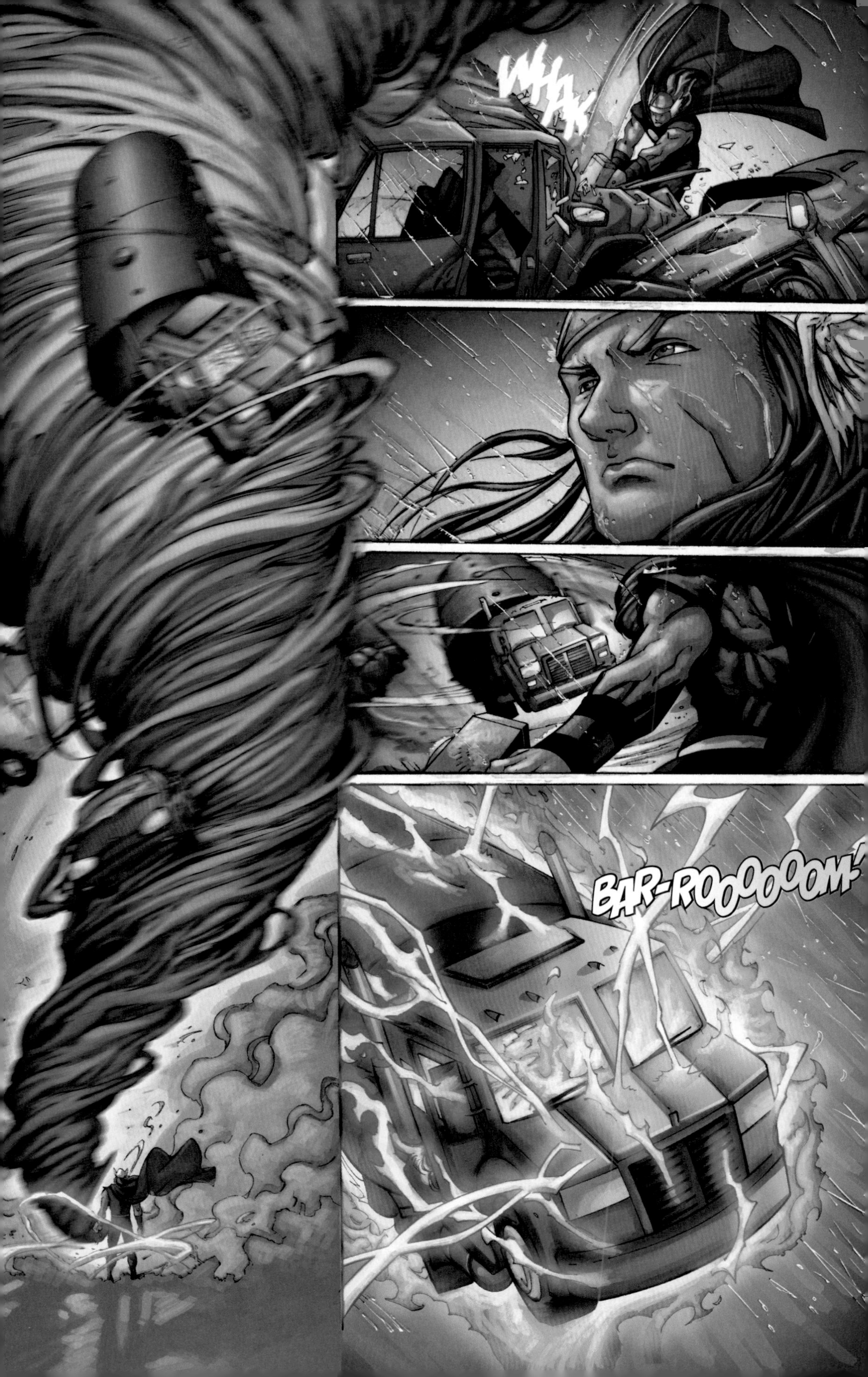
WHAK
BAR-ROOOOOOOM!

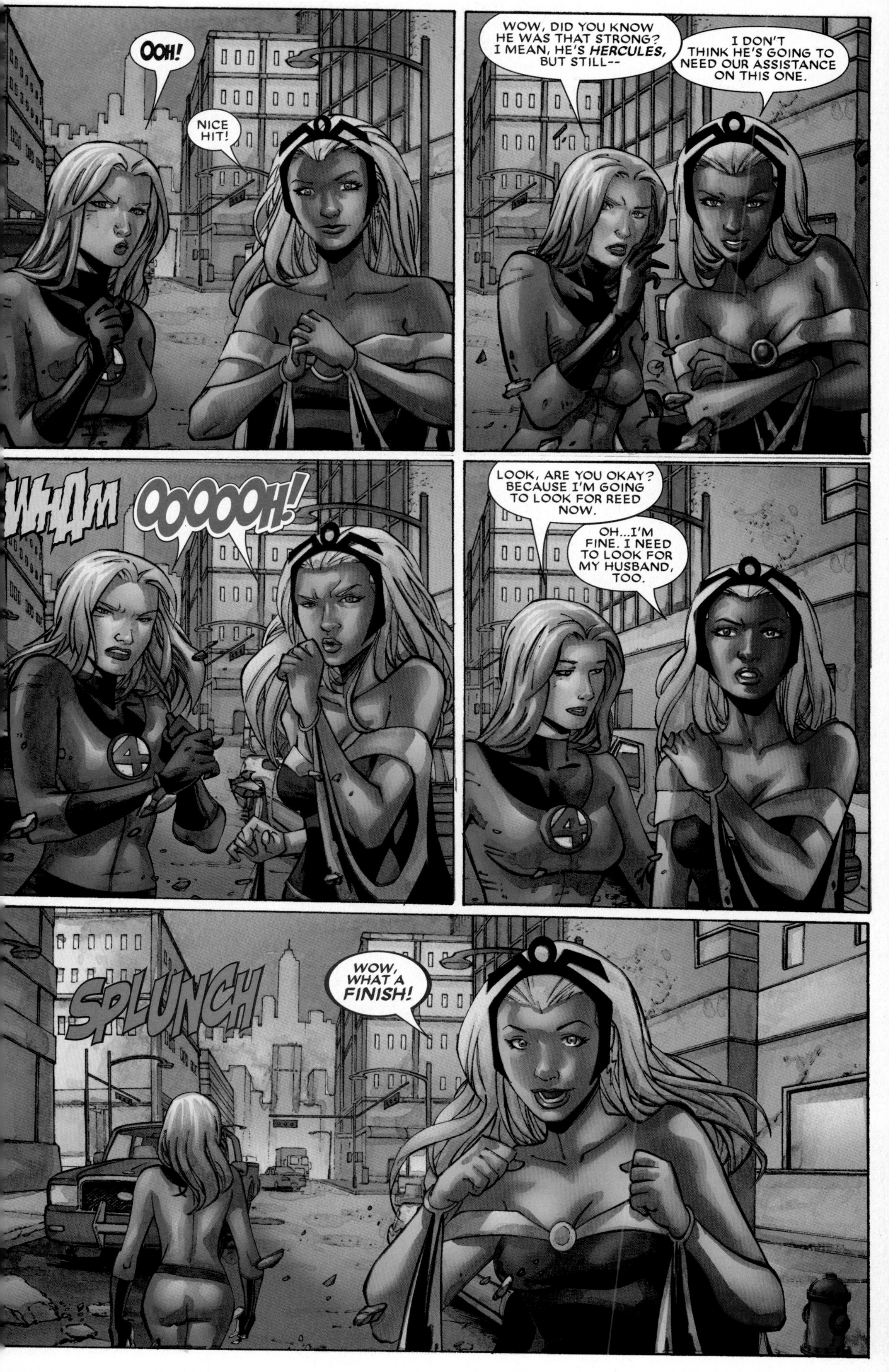
OOH!
NICE HIT!
WOW, DID YOU KNOW HE WAS THAT STRONG? I MEAN, HE'S HERCULES, BUT STILL--
I DON'T THINK HE'S GOING TO NEED OUR ASSISTANCE ON THIS ONE.
WHAM
OOOOOH!
LOOK, ARE YOU OKAY? BECAUSE I'M GOING TO LOOK FOR REED NOW.
OH...I'M FINE. I NEED TO LOOK FOR MY HUSBAND, TOO.
SPLUNCH
WOW, WHAT A FINISH!

...THE STREETS OF NEW YORK WERE AS VIOLENT AS THE FIELDS OF GETTYSBURG AS THE FINAL BATTLE IN THE "CIVIL WAR" BETWEEN SUPER HEROES SEEMS TO HAVE PEAKED TODAY. BUT IT WAS ANYTHING BUT CIVIL IN THE CONFLICT BETWEEN SUPPORTERS AND OPPONENTS OF THE SUPERHUMAN REGISTRATION ACT....

ANOTHER HOME LOST. I HOPE IT WAS WORTH IT TO END THIS STRUGGLE BETWEEN FRIENDS.

OH! THERE YOU ARE!

HOW DO YOU DO THAT?

WE HAVE A PROBLEM.

I KNOW. IT'S GOING TO TAKE MONTHS TO REBUILD--

NO. A BIGGER PROBLEM.

WHAT?

CAP QUIT.

WHAT? YOU CAN'T BE SERIOUS. HE--

I'M DEADLY SERIOUS. CAPTAIN AMERICA... *SURRENDERED*...

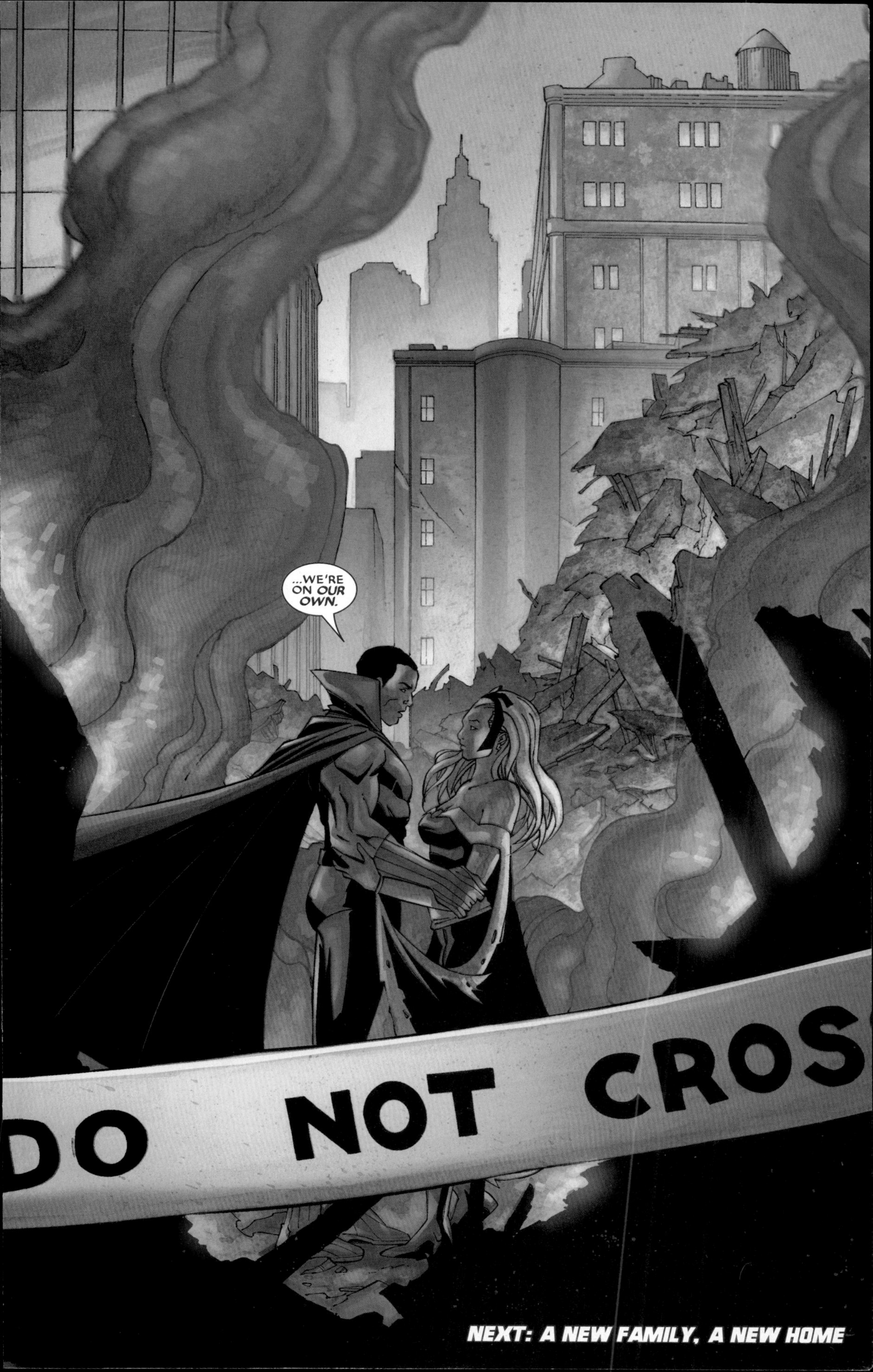
...WE'RE ON OUR OWN.
DO NOT CROS
NEXT: A NEW FAMILY, A NEW HOME

22

UNUSED COVER BY MANUEL GARCIA

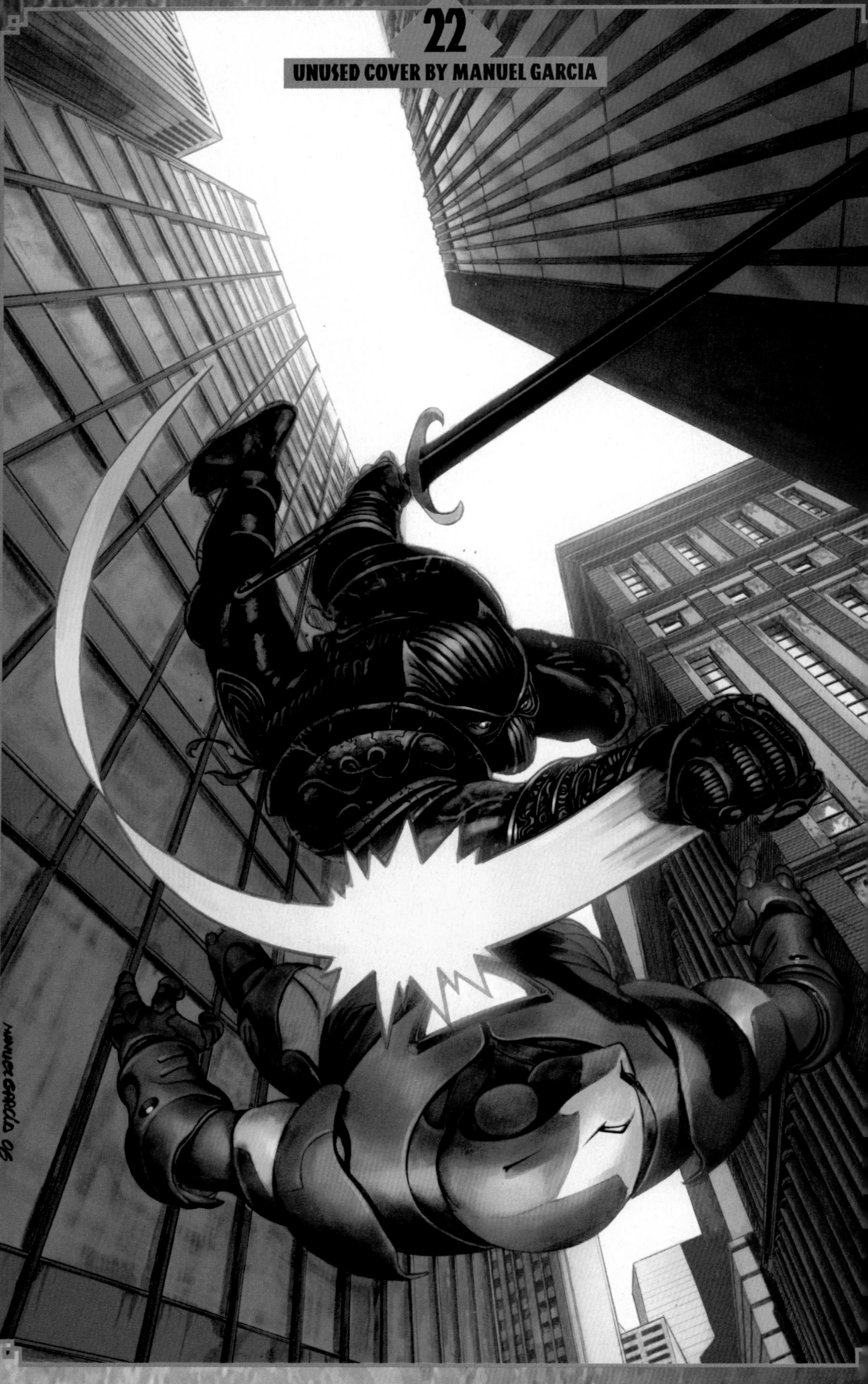